WITHDRAWN FROM
TSC LIBRARY

TALLAHASSEE
LIBRARY
COMMUNITY COLLEGE

D1447127

**The 57 Club**
Florida Government and Politics

UNIVERSITY PRESS OF FLORIDA

Florida A&M University, Tallahassee

Florida Atlantic University, Boca Raton

Florida Gulf Coast University, Ft. Myers

Florida International University, Miami

Florida State University, Tallahassee

New College of Florida, Sarasota

University of Central Florida, Orlando

University of Florida, Gainesville

University of North Florida, Jacksonville

University of South Florida, Tampa

University of West Florida, Pensacola

**University Press of Florida**

Gainesville · Tallahassee · Tampa · Boca Raton · Pensacola

Orlando · Miami · Jacksonville · Ft. Myers · Sarasota

# THE 57 CLUB

## My Four Decades in Florida Politics

*Frederick B. Karl*

Foreword by David R. Colburn
and Susan A. MacManus

Copyright 2010 by Frederick B. Karl
Printed in the United States of America. This book is printed on Glatfelter Natures
Book, a paper certified under the standards of the Forestry Stewardship Council
(FSC). It is a recycled stock that contains 30 percent post-consumer waste and is
acid-free.
All rights reserved

15   14   13   12   11   10      6   5   4   3   2   1

**Library of Congress Cataloging-in-Publication Data**
Karl, Frederick B.
The 57 club : my four decades in Florida politics / Frederick B. Karl ; foreword by
David R. Colburn and Susan A. MacManus.
p. cm.—(Florida government and politics)
Includes index.
ISBN 978-0-8130-3463-8 (alk. paper)

1. Karl, Frederick B. 2. Legislators—Florida—Biography. 3. Judges—Florida—
Biography. 4. County officials and employees—Florida—Hillsborough
County—Biography. 5. Florida. Legislature. House of Representatives—
Biography. 6. Florida. Supreme Court—Biography. 7. Florida—Politics and
government—1951– 8. Hillsborough County (Fla.)—Politics and government—
20th century. I. Title. II. Title: Fifty-seven club.
F316.23.K37A3 2010
328.73'092—dc22 [B]     2009051041

The University Press of Florida is the scholarly publishing agency for the
State University System of Florida, comprising Florida A&M University, Florida
Atlantic University, Florida Gulf Coast University, Florida International Uni-
versity, Florida State University, New College of Florida, University of Central
Florida, University of Florida, University of North Florida, University of South
Florida, and University of West Florida.

University Press of Florida
15 Northwest 15th Street
Gainesville, FL 32611-2079
http://www.upf.com

*For Merci*

# Contents

# *Foreword* •————————————————————————————

Florida has held a unique place in the American mind for over six decades. For many retirees, its environment has been like a healthy elixir that allowed them to live longer and more robust lives; for others, Florida is a place of renewal, where all things are possible; and for immigrants, it is a place of political freedom and opportunity. Historian Gary Mormino describes the state as a "powerful symbol of renewal and regeneration." It has been suggested that, if Florida had not existed in the post-World War II era, Americans would have been the poorer for it. Others who watched the 2000 presidential election wondered if that were so.

During World War II, Americans from all walks of life discovered Florida through military service, and it opened their eyes to the postwar possibilities. With the end of the war in August 1945, Florida veterans returned home, where they were soon joined by hundreds and then thousands of Americans who were ready to pursue a new life in the Sunshine State. In the sixty years between 1945 and 2005, 17 million people moved to Florida, increasing the state's population to 18.5 million people in 2005.

Florida's population growth, the settlement patterns of new residents, and their diversity had a profound effect on the state's place in the nation as well as the image Floridians had of themselves. Prior to 1940, Florida was the smallest state in the South and one of the poorest in the nation. Its society and economy were rural and agricultural, biracial and segregated, and most residents lived within forty miles of the Georgia border. These demographics and the state's history shaped the public's racial and cultural mindset as well as its politics. Florida was a one-party state, controlled by the Democratic Party since the end of Reconstruction in 1876.

All that changed in the fifty years following World War II. By 2005—in less than an average life span today—Florida became the largest state in the region, the fourth largest in the nation, a senior haven, and a dynamic multiracial and multiethnic state. Most Floridians now reside closer to the Caribbean than they do to Georgia, and, for most of them, their image of themselves and their state has been significantly influenced by this new geographic orientation. By the twenty-first century, demographers viewed Florida as a microcosm of the nation because of its size and population complexity.

As Florida changed, so too did its politics. Voters threw out the constitution of 1885 in favor of a new document which would speak to the needs of a new state in 1968. They then gradually abandoned the Democratic Party in favor of a dynamic two-party system. By the 1990s, Republicans used their expanding constituency and control of the districting process following the 1990 census to take control of the state legislature and the congressional delegation. These were remarkable developments and reflected the dramatic changes taking place in the state's population and demographics. By 2008, Republicans controlled all state offices which were districted. However, in statewide races for governor, U.S. senator, and elected Florida Cabinet positions, as well as in presidential contests, Democrats frequently won and held a 6 percent lead over Republicans in registered voters (42 percent to 36 percent).

Such a politically and demographically complex and diverse population has made Florida today something other than a unified whole. The political maxim that "All politics is local" is truer of Florida than most other states. For example, those who reside in north Florida share little in common with those living in central or south Florida and vice-versa. While those in southeast Florida see themselves as part of the "new America," those in north Florida view Miami as a foreign country. Ask a resident what it means to be a Floridian and few, if any, can answer the question. Ask a Floridian about the state's history, and even fewer can tell you that it has operated under five different flags, or that its colonial period began much earlier than that of New England or Virginia. Perhaps one in ten or twenty residents can tell you who LeRoy Collins was, despite Republican Jeb Bush's recognition of this Democratic governor as the model for all others who followed. It is literally a state unknown and indefinable to its people. Such historical ignorance and regional division become major obstacles when state leaders try to find consensus among voters and solutions that address the needs of all citizens.

An essential purpose of this series is to put Floridians in touch with their rich and diverse political history and to enhance their understanding of the political developments that have reshaped the state, region, and nation. This series focuses on the Sunshine State's unique and dynamic political history since 1900 and on public policy issues that have influenced the state and the nation. The University Press of Florida is dedicated to producing high quality books on these subjects. It is also committed to publishing shorter essays of twenty-five to fifty pages in this series that address some of the immediately pressing public policy issues confronting Florida. As part of this series, the University Press of Florida also welcomes book manuscripts on the region that examine critical political and policy developments that impacted Florida.

This particular volume, *The 57 Club: My Four Decades in Florida Politics*, by Frederick B. Karl offers a superb view of what every aspect of legislative life was like for the thirty-nine legislators (all white males) who were first elected to the Florida House of Representatives in 1957. Karl and his colleagues came to office as the state began to transition away from its rural, segregated, Deep South roots. Over the course of their careers (the last one left the legislature in 1988), many of these Club members played major roles in modernizing the governance structure of the Sunshine State, writing a new state constitution and transforming public policies in the areas of civil rights, education, environment, and taxation.

Karl gives a very detailed, highly personal, emotional account of the hard-fought battles over two major issues—desegregation and reapportionment. These issues divided legislators (the large majority of whom were Democrats), along ideological and geographical lines. Ultimately, power was wrested away from the very conservative "Small County" bloc, heavily concentrated in rural North Florida. Particularly intriguing is Karl's portrayal of the anguish that these lawmakers felt as the state transitioned from a rural-dominated, county-based representational system to one structured in accordance with the "one person, one vote" law. Equally fascinating is his description of the courageous stances made on racial integration by colleagues and governors, knowing full well the political consequences of taking such positions.

Rarely do we get such a close-up view of how legislative coalitions are built among legislators from vastly divergent backgrounds, particularly during tumultuous times. Karl's major premises are that it was done with strong, principled leadership and with a belief by a critical mass of legislators that "one can disagree with others—even those in control—and if done honorably, can continue to have their respect." As he notes, "One should not lose confidence in a colleague who votes differently. And one should not nullify a friendship over any one issue or vote."

Karl's descriptions of various aspects of the legislative process are superb—the politics of committee assignments, legislators' savvy use of rules on the floor, the effectiveness of colleagues' speeches and debating skills, the role of humor in calming down angry exchanges, polite ways of punishing unethical colleagues, the power of social invitations, the usefulness of lobbyists, and the interface between the press corps and legislators. His candid discussions of what it feels like to be on the losing side of a legislative vote or an election (in his case for governor) and how to move on afterward should be read and taken to heart by those contemplating political careers.

*The 57 Club* is a unique book reflecting the author's unusual resume. Mr. Karl has had experience in all three branches of government and at both the state and local levels. He offers a very rich perspective of Florida politics at a critical turning point in our state's history—a period for which we have few firsthand accounts.

David R. Colburn and Susan A. MacManus

# *Preface* •————————————————————

This is a story about the Florida Legislature during the tumultuous sessions of the late 1950s and early 1960s, with an emphasis on members of a unique and informal fraternity called the 57 Club. It is told through anecdotes of that time as I remember them.

Those were exciting times for legislators and for everyone who lived in Florida. The inexorable and painful movement to racially integrate Florida's public schools as well as the crying need to fairly apportion legislative representation were two issues on the minds of all public officials. These were important issues, and they were politically dangerous to those involved with them.

I've written this book for those who are curious about the past and have an interest in how the past has shaped what they know as the present.

Readers who persevere through the following pages will see, from a somewhat different perspective, a bit of the history of Florida politics as they learn about the 57 Club, its members, and the issues we were obliged to face.

As I recalled and memorialized the anecdotes, my goal was to preserve an account of happenings that are worth remembering but that otherwise would have fallen unnoticed as crumbs from the table of history.

# PART 1

*The Club, the People, and the Environment*

# 1  *The Club Is Born* •————————————————

There's an old saying in north Florida that when a baby boy is born he is put on the floor, and if he doesn't crawl toward the state capital they send him away. For all its humor, the saying speaks volumes about the political climate of Florida many years ago and the long-term effects—both good and bad—of the tight-fisted control exerted by Florida's small northern counties.

Every time there was talk about how the sparsely populated counties dominated the legislative branch of government, that saying surfaced. It was one of the first things my colleagues and I, as freshmen members of the Florida House of Representatives in 1957, learned when we arrived in Tallahassee. It voiced the degree of concern over giving up even a scintilla of that control. It also makes the story of the 57 Club more understandable.

I was an original member of the 57 Club of the Florida Legislature. Actually, those of us who were elected to the Florida House of Representatives in 1956 and served for the first time in the regular legislative session of 1957 were automatically members of the organization.

There were no forms to fill out, no initiation rituals to endure, and no dues to pay. My qualifying credentials were satisfied when I was declared the winner of a hard-fought, countywide election as state representative in Volusia County.

There were thirty-nine of us in the state who met the membership conditions for the 57 Club, and we began our political ventures together. Each one was distinctive, but surprisingly we also had similarities.

By sharing my own experiences and reactions, describing what I witnessed or heard along the way, and telling stories about friends and colleagues, I hope to present a better understanding of how the Florida Legislature functioned, as well as a fresh and intimate look at an important period in Florida's history.

My 1956 campaign photo.

## The Club

The 57 Club came into being following a custom in the U.S. House of Representatives, where a club or class is formed after each general election for all newly elected members of Congress. When someone suggested that the freshmen members of the 1957 Florida House of Representatives ought to emulate Congress and organize a similar "club," it was thought to be a good idea. Its purpose would be to provide freshmen representatives with an opportunity to know one another quickly and to begin our respective legislative careers on a harmonious note.

Not everyone favored the organization. There were those who worried that we were forming a base of power, or that somehow we were preparing to challenge the entrenched control structure. The question often heard in the halls was: "What in the Hell are they doing?"

Although Florida was beginning to show signs of maturity, it should be noted that because it was a one-party state (almost everyone who wanted to vote registered as a Democrat), almost all thirty-nine of us were Democrats. Florida was also a rather traditional state, so neither females nor African Americans were elected to serve with this group. Perhaps it was a sign of the times—almost everyone was uptight about race or feminism. In my election, for example, all three candidates were white males. No one else ran.

Since membership in the 57 Club was limited to the winners of the 1956 election, there were no women or blacks in the Club. Because many of the members later became registered Republicans, a meeting today would not be attended only by Democrats. However, at the time the Club was formed there was plenty of diversity other than in political parties, gender, and race.

Financially, members ranged from Ben Hill Griffin Jr. of Polk County—said to be one of the richest men in the country—to most of the rest of us who were young business or professional folks living from paycheck to paycheck, and all the way to a small number who had precious little in the way of monetary assets.

There certainly was intellectual diversity, with Bob Mann of Hillsborough County holding several graduate degrees, while the rest of us had less formal education. Others were doing well if they had any college training. Occupations included lawyers, businessmen, insurance agents, farmers, teachers, a commercial mullet fisherman, and a Greyhound bus driver.

In matters of race relations, attitudes covered the entire spectrum, from advocacy of integration to outright hatred of the idea and a belief in the righteousness of segregation.

Similarly, there was diversity in thinking about all aspects of government, education, and social behavior. There was so much political, educational, financial, and philosophical diversity that some of us worried that we wouldn't even be able to muster a majority vote to pass the annual Mother's Day Resolution.

## World War II Military Service

Even with all of that diversity, our group of thirty-nine males had an underlying tie that tended to bind us together. Most of us had been in military service during World War II. The exceptions were those who were either too young or too old to participate.

Military service during that war was so universal that conceptually it was more like being a registered Democrat in a one-party state than it was like being a member of an exclusive club or lodge. That is to say, it was sort of taken for granted that those who were near your age were veterans. In conversations where two or more were getting acquainted, the subject would often come up in some casual way, and it wasn't surprising to learn that the person you were visiting with had served in the Army, Navy, Air Force, or Marines. Because the war permanently marked so many of us, there was something of a comfortable environment that grew up between two or more former servicemen when they came together. In some ways it was similar to the feelings a member of the Armed Forces experienced when seeing a hitchhiker by the side of the road using his thumb to ask for a ride. Certainly there was an awareness of

My tank and I take a break in Berlin shortly after the war ended.

the danger of allowing a total stranger into his car, but he was apt to discount the danger somewhat and offer a ride if the hitchhiker was in uniform.

The war ended in 1945. Our election to public office was only about eleven years from the cessation of hostilities, and less than that if measured from our respective discharges or separations from the service. In my case, for example, I was late getting home because my division was selected to be the first American troops to enter Berlin following its conquest by the Russians and to serve there during the Potsdam Conference, where Winston Churchill and Josef Stalin met with Harry S. Truman, who had become president upon the death of Franklin D. Roosevelt. Then, after I was back in this country, I was hospitalized to be treated for the effects of the wounds I received in combat. So I was elected to the legislature only ten years after the end of my service. Consequently, my colleagues and I still were under the influence of the experiences we had during the months or years we had been exposed to that alternate lifestyle.

We were a fraternity of lucky people. We had survived whatever our respective ordeals had been. We were proud of our individual and/or collective victories. We had a residue of patriotism left over from the propaganda and serious lessons we had been taught. While we seldom discussed specifics, we knew something of the military record—or non-record—of every colleague. This subject was always with us, and it helped shape our relationships and our political philosophies.

## The Political Environment

Any description of the political environment in Florida must include some comment on the way the state was affected by certain national and international activities. One such program was the exploration of outer space, or as it became known, the "race for space."

Although the Florida Legislature had little or nothing to do with the competition between the United States and Russia for dominance in outer space, we certainly were aware that early on Communist Russia was ahead of our country in rocket technology. America's primary space center was in our state, and the daily newspapers were full of stories about the space race. Every significant rocket launch, such as Alan Shepard's ride into space and return to earth down range—which occurred while we were in session—caused a pause in legislative business. And John Glenn's success as the first American to orbit the earth made us proud and helped ease the torment we were experiencing as a result of Russia's early superiority in rocket technology.

There were legislators who suffered from paranoia with respect to Russia's achievements in space and thought Communists were responsible for all the unrest in this country, including the efforts to eliminate racial segregation in the schools and elsewhere. Those concerns were no doubt partially responsible for the birth of the Johns Committee, a U.S. Senator Joe McCarthy-like group of legislators that caused upheaval on the campuses of colleges and universities, the effects of which are still being felt.

The Cold War with Russia, including the space race, was an integral part of the political environment into which the members of the 57 Club were thrust.

Also, it must be recognized that the members of the Club were maturing politically during the Dwight Eisenhower presidency and the early days of the John F. Kennedy administration. Florida's racial tensions were not unlike those of the nation's, and they were intensified by the assassinations of President Kennedy, the Rev. Martin Luther King Jr., and Robert Kennedy. They certainly shook each one of us to the core and affected the political environment in which we grew up.

Warren Cole and I were diligent supporters of Senator John F. Kennedy when he ran for president in 1960.

Later, when George Wallace of Alabama was shot, I had more of the same kind of sadness. I had met him a time or two and did not like him, but I still could not believe such things could be happening. Just the fact that those assassinations could occur in America depressed me.

But I also had a special set of feelings about the assassinations. Shortly before the Battle of the Bulge, in December 1944, I had a talk with another young lieutenant who was a fellow tank platoon leader in the same company in which I served. He asserted that there would never be a dictator in America like Adolf Hitler because if anyone started to act like a dictator, he would shoot him. I had seen my friend in combat, and I knew he had the determination and the skill to do what he said. Personally, I didn't think any of the leaders who were shot in America were potential dictators, but I didn't know what my lieutenant friend considered to be politically offensive. However, I confess that I was relieved when the assassins were identified and he was not one of them. I talked with my Army buddy years later when we were approaching "old soldier" status and he agreed that there had not been a real threat to our freedom yet, but he assured me he was still on guard.

## A One-Party State

In 1956 the Democratic Party was dominant in Florida. Virtually all voters were registered Democrats. There were pockets of registered Republicans, particularly around St. Petersburg and Sarasota on the west coast, but state and most local elections were settled in the Democratic Party primaries. If one wanted his vote to count in one of those races, he became a Democrat, even if he had no love for the party or did not intend to vote for the party's nominees for national offices. That had pretty much been the case since the days of Reconstruction following the Civil War.

There was also a history throughout the South of attempts by the Democratic Party to deny certain potential voters, primarily African Americans, access to the voting process. Various schemes were tried, such as erecting financial barriers through the use of the poll tax, which required payment as a condition of voting. Another scheme established an intellectual barrier by requiring a would-be voter to pass a test on the U.S. Constitution, which allowed for subjectivity and unfairness.

The poll tax was two dollars, which seems to be a pittance today, but at that time it was a substantial amount to pay if a person was living on the edge of poverty. It may be hard to envision, but when the poll tax was two dollars, one could hire an African-American woman as a full-time maid and baby sitter for eight dollars a week. To put it in perspective, a two-dollar poll tax equaled almost two days' pay for the maid. No such inhibitors existed in Florida in 1956, but the memory of them was fresh and still bitter.

## An Important but Weak Office

While those of us who were to become members of the 57 Club were busy with our own campaigning, a larger election battle was looming—that of the Governor of Florida, the most important state office filled in 1956.

Realistically, the position was weak because Florida's governor was limited to one four-year term, and the executive power had to be shared with the elected members of the Florida Cabinet, who had no term limits and operated generally in the same way a corporate board of directors functions. The person elected had to be a strong leader and popular with the electorate to govern effectively.

Under normal conditions, the weakness of the Office of Governor would not have mattered too much to the people of Florida, but in the 1950s and

1960s, when the state was in turmoil about imminent integration of public facilities, problems resulting from growth, and the effects of neglect in the areas of education and social programs, the official weakness worried those who understood the cumbersome diffusion of power. It made necessary the selection of bold and resourceful governors who could lead effectively even without a full measure of executive power.

In the election of 1956, the year the 57 Clubbers sought election for the first time, LeRoy Collins was the leading candidate for governor. Because of a historically important set of circumstances, Collins was running as an incumbent, something that wasn't done previously in Florida.

Here's how that occurred: In 1952, Dan McCarty was elected to a four-year term as governor, but he died shortly after his inauguration. The Florida Constitution did not authorize a lieutenant governor at that time, but provided that in the event of a vacancy in the Office of Governor, the president of the Florida Senate would automatically become the acting governor and serve until the end of the term or until the next general election, whichever came first. Should the senate president be unable to step up and serve, the next in line of succession was the Speaker of the Florida House of Representatives.

This order of succession was patently unfair to the people at that time. Governor McCarty was elected statewide, but when he died in office, his unexpired term was in the hands of a senator who was elected by a relatively small group of voters in a small district in the mostly rural part of north Florida. That senator was Charley Johns of Bradford County.

The next general election was in 1954, and by then Collins, also a senator at the time, was challenging Acting Governor Johns for the next term. Collins was seen by many as a better choice—with respect to the size and character of his Senate district—to occupy the important office, even though he was also a resident of north Florida. That was because Collins represented Leon County, home of the state capital, which was a bit more cosmopolitan than the area represented by Johns. Moreover, in the election of 1954, the people would elect their governor in a statewide vote, thereby ending governance by someone from a sparsely populated area who was not elected by all the people but was seated by operation of law.

It should be noted that the rules of succession to the Governor's Office were corrected the next time the Florida Constitution was revised, so in December 1998, when Governor Lawton Chiles died in office, Lieutenant Governor Buddy MacKay, duly elected by the people, moved up into the office and served out the unexpired term.

## Collins Takes Over

In the 1954 gubernatorial race, Senator Collins defeated Johns in a bitter, intra-party campaign that pitted one group of Democrats against another. Collins conducted a well-organized campaign out of necessity, because that was the only type of campaign in which there was a possibility of taking out a strong and entrenched incumbent.

After taking office, Collins sought an opinion of the Florida Supreme Court on the question of whether the one-term limitation would prevent him from having his own four-year term immediately following his service as governor during

LeRoy Collins was the voice of moderation during emotional times. (Photo courtesy Florida Archives.)

the unexpired term of Dan McCarty. Otherwise, Collins would have to leave office after two years. The court held that he was not prohibited from running for governor again in 1956. Consequently, he would have the unique, unprecedented opportunity of being governor for six years if the voters were willing to reelect him, and they did just that in 1956.

Collins was completing his first two years in office (1955–57) when he announced that he would seek reelection, and the campaign began. In that 1956 election, he had opposition in the primary but he defeated the field, including Farris Bryant of Ocala, who would run again four years after that and win the right to be governor from 1960 to 1964.

There were numerous issues confronting Collins, but racial issues were by far the most important and certainly the most controversial. It was not surprising that in the campaigns of '54, '56, and '60, racial issues were a priority on all political agendas. Florida was severely tested to see whether its political leaders could be subjected to extreme racial tension and still be able to address major decisions in other areas of government with calm and thoughtful consideration. Because of sensible, moderate leadership, our state survived the test without significant permanent injury or scars.

It was during this crucial and emotional time that I entered Florida's political stage. I had returned to my home in Daytona Beach following service in World War II and then received my law degree from Stetson University in

December 1949. As I practiced law, it became increasingly difficult to restrain my urge to run for public office. I had been infected with an interest in the political process by my parents, who believed deeply that there was no higher form of public service than the honest practice of politics, and they were convinced it would be an honorable and satisfying way to live. They also taught me that it is always best to tell the truth, and I picked up on that lesson, too.

However, as long as we are on that subject, I must say that along the way I learned the hard way that the old philosophical saying is also true, and that is: Anyone who tells the truth should have one foot in the stirrup.

For more than five years, after graduating law school until 1956, I tended to my law practice and fought off all temptations to run for office. But in early 1956, Thomas T. Cobb, who had been one of the state representatives from Volusia County for ten years, announced that he would not seek re-election. His action created a vacancy in our legislative delegation that had to be filled by an election. My instincts told me that as a novice, I would have a better chance of winning the seat if there was no incumbent that would have to be taken out.

I could not pass up this chance to launch my political career. My desire was intensified by a serious, decisive conversation with Dan Warren, a friend who sought me out and convinced me that I had a duty to run and thereby prevent the important position from falling into the hands of a person who, in his opinion, was not worthy of the honor of serving in that capacity.

Dan Warren was later elected as State Attorney for the Seventh Judicial Circuit. He was in office when Dr. Martin Luther King Jr. visited St. Augustine and was met with threats of violence and the arrest of many of his followers. Warren's book, *If It Takes All Summer*, includes an excellent, blow-by-blow account of the St. Augustine experience.

It is fair to say that had I been more experienced in politics, I probably would not have run at that time. I didn't know it, but most of the political power in Volusia County was already committed when I announced my candidacy. I discovered that Tom Cobb, the incumbent who opted to step down, had groomed and was supporting Dick Stanier, one of my opponents; the local newspaper was also supporting Cobb's choice. Meanwhile, the "Courthouse Gang" (county officials who were active in elections) as well as the labor unions were supporting Bob Durden, my other opponent. Because of evidence of strong support for the two of them, there was little hope for me. I had no real choice but to put on my brave face and do the best I could. I began by saying, "There is nobody left to support me but the voters, so I will go directly to them."

Dick Stanier was a lawyer, and he had married a woman whose family owned and operated Gardner's, a seafood restaurant in Port Orange, a small town south of Daytona Beach. He helped operate the very popular restaurant and his work there was less confining than the practice of law, so he could prepare and run for state representative without creating a financial hardship for himself and his family. He had no trouble raising the money to finance his campaign.

Bob Durden, the other opponent, was someone I had known for years. In fact, we ran into each other in a Red Cross facility in London during World War II, when I was on my way from the hospital back to my unit, which was preparing to fight its way across the Rhine River. He was a glider pilot who flew troops across the English Channel and landed behind enemy lines.

The fact that we had a friendly relationship did not prevent either of us from challenging the other. He apparently knew of my intentions, but beat me to the courthouse and entered the race shortly before I qualified. Durden was better known in political circles than any of us in the race. In addition, he was a few years older than I, and had all of the attributes of a natural politician. These qualities helped make him a formidable opponent.

What also made Durden a fearsome adversary was his experience and contacts in the political community. His father was a constable in a Justice of the Peace district, and Bob had grown up in a political environment which benefited him because he knew all of his father's political friends. Campaign money was as readily available to him as it was to my other opponent.

## My Political Reservations

I confess that I had certain reservations about running for public office, not the least of which was a part of politics that bothered me at the beginning of my public life. I questioned how I would react to personal and political attacks when they came. Would I hold grudges too long, or be able to work with those who politically ambushed me? What if they were friends of some sort?

Could I hold my temper? Could I work with those who didn't like me politically or otherwise? I did not let those questions hold me back, and I ultimately figured out how to cope with all kinds of attacks and other adversities.

The campaign was exciting, attracted a lot of attention, and seemed to go on forever. In the first primary election, the top vote getter was Dick Stanier who, as I mentioned, had the support of the local newspaper. I was a close second, and Constable Durden's son was the low man on the political totem pole. Then, in the runoff, I emerged the winner. In retrospect I can say that

I am glad the primary election provided for a runoff between the first- and second-place finishers, because I came in second. If the rules then had been what they are today, in which the one with the most votes wins even if he or she doesn't have a majority of the votes cast, my political career would have ended right there.

## An Office Worth Having

It would not be hyperbole to say that the Office of State Representative was an important one and, in many ways, it was more important in 1956 than it is today. In the first place, there were 95 representatives then as compared to 120 today. The weakness of the Governor's Office was an additional reason that legislative positions were considered to be so critical, but perhaps the most significant factor was that Home Rule had not come to the counties of Florida.

Home Rule is the name given to a dynamic in which the county governance apparatus is vested with the power to make most of the relevant decisions at the local level without legislative approval. Historically, counties were extensions of the Florida Legislature, and as such had only those powers granted to them by the legislature. Human nature being what it is, those with the power tended to guard it with a vengeance. The Florida Constitution at that time did not authorize counties to have charters that contained even a small measure of delegated power.

In 1957, sixty-six of the sixty-seven Florida counties did not have charters or Home Rule powers because the legislature was unwilling to relinquish its control of local politics. The only county with a charter and Home Rule powers was Dade County, because it had been successful in putting a constitutional amendment on the ballot to let the people throughout the state decide whether a county should have that power. The amendment authorizing a charter for Dade received a favorable vote in 1956, and the charter itself was approved by Dade County voters in May 1957.

That cumbersome process of amending the constitution every time a county wanted to try the new way is no longer necessary, because the 1968 constitution granted Home Rule to all counties and provided the authority for each of them to have a charter without a statewide vote.

It is interesting to note that from their inception, Florida's cities—also known as municipal corporations—were chartered, and the charters authorized a measure of Home Rule. Cities were in an advantageous position compared to counties, and their autonomy made them stronger and more effective, even though the grants of power to the cities were limited in various ways. First, the legislature limited the power of cities by reserving the right to amend or completely revoke all charters. Statutes were created that in one way or another narrowed the scope of granted power. And finally, the charters themselves had restraints on powers written right in them.

When a group got together to form a new city, they typically found the legislature unwilling to grant absolute Home Rule. A compromise had to be reached or the bill containing the charter would die from legislative abandonment. Nevertheless, it was said that the cities had Home Rule.

The legislative delegations from most counties in 1956 had complete control over county government until the 1968 constitution became effective in 1969. The delegates exercised this power in such things as fixing the amount of compensation paid to county commissioners and paying salary supplements to circuit judges. The delegations even had the power to establish new courts in their counties. County commissioners could not name roads or bridges and had to go, hat in hand, to the legislators for permission to honor someone in that way. Those legislative positions were coveted by up-and-coming politicians because, for one thing, they were so critical to the operation of local governments.

## Unfair Legislative Apportionment

Another unfair situation was that on a statewide basis the legislative representation was not fairly apportioned. The Florida Constitution provided for periodic reapportionment but paid lip service to the notion of a fair distribution of legislative power. Since reapportionment was strictly a legislative function, there was no way to force appropriate action as long as the courts did not intervene. There were those of us who saw the need to correct the distribution of power, but we were in the minority, and, therefore, impotent. It was not a good situation.

The reapportionment issue was a combination of a fight for power on the one hand and the economics of politics on the other. In 1957, Florida's constitution authorized thirty-six senators and ninety-five representatives. They had previously been apportioned in a manner calculated to vest actual control in the small counties—that is to say, the counties with small populations. Each senator represented a single-member district, and the constitutional mandate that all districts be as nearly equal in population as practicable was all but ignored.

The representational inequity of that time is well illustrated in the comparison of Jefferson County in north Florida, which had a population of about 9,000, and Dade County in south Florida which had around 900,000 residents. However, each county was a senatorial district and each had one senator. That made Jefferson County's vote in the Senate equal to Dade's. (A factor that tempered the effects of this particular mal apportionment was that the senator from Jefferson County was Dill Clark, an elderly, beloved, strong man who wielded his significant power wisely.)

The House of Representatives was nearly as badly apportioned. The ninety-five representatives were disbursed among the sixty-seven counties in a way that also vested control in the sparsely populated counties. The five counties with the greatest population had three representatives each, the next sixteen largest had two representatives, and all other counties had one each. Liberty County, for example, with only about 3,000 residents, had its own state representative—or one representative for 3,000 residents—while Dade, with its 900,000 people and three representatives, had one representative per 300,000 residents. Liberty County had nearly 100 times more voting strength than Dade.

Representatives of the small counties enjoyed this control and intended to keep it. They did not hesitate to use whatever means were available to retain their position of power. Fear of political retaliation for any act of disloyalty was always a factor. Good fellowship and seemingly solid, everlasting friendships were at the opposite end of the persuasion methods used by the leaders of the small counties. In this way, the leaders insured continuation of their conservative agenda.

These tactics were not for the exclusive use of the small counties, of course, and almost all legislators used them to some degree. However, the small county members and many of their leaders were highly skilled in these tactics and used them regularly and effectively.

Money was another major incentive for keeping power. Those small counties greatly benefited from a state law that required tax money from gambling facilities in the large counties to be distributed in an equal amount to each of the sixty-seven counties. As a result, the delegates of small counties stuck together to protect that precious stream of revenue which helped keep property taxes low.

Governor Collins was a strong advocate of fair apportionment. He kept the legislature in special session for the better part of a year between the 1955 and 1957 general sessions in an effort to force legislative leaders to take appropriate action, but that strategy did not work. Since the courts had not yet intervened, the issue continued to fester and present an ongoing problem.

## Continuity of Legislative Service Led to Control

It was self evident that control of the legislative branch of state government was worth the enormous time and talent required to attain it. Political dominance could be acquired and retained by the smaller counties if they were willing to work for it and then guard it with their political lives. One way they were able to gather and hold on to power was through continuity of service by their legislators, which gave them seniority and superior institutional memories. That was a small price to pay for control, which is always an advantage. They had no intention of giving it away.

In north Florida, where there are many rural, sparsely populated counties, the urge for preservation of representational control was particularly strong. There were many stories to illustrate that point, but the one that always grabbed attention was the old saying I recounted at the beginning of this book about the way baby boys were tested to see whether they had an interest in politics. There was a lot of truth to that message.

## Getting an Early Start

Following the 1956 primaries, when we were certified as the official nominees of the Democratic Party, political folks began treating us as though we were already elected and in office. I thought it was a bit premature because it was still six months before the general election, at the end of which we would be considered officially elected. I had a Republican opponent to face in November, as did several others. Nevertheless, we just went along with the fiction. It was a busy time as we transitioned into public life. There were three events that took place between May and the November general election that deserve to be mentioned.

## Special Session on Race Strategy

The first was a special session called by the governor to develop a strategy for Florida's reaction to the U.S. Supreme Court's opinion in *Brown v. Board of Education*, handed down in May 1955. That historic opinion struck down the longstanding plan for the nation's school systems that operated on the theory of "separate but equal facilities" for minority students.

Governor Collins refused to adopt a hard line, anti-integration position for the state, but he was aware of the intense feelings of the many folks who were opposed to integration, so he went only as far toward immediate integration as was politically possible. It was in that environment that he appointed a blue-ribbon committee with the mission of developing a plan to delay and obstruct the mandated integration of public schools. Any proposal would have to be crafted to pass the test of constitutionality. And, if it was to have any chance of achieving its goals, it would have to be led by someone with the credentials of a skillful, knowledgeable, and believable public person with a moderate philosophy. Such an individual was retired Circuit Judge L. L. Fabisinski of Pensacola, who had distinguished himself during his active years on the bench. The group he chaired quickly became known as the Fabisinski Committee.

In the summer of 1956, when the prospective members of the 57 Club were nominees for thirty-nine seats in the House of Representatives but not yet elected, the incumbent legislature was called into special session to receive and react to the committee's report and recommendations.

Attendance at a special session could be required by the governor through unilateral action on his part. The President of the Senate and the Speaker of the House, acting together, also had the power to call legislators into session. Of course, the members had residual power to call themselves together, but that was such a cumbersome procedure that it was seldom used.

The special session would be a meeting of a lame-duck legislature, and it appeared likely to make decisions that would bind us as we worked through racial issues in the future. We were told that attending the session as observers would give us a chance to see how their decisions might affect our duties, and help us get up to speed on the racial dispute. One of the issues we would be facing as soon as we were elected was how we could accommodate to some extent the advocates of integration without provoking everyone else or encouraging the use of force.

I attended the session, and it was an eye opener. I developed fundamental knowledge of the way legislative business was conducted. I also learned the pros and cons of the racial issues, and I could feel the tension that the issues of racial integration generated.

The essence of the committee's recommendations was that the state should develop a plan that would, at the very least, slow the integration movement by assigning pupils to available schools based on subjective criteria. The hope was that those who objected to integration would not be assigned to an integrated facility, while at the same time it could be said that the state was in compliance with the "Law of the Land."

Moderate leaders felt that such a compromise was as far as we needed to go, but that conclusion was not satisfactory to legislators with a more conservative point of view. They could not rest until they passed a bill or bills that reflected the heat and passion they felt about the possibility of black and white children being together in schools. Accordingly, after the special session, they prepared major bills to be considered when the legislature convened again.

## The Courage of Jack Orr

Those of us who attended the special session were also treated to personal and unexpected lessons in subjects related to the political environment and the meaning of the term "political courage."

The best example of political courage came from Jack Orr, representing Dade County. He received permission to speak from the chamber's lectern, known as the "Well," and spoke eloquently about the reports which recommended, among other things, a pupil assignment law.

Orr announced that he had written his remarks and would read them. He said that they would constitute the explanation of his vote and that he was doing so because the subject matter was so delicate. But I always believed that there was a different reason that Orr read his statement that day. Here's why: Members' remarks made in debate were not published in the House Journal. That decision had been made previous to the special session because of the enormous volume of talk in routine debates. Also, any observer could notice the repetition that occurred in every major debate. The cost of recording and printing those volumes of statements was deemed to be excessive, given the benefits to be expected. Stated another and more direct way: it just wasn't worth it.

Although there was a way to have a particular speech or set of remarks published verbatim in the Journal, it required unanimous consent of all members present. Because any one member could prevent the printing, it was unpredictable and could not be planned with any degree of confidence. Therefore, this method was seldom used.

However, the rule with respect to an explanation of a vote was quite different. Each member needed a way to explain his vote on any given issue, and there was sympathy for an elected representative who had

Jack Orr demonstrated great political courage.

to cast a vote that could be misinterpreted and used against him. Therefore, the rule provided that any member who wished to explain his vote could do so by writing the explanation and handing it to the clerk within a specified time, and the statement would be printed verbatim in the Journal with the overall vote of the House on the bill.

Today, Orr's remarks can be found in the House Journal in the form he delivered them, but they are labeled as his explanation of his vote. Had he not written and filed them as he did, there would probably be no official record of what he said that day.

Jack Orr stunned everyone when he boldly announced that he would be voting against the proposals because he believed segregation was morally wrong and that the state should not engage in such delaying tactics. Among other things, he said:

> First, I favor the gradual integration of our public school system. In view of the fact that our custom of segregation is one of long standing, I realize that this cannot be changed overnight as the consequence of governmental edict, but I do not understand the decision of the Supreme Court of the United States to require that abrupt a change. I believe, moreover, that had we devoted as much energy, time, and talent to discovering means to live under the law instead of in defiance of it, we could have discovered a way.
>
> I believe segregation is morally wrong. The existence of second-class citizens is repugnant to our great democratic principles.
>
> I predict that none of the measures passed or proposed will accomplish the result you seek. Despite the clever language employed, the Supreme Court will surely see through the Fabisinski Committee bills and will strike them down.
>
> When we finally have to face up to this problem, and we surely will be required to, I hope that God gives us the wisdom and strength to conquer prejudice and bigotry and to renew our faith in our Constitution.
>
> Meantime, I will take solace in the prayer our chaplain delivered last Tuesday: "Help us, thus, to see that it is better to fail in a just cause that will ultimately succeed, than to succeed in an unrighteous cause that will ultimately fail."

Jack Orr stood alone that day. His was the sole vote against the pupil assignment proposal and other segregation bills. The next time he ran for re-election, he was soundly defeated.

A copy of his eloquent remarks is included in the Appendix because of the importance of what he had to say, and so that more than fifty years later, one can judge whether his remarks would cause such a stir today.

Jack Orr's integrity and eloquence set the tone for those of us at the threshold of legislative service. Frankly, it was an inspiration to many of us and helped us find our own courage when the emotionally charged issue of race relations forced many of us into situations similar to the one he had faced.

## The Party Caucus

The second important happening while we were still nominees in 1956 was the receipt of an invitation to a weekend party in St. Augustine. It was referred to as the Democratic Party Caucus to make it official. Those in the know advised us to go. I went.

It was truly a nice affair. The old-but-elegant Ponce de Leon Hotel provided us with an impressive ambience. My home was just fifty miles or so to the south, but I had never been inside that grand hotel built by Henry Flagler. The setting was outstanding, as were the food and drinks, and all the trimmings.

It was a chance to meet and begin relationships with those with whom we would be working. Governor Collins was there, fresh from the election victory where he had won a full four-year term. Members of the Florida Cabinet were at the caucus as well. In those days, the Florida Cabinet consisted of the Secretary of State, Attorney General, Commissioner of Education, Comptroller, Treasurer, and Commissioner of Agriculture. They were each elected statewide with no term limits, and they shared the executive power with the Governor of Florida. They were important and powerful.

The President of the Senate and a few of his leaders attended. They were members of the "Pork Chop Gang," a group of about fifteen seasoned politicians who ran the Senate. And, of course, the leaders of the House were there. They were the official hosts.

The caucus was an introduction to power in that it was a taste of what was in store for the future. Being guests of honor at such an affair and being treated as though we were important was good for the morale of most of us who were on our first political venture. On the other hand, the meeting was designed as a lesson in protocol and the rules of the game, including the discipline expected. Those rules and expectations were dressed up as fellowship, loyalty, and tradition, but there was no room for doubt about the existence of control or who was holding the reins.

Robert T. (Bob) Mann of Hillsborough County was a first-term representative. Yet he made himself known to all of those in attendance at that caucus of Democrats by injecting himself into proceedings which had been carefully scripted. Leaders knew who would be speaking, what they would say, and the order in which the speakers would appear. Above all else, there were to be no surprises. The meeting was for the orientation of the newest kids on the block and nothing else.

Bob changed their plans. He took issue with a resolution that would appropriate funds in a manner he felt was unethical. Surprise, then shock, and finally outrage were the unscripted reactions to the young upstart's comments. Then it was over, but we all knew Bob Mann.

If a lesser man had committed that mortal sin of protocol, he may have suffered permanent political damage. Not so for Bob. He was very bright and very well educated. His debating skills were outstanding. I don't believe anyone in the House ever got the better of him in debate.

The caucus was a success in spite of Bob's intrusion. Everyone had a good time and got their political lives off to a fast start. The lobbyists who attended were discrete and did not give the appearance of being in charge. We were never told who paid the enormous bill for our rooms, food, and all the rest.

## A Test by Lobbyists

The third event worth noting in that summer of 1956 was a test by lobbyists. I didn't recognize it as a test at the time, but later on when I looked back and thought about all that happened, I realized that what I experienced was undoubtedly a part of the lobbying strategy in which lobbyists needed to know as much as possible about each legislative member. The test was not as formal or structured as one might think it was based on my description, nor was it the only such appraisal and evaluation to which I was subjected. It does, however, illustrate just how thorough and subtle a process the test was.

After the Democratic primary, I was back in the firm practicing law. One day I had a visit from a person who told me he worked for a company interested in the laws regulating so-called small loans. Those loans were exempt from usury laws and could bear interest at more than 20 percent.

My visitor was subtle and explained that he knew of the good reputation both my firm and I had for high quality law work. His company needed such legal service and was willing to pay a monthly retainer for my availability. I would be paid whether I was asked to do something or not.

I declined. No doubt word of that meeting was shared and added to other data. I was never approached again, nor was I invited to some of the ongoing hospitality facilities where lobbyists provided free food and drinks. The "price" a guest paid was having to listen to the lobbyist's point of view, while feeling a bit indebted. I feel certain that I was passed over for other perquisites as well.

Bob Mann took legislative leaders by surprise. (Photo courtesy Florida Archives.)

As strange as it seems when reviewed today, retainers of the type offered to me were not considered bribery. There was a different standard in the '50s and before. For example, a legislator named Roy Surles of Polk County was general counsel to a company that sold Green Stamps to retail merchants. The stamps, popular at that time, were given to customers who could redeem them to buy small items. Surles not only represented the company, but at the same time was also involved in their affairs as a legislator.

My colleague from Volusia County, Jim Sweeny, a respected representative and chairman of the House Finance and Taxation Committee, was openly very close to Florida Power and Light Company, the largest electric utility in the state. He frequently flew in the company's airplane and spent much of his free time in the company of a Florida Power and Light officer. Neither of those situations would be acceptable today, but in 1957 it was commonplace. However, it should be noted that about the time of the 57 Club, the tide began to turn. LeRoy Collins talked of an ethics code and of outlawing conflicts of interest.

Many of us lived by a higher standard of ethics than was required and began agitating for openness in government and disclosure of conflicts. By the time the 1968 constitution was offered to the people, everyone—with the possible exception of a few who were still on retainers of some sort—was ready for the new way.

And so it was that the thirty-nine young men would be forever linked to one another by the 57 Club.

## 2 *Club Members and Others* ─────────

That old saying in north Florida about putting baby boys on the floor to see if they are interested enough in politics to crawl toward the state capital was not that far from the truth in the '50s and '60s. It was a pretty fair indication of how serious the rural part of Florida was about maintaining control of state politics.

### Dempsey Barron, Master Politician

Dempsey Barron of Panama City surely crawled toward Tallahassee, because when he arrived at the state capital in 1957, newly elected to the Florida House of Representatives, he was already a master politician. He was also instantly popular, so the other freshman representatives elected him chairman of the newly formed group called the 57 Club.

Dempsey Barron displayed his political skills at the St. Augustine caucus. He worked the crowd like a pro. Consequently, it was no surprise when he was elected to lead our club. He enjoyed legislative service from the first day, and he stayed in it longer than any other Club member.

Those of us who lived south of Florida's Panhandle referred to that part of the state as north Florida. Dempsey was from Bay County, which aligned with the sparsely populated counties that formed what was informally known as the Small County Bloc. Almost everyone living in one of the small counties seemed to be interested in—and to understand—what was going on in the legislature. They had a commonality of interests and institutional memories which helped make them politically strong.

Dempsey Barron fit right into that political environment. He knew his constituents and just how far they would go with him. He certainly was not a liberal, but neither was he an extreme conservative. He opposed some of the anti-integration bills and supported education funding as well as a few social programs. And yet, when Barron was a leader in the Senate during the 1970s, he almost single-handedly prevented Florida from ratifying the Equal Rights Amendment.

Anyone who visited Dempsey's Senate office during his later years will remember seeing a sign on his desk. It was a blunt caveat in a brief but telling message about him: "Assume Nothing."

He was an excellent debater who knew how to use humor to make an important point. He could make us laugh as he told a tale about trying to force a pill down the throat of a cow and how she bit his hand. And, when a member offered an amendment that was incompatible with a bill, or if a political situation caused the proverbial strange bedfellow syndrome, he was likely to explain that the mismatches were like trying to mix sugar and manure: It did nothing for the manure, but it absolutely ruined the sugar.

Dempsey Barron surely "crawled toward the capital." (Photo courtesy Florida Archives.)

Then there was the time Dempsey arranged a party in my honor. He invited a select group of our mutual friends to have dinner at Tallahassee's well-known Silver Slipper Restaurant, and he acted as master of ceremonies all evening. The climax was a made-up story he told about me. He used his best speaking technique and skillfully demonstrated what he was describing.

According to Dempsey's tale, I went to a clothing store to buy a new suit. The manager was a great salesman, so when he couldn't find a suit that fit me he proceeded to convince me to buy one that didn't fit. He did that by having me reach around the back of my neck and awkwardly hold a wad of coat and then gather the waist of the pants with my other hand so they would stay up.

He continued with other adjustments that required me to bend over, use my elbows, and keep my knees bent and together.

Dempsey proceeded to demonstrate each of these ridiculous movements and ended up all bent over and hunched up in an unbelievable position that made it barely possible for him to walk by shuffling along. He then explained how I left the store in that posture, trying to walk along the sidewalk, when I came upon a couple walking in the opposite direction. The woman whispered to her husband, "Look at that poor, crippled man, isn't he pitiful?" The husband replied with a sigh, "Yes, but don't his clothes fit nice?"

In terms of credentials, Dempsey Barron was a pretty typical freshman representative in 1957 in that he was a veteran of World War II who received his education, including law school, under the GI Bill of Rights. He was married and had a young family.

Ultimately, he was elected Senate president and received just about every honor awarded to a senator by those who watch legislators in action.

Dempsey was an attorney, a rancher, a Democrat, and later a Republican. But those who knew him believed that his first and best love was the Florida Legislature. His county was large enough to have two representatives, and the people who elected them approved of their legislators' aligning themselves with the small counties. It was a typical Panhandle county.

Every politician who wants to stay in office must know his constituency. How does one get to know what the people he serves would want him to do and what margin of deviation they will tolerate? There is no easy answer. The elected official must have that certain sensitivity that allows him to "feel" the attitude of his people. On a handshaking afternoon he will pick up the signals, because, as every politician knows, a special relationship develops between the shaker and the shakee.

Then there is the mail. The collective letters and telegrams (now e-mail messages) give off a telltale aroma that delivers the message about a community's attitude. I am not suggesting that one count the number of messages for and against a given issue, although some did just that when facing a decision on a contentious vote. However, there is no true need to count. The essence of the collective attitude is there for the sampling, and the successful politicians of the 57 Club era knew how to do it. Dempsey was a master at that art. He knew just how far he could go on the issues before him.

It must be admitted that he lost that touch in his later years and was finally defeated after more than thirty years of public service. By the end of Dempsey's time in office, political pollsters had become important in every race, and communication had developed to the point at which the candidate's reading of his constituency did not seem so important. Moreover, Dempsey himself seemed to lose some of his interest and a bit of his old spirit.

However, before that time, and as he matured and gained experience in the legislative halls, Dempsey turned into the genuine "Dean of the Senate." He fished the ponds around Tallahassee with Senators Verle Pope of St. Augustine and Wig Barrow of Crestview. Ultimately, Dempsey became something of a kingmaker. He supported various representatives who aspired to be the Senate president. The candidates he supported usually won, which allowed him to continue to play a major role in the business of the state.

One such person Dempsey supported was W. D. Childers, a bantam rooster of a man from Pensacola. During his term as Senate president, Childers was aware of the fact that he owed Dempsey for the opportunity to preside for the two-year term. Nevertheless, Childers felt that he should establish his independence. Throughout the term, Dempsey kept Childers in a subordinated position. State newspapers had a field day with the Barron/Childers alliance. The notion of Childers' being a "dummy" sitting on Barron's knee and repeat-

I speak to members of the Senate, which included Dempsey Barron (third from right) and W. D. Childers (second from right), who received Dempsey's support for President of the Senate.

Dempsey Barron and I in later years, when we served in the Florida Senate.

ing what Dempsey said soon surfaced and became quite popular. Dempsey defended his power to control W. D., and the entire Senate for that matter.

It was early in that time period when Dempsey had a dispute with governor Reubin Askew. When Askew attempted to lobby senators in opposition to the Senate president's position, Dempsey was offended and reacted angrily. At just the right moment, when Dempsey was presiding and the TV cameras were turned on, he publicly told Governor Askew to "Stay the Hell out of my Senate."

From his first day in the legislature, Dempsey displayed a unique set of skills. He was smart enough to fully comprehend the details of what was going on at all times. He was interested enough in what was happening to persevere and live off of a seemingly endless supply of energy. When others were tired, he was not. He could think on his feet, and his quick wit served him well. He was capable of being a considerate friend, but he could also be as hard as nails with anyone who opposed or otherwise offended him. Dempsey was a natural-born legislator. For that reason, he was the logical person to head the 57 Club.

I considered Dempsey to be a friend. That means, to me, that I knew him to some extent, and that he was not an enemy. I hardly knew his wife or his children. Our conversations were mostly about the main interest we had in common, and that was legislation. We were often on opposite sides of an issue, but occasionally we had the same views on a bill or part of a bill. We each expected that the other would not lie or steal or take an unfair advantage, but not much more was expected. However, over time we came to respect one another on a professional level, and we drifted into a comfortable relationship in which each knew pretty well what the other would do in a given circumstance.

Dempsey never broke a promise to me, nor did he ever ambush me on legislation. If he was against a bill I was managing, he made sure that I knew what he was doing. There were no unpleasant surprises. I treated him the same way. We did not correspond after I left the Senate, but his door was always open to me. I asked him to vote to sustain a veto and he did it—and not just because I asked him to do so. I once went to Panama City at his request to help in his campaign for reelection. We were friends.

Defining Dempsey Barron was never easy. He was part redneck, part politician, part statesman, and part friend. He worked hard and played hard. There were rumors of misconduct, but I never saw evidence that he was breaking the law or violating Florida Bar rules. It truly is hard to define him, but happily, that is not what this is all about.

## Jack Mathews

One member of the 57 Club who understood the legislative environment better than the rest of us and who was always ready to debate a bill was John E. (Jack) Mathews. There were two reasons for the advantages he had. First, he was a constitutional scholar and never stopped studying and researching both the U.S. and the Florida Constitutions. The second reason was that his father had served in the legislature and as a member of the Florida Supreme Court.

Jack grew up in a politically prominent family, where he was exposed to important political people and major issues. He became familiar with and comfortable in the legislative environment, which put him out

Jack Mathews followed in his father's footsteps by serving in the legislature. (Photo courtesy Florida Archives.)

in front of the field of freshmen as we left the starting gate. Representative Buck Vocelle was the only other member of the 57 Club whose father left him such a legacy.

From the beginning of our respective political careers, Jack Mathews and I built similar voting records. Perhaps his was a bit more conservative than mine, which was understandable. One of the other state representatives in Jack's Duval County delegation was a serious advocate of segregation and always outspoken when the racial issue surfaced. Another reason Jack's voting record smacked of conservatism was the known attitude of his constituents. They seemed to have much in common with the citizens of sparsely populated counties. It was said that Duval was the largest small county in Florida.

During debates, Jack and I usually spoke for the same side. There were issues upon which we disagreed, but the disagreements were not drastic. Neither of us tried to secure an advantage at the expense of the other, and although we seldom socialized or spent time together visiting about our respective families or law practices, I felt that I knew Jack quite well and that I could predict what he would do in any competitive situation in which we found ourselves.

Nevertheless, I always felt a bit uneasy when Jack and I were adversaries. I wasn't paranoid about it, but my little voice within would whisper to me once in a while and warn me to remember that legislative friendships were not the same as regular friendships.

I admired Jack's skill when fighting an emotional issue. He always seemed to find some technical defect and focus on that rather than attack the substance. I felt that he was preparing for his political future, where he would meet people with strong views on subjects filled with emotions and would be able to deny his philosophical opposition.

Jack was no coward. He had both the courage and the knowledge to hold his own in almost any situation, but he was no fool either. Why should he take a stand and bring down the wrath of the opponents on an issue if not necessary? I felt that this was the most common approach to controversial issues in both houses of the legislature.

Jack did good work in the House for three two-year terms, then ran for the Senate and won. He was a candidate for governor in 1964, and so was I.

During that race, Jack's campaign people damaged me and my campaign. I was angry and disappointed in Jack, and felt that he knew what his people were doing and condoned it. However, we were competing in a political contest and often, in desperation, the rules of common decency are temporarily suspended. There was nothing I could do except try to control the damage they caused.

I am not a vengeful person in situations like that one, so I put the past behind me and was cordial when the race ended and we were both in the Senate. Jack, as the Senate president, gave me an important assignment and I did it well. He told me how much he appreciated what I had done, and he supported me all the way. We developed a measure of mutual respect, but as mentioned earlier, we never had a social relationship. Jack and I shared some form of professional, legislative friendship.

Regarding the race for governor, Jack and I finished last and next to last in the Democratic primary of 1964. Our friends seemed to think that it would make us feel better about our defeat if they said that the candidates finished the race in inverse order of their competence. It didn't help.

I stayed out of the legislature for four years after that, but Jack held on to his Senate seat. His maturity and experience made him a strong leader and he developed a commendable record. Later, he tried again to be elected governor, but failed.

Sometime thereafter, Jack contracted a rare disease that took his great mind. He died in the Veterans' Hospital in Gainesville.

There are many things that could be said or written in retrospect about Jack Mathews, but they can be summarized in two sentences. First, it is a tragedy that he wasn't elected and allowed to serve as governor—he would have been a good one. Second, it was also a tragedy that he died so early and deprived the people of Florida of the benefits of his wonderful mind.

## A. J. Ryan

I was never able to get to know A. J. Ryan very well, and that is one of my great regrets. He was a 57 Clubber, having been elected in 1956 in Broward County. We served together in the House for eight years and I had contact with him during the days, but we were seldom at the same after-hours events.

We had a friend in common whose name was Jack Peoples. Jack was close to Governor Collins and had lobbied for him at one time. Collins appointed Jack to head the State Beverage Department, and he represented that agency before the legislative committees. For those reasons we saw Jack quite often, and he always wanted A. J. and I to work together, particularly on matters that were of interest to Governor Collins. We did that—not just because of Jack, but because we both respected the governor and wanted to be a part of what he was doing for Florida.

When we worked together we were very much in harmony, and I found A. J. to be interesting and impressive. He supported me wholeheartedly when

I ran for governor, and later requested me as a character witness when he was being investigated for failure to file his federal income tax returns, which I willingly did for him. I felt certain that A. J. was not trying to defraud the government when he failed to file his tax return, and that is what I said when I testified. Actually, I characterized him as a young, absent-minded professor who, because he was so bright, took short cuts and occasionally lost his way. I speculated that he had nothing to hide from the IRS and that he was not impoverished. He had intended to file, but procrastinated instead.

A. J. Ryan was notable for his infectious laugh. (Photo courtesy Florida Archives.)

Incidentally, the IRS didn't think much of my theory of why A. J. hadn't filed his tax returns. He was sentenced to ten days in jail. That was bad and very painful, but it could have been much worse.

Ultimately, both of us suffered from Parkinson's, that insidious disease which, once contracted, progresses inexorably throughout the remainder of one's life.

I knew A. J. was smart. I could tell that from his debates and from the conversations we had. My conclusions about his intelligence were reinforced by Jack Peoples, who told me that A. J. had gone all the way through law school without ever purchasing a textbook or casebook. A. J. was able to pay attention to the classroom lectures, and with a little review of what he heard he could pass the tests. Actually, he did better than that, as he finished second in his class.

As I mentioned previously, we never developed a deep and lasting friendship. What we had was similar to the relationships that arise in combat during a war. Two people can fight side by side, rely on each other, and have the deepest respect for one another, but when the fighting stops, each goes his own way and there is no lasting bond beyond the one formed while the shooting is going on.

A. J. was full of stories, and he laughed out loud at his own jokes. He had an infectious laugh that was loud and heartwarming. His personality made him easy to like. He was popular, and everyone was eager to hear his stories, like the one about an old man who he knew quite well.

As the story went, the old man met him one day with a prolonged sigh and said, "God I'm depressed." A. J. asked him why he felt so down and he answered, "Well I'm retired, you know, and very comfortable money wise. I live in a beautiful home in a fine section of town. I married a younger and very beautiful woman, and she truly loves me very much." A. J. stopped him and said, "If you have all of that, how could you possibly be sad?" With another pitiful sigh, he said, "I can't remember where I live."

## A Few Who Came Before '57

Every two years there is a general election, and all members of the House must run or get out. Thus, new faces appear every two years. Typically, there are fewer than there were in 1957, when thirty-nine newcomers showed up in Tallahassee. At that time, many incumbents were tired out from the endless responsibility of trying to fairly reapportion the legislature. However, the turnover is high in any given year. Some are defeated, some quit, and occasionally someone dies in office. The few fatalities are usually explained by legislature watchers with the old saying, "Only the good die young."

When we in the 57 Club joined the House, there were fifty-six survivors already there. They had been elected at least one session before us, and had been through at least one reelection. There were some outstanding people among the fifty-six, and in many ways they helped us. We won't belabor the subject, but to understand what life in the Florida Legislature was all about, and to have some feel for how it functioned at the time, we should take a look at a few of the people who joined the legislative family shortly before the 57 Club was formed.

## Doyle Conner

By the time we arrived, Doyle Conner had already been selected to be Speaker of the House for the 1957 session. That was interesting because those of us who came in for the '57 session were destined to serve two years under his leadership, but we had practically no voice in his election.

That would not matter much if the Office of Speaker was not so important, but it was—and still remains—a very important position. Not only was the speaker second in line, behind the Senate president, to be governor if a vacancy occurred (unlike today, in 1957 there was no lieutenant governor), but also the speaker had nearly total control of committee assignments and all bills introduced. With that kind of power and influence, the speaker could politically make or break any member of the House.

It is true that a vote was taken on Doyle's selection when we met in caucus in St. Augustine, but that was just a ministerial act. We understood that Doyle had enough pledges in his pocket to elect him at that time. We also confirmed him when the House was being organized following the general election. But, here again, the selection was already locked in. Our vote was a mere formality.

We met Doyle at the caucus, and he attended the special session, of course, but it took a while to get to know him well enough to be comfortable under his leadership. He was very young. It was said that he was the youngest person ever to be speaker. I could empathize with him about the problems his youth generated, because a few years earlier, during my service in World War II, I went through Officer Candidate School and became a commissioned officer when I was only eighteen years old. Every man in my tank platoon was older than I was. It took a special kind of leadership to induce older men to follow me into battle, so I could understand his problems in leading older people through the legislative experience.

Doyle's home was in Starke, a small town in sparsely populated Bradford County in the northern part of the state. As a young student he was active in youth programs related to agriculture. He was the national president of the Future Farmers of America, which stands as early proof of his ability, his likeable personality, and his political skill. He was elected to the House just after attaining the minimum age for membership. Even though he was younger than most of his fellow members, Doyle soon became a leader of that group. He was still in his early twenties when he was elected speaker.

Doyle was an excellent speaker of the House, and when his duties were finished, he ran for and won the cabinet office of commissioner of agriculture. That office was his apparent goal in political life, for he stayed there until retirement. Thereafter, he concentrated on his farm in Leon County.

One could not properly refer to our relationship as a friendship. It was an acquaintanceship. We had practically nothing in common, and neither reached out to the other in an effort to develop a friendship. There were no ambushes, betrayals, or deliberate offenses perpetrated against the other. It appeared that we each respected the ability of the other.

Doyle would have made a wonderful member of the 57 Club, if only he had been eligible.


## Election of Future Speaker

After we had been nominated, but before the general election of 1956, we were all approached by various veteran legislators seeking our pledge of support for one of the candidates for the Office of Speaker to succeed Doyle Conner and preside in 1959. It seemed awfully early to ask the members to commit. After all, we had just finished the formalities to put Doyle Conner in the seat for 1957, and here we were starting the process all over again for the session that was two years away. Our mild protests failed to move anyone in a leadership position, so the process continued.

The race for speaker had boiled down to a contest between representative Tom Beasley from DeFuniak Springs in Walton County—the candidate of the small county group—and Sam Gibbons of Tampa, who was supported by representatives of the larger counties. The experienced members were very patient with the newcomers as they tried to persuade us to vote for whichever candidate they were working to install as the speaker. Any doubt about the importance of the position was dispelled by the diligence and intensity of the supporters.

Representative Jim Sweeny, my colleague from Volusia, was asked to talk to me. It was a low-key discussion, but Jim used all the ammunition he had. I guess his strongest argument was that Tom Beasley would probably win, and it would be in my best interest as a new member to be with the winner. Certainly that would be better than being pegged as an opponent of the speaker, he argued.

I was also approached by the other side. They told me all about Sam Gibbons, including his war record, his strong stand for fair apportionment, and other significant issues. They also stressed the need to stick together and make a powerful showing by those of us who believed that the right things to do were to avoid a radical position in racial matters, improve education, advocate fiscal responsibility, and support fair apportionment. I was more comfortable with Sam and his supporters than with the Beasley people, so I made my pledge to the Gibbons side. But just as Jim Sweeny had predicted, Tom Beasley won.

## Sam Gibbons

I found Sam Gibbons to be particularly interesting. I learned early on that he truly was a World War II hero. He had been a paratrooper and had jumped into Normandy in the darkness the night before the Allied invasion of Europe in 1944.

Jumping out of an airplane into enemy territory was enough to qualify one as a hero, but U.S. paratroopers in Normandy also had to try to locate one another and then attack enemy installations to weaken resistance to the invasion. If the invasion was delayed, or if it failed, they were on their own in what would have to be described as a life-threatening situation. Sam survived that ordeal and was still serving, but in a different and less dangerous capacity.

Sam soon ran for the Florida Senate and won. A few years later he won a seat in Congress and served there with distinction until he retired. His entire record of public service is a good one, and he accomplished a great deal during his work in the Florida Legislature and U.S. Congress.

I was impressed by Sam's accomplishments with respect to local government. He consolidated several municipalities into the City of Tampa, which was very progressive. It was also politically dangerous. Generally speaking, people abhor change and tend to resent disturbances to the status quo. Moreover, I was always a little surprised at the intense feelings about bills that only applied in one county, especially when they related to matters changing or establishing boundary lines.

Sam Gibbons' public service included the Florida Legislature and the U.S. House of Representatives. (Photo courtesy Florida Archives.)

Sam also passed enabling legislation for a massive urban renewal program that resulted in the elimination of slum-like areas along the river in downtown Tampa. He felt confident that the time would soon come when people would demand the right to see and use the public waterway. I was so impressed with his urban renewal bill that I had similar legislation prepared for Daytona Beach, and I introduced and passed it. I hasten to add that I had Sam's permission to copy his work product.

There were no overt, adverse effects from my decision to support Sam Gibbons. However, there is no way of knowing what might have been if I had started my legislative tenure by joining the Small County Bloc and pledging my support for the people and issues supported by them. It is possible that I could have received advice, counsel, and meaningful support for myself and my causes.

There have been times since 1957 when my mind has ventured close to the threshold of that speculation trap, but it always stops short and never actually goes there. I have no regrets about the path I took. I did pretty well considering that I was on the minority side, so as usual, I tend not to dwell on things that might have been. However, this is a special, once-in-a-lifetime situation, and perhaps I have been waiting for this opportunity to step across that traditional boundary of mine.

## What If . . . ?

What if I had decided to join with the representatives of the small counties? Was there a place for me in that group? Would it have been helpful to me in achieving my political goals? Would the county I represented have fared better?

It is probably reasonable to say there would have been certain advantages for me in my political life had I joined them. They were in control of the legislative branch and politically strong in every county, but especially strong in the counties they represented. They had the reputation of taking care of their own. Actually, the small counties constituted an effective political organization.

I think it safe to assume that if I had joined them and they had accepted me, I would have had the support of a fine-tuned political machine. Belonging to that group meant generous campaign funding and other helpful assistance. Acting governor Charley Johns had support from the small counties yet lost the governor's race to LeRoy Collins in 1954, so they were not invincible. However, Farris Bryant later won the post by beating Doyle Carlton Jr. in 1960, and a big factor in that race was the help he received from the small county organization.

My membership in the small county group could very well have enhanced my political fortunes. Moreover, if I lost the one race—as I did in reality—those veteran politicians would have made it easier for me to run again, or ride again the horse that threw me. Yes, those were some of the positive aspects of the issue, but all of that begs the question as to whether I could have afforded the cost of joining the Small County Bloc.

That bloc could not be effective unless there was solidarity in the ranks of the small counties. Discipline was absolutely necessary. When the leaders agreed to support a person or an issue, they had to deliver on the promise or suffer the loss of credibility. No doubt this is the juncture at which the leaders would have asked me to disembark. I put a high value on my independence, which would have made it hard for me to vote "right" whenever the leaders needed my support. Not even in my wildest dreams could I have voted contrary to my beliefs. I am convinced that I could not have maintained a personal, mutually beneficial membership. Most likely I would have been cast out the first time a vote was taken and I broke ranks because I couldn't vote "right."

There is another interesting question that has never been answered to my satisfaction, and that is: How was Farris Bryant able to maintain his position with the small counties, advocate the small county agenda, and enjoy their effective support in his statewide race that led to the Governor's Office? Did he really believe in the positions that he took, or was it all political expediency?

I did not know Farris well enough to judge him on his loyalty to his beliefs. I knew him by reputation before his political prominence, and watched him as he entered the political arena, but I cannot say with any confidence what he believed with respect to the pending racial issues or any other major set of issues.

When I first became aware of Farris I had the impression that he was a moderate in racial matters and conservative in fiscal issues. There was nothing in what I saw or heard about him that gave me any warning that he would take the lead in the passage of an infamous resolution interposing state rights. I tend to give everyone the benefit of the doubt, so I assumed that I just didn't know him very well, and that he believed in the righteousness of the positions he took. If I was correct in my conclusions, there was really no mystery as to how he worked so well with the small county people: he was one of them. I am comfortable with that finding, and it reinforces the notion that I could never have made it in the bloc. My political philosophy was different from theirs, and I couldn't vote with them and repudiate my established set of beliefs.

There were several issues that provided justification for working so hard to have solidarity in the group. The tax issue was important to the less populated counties because they each received the same amount of money from certain gambling taxes as every other county. That political prize was always at risk and had to be guarded by a strong and dedicated alliance of small counties. My county would have been better served by a more equitable distribution, so promising to fight to retain the equal share plan would have pitted me against my own constituents.

Control of the legislature meant control of such entities as the Appropriations Committee. If a county was not paying in taxes as much as it was receiving from the state in benefits, it was important to have the Appropriations Committee on its side to protect these benefits. Here, again, my county was not paying less than it received, and Volusia County had no need to exert special control over the committee. Of course, it was necessary to protect the small counties from new taxes that would adversely affect them.

Then there were the more subtle issues like influence with respect to where improvements would be placed. Highway patrol stations, state hospitals, prisons, new state buildings, roads, bridges, parks, and much more were important to those small counties, and the leaders of the bloc had a lot to say about where they were placed and what priority they received. Having a measure of that influence would have been somewhat beneficial, but in truth, my county was large enough and it had enough revenue to meet its needs, so having access to such influence was not an economic necessity.

Furthermore, it goes without saying that the pure appetite for power was an effective driving force. I would probably have been expelled from the bloc the first time I challenged the fairness of one or more of the protective devices enacted for the benefit of members of the bloc or their interests.

As was my habit, I watched the entire operation of the legislature and developed the notion that the most powerful lobbyists seemed to be very influential with leaders of the bloc. I was never aware of any specific misconduct, but there was always an underlying suspicion among the large county representatives and certain members of the media that something unsavory was going on. I was not all that suspicious or cynical, so I didn't go around suggesting that all was not well. I didn't like the idea that everyone who belonged to the small county group was painted with the same brush of suspicion. I had friends in the group, and I joined with them in resenting the rumors. Had I been a member I would have been sensitive about that situation. Wherever I was standing, I made a concerted effort to separate myself from any suspicious activity.

I believed at the time of the 57 Club that my attitude toward racial integration would have been a deal breaker and locked me out of the bloc. Perhaps it would have, but events since then tend to persuade me that the leaders of the bloc might have tolerated more of my ideas than I thought. A group of bloc members offered to support me for Speaker of the House, and they did so with full knowledge of my advocacy record. I was able to develop cordial relationships with individual members like George Anderson, Jim Sweeny, and Tom Beasley.

It must be noted here, however, that I was not so sanctimonious or so sure of myself that I publicly avoided those who took routes different than mine. A few in the large county camp avoided those who joined the bloc because they felt that their own positions represented the only valid set of beliefs. Most of the small county people believed that the interests of their respective counties would be best served by following the bloc, particularly when they perceived the bloc's legislative positions as bona fide and best for the state. In my way of thinking, both positions warranted fair consideration.

The obvious conclusion is that I might have fared better in my political ventures had I joined the small county representatives. I can't go back to do so, and even if I could go back I wouldn't do anything differently. I did what I thought was best, all things considered, and I would do the same again.

## Mallory Horne

Another member of the House who was there when the 57 Clubbers arrived and who immediately caught our attention was Mallory Horne. He was destined to become speaker of the House and, in due course, the president of the Senate. Horne was outgoing and friendly, and because he represented Leon County—the home of the state capital—he assumed the role of host. We were living in his district for the sixty-day session, and he made us all very com-

Mallory Horne served as Speaker of the House and later as president of the Senate.

fortable. His concern for every one of us seemed genuine. He worked hard at helping us with housing problems. He was always available to answer questions about places that served food or sold clothing, or anything else that we needed or wanted.

We soon learned that Horne had been a military pilot during the war, and that he was good at that, too. He kept a small airplane at the municipal airport in Tallahassee, which he used in connection with his law practice as well as for pleasure.

Mallory was close to the small counties, and he regularly voted with them. I always assumed that the location of his district in north Florida was one of the reasons he did so. Perhaps a better reason was that since the small counties were in control of the legislature and the legislature met in his district, he had a duty to work closely with the leaders. He could hardly do so if he was at odds on issues of importance to them.

During our early years in the House, Mallory contributed heavily to the progress of the legislature, and each speaker used his skills. As a newcomer I found him helpful as a source of information and legislative history. Over the many years we served together we grew friendly, and I always respected him and his attributes. Nevertheless, we often took opposite sides on issues.

I had no trouble opposing one or more of my colleagues, nor did I have any qualms about being opposed, so long as the opposition was fair and conducted honorably. I could never understand members who believed in using surprise or other cute tricks to try to win a debate on a bill or a motion of some kind. They never knew what the fallout might be.

Mallory did not resort to such tricks to make a point or win a debate. He was an excellent orator, and he could speak on almost any subject with eloquence. His vocabulary was larger than most people's and his philosophy seemed moderate, so his speeches were well received by almost everyone. More important, he was an expert on the subject of the rules of the House. He not only knew the rules, but also their history and origin, including precedents. He also understood their importance and how to use them effectively in debate. His skill was unmatched, and I for one did my best to duplicate his knowledge of the rules.

## Rules of the House

Each house of the legislature adopts its own rules. Usually it is one of the first orders of business, if not the very first. Those rules are critical to the operation and control of the House and Senate. They are comparable to the bylaws of a corporation or civic organization, but understandably, are much longer and contain much more detail. Every time a new term begins, the rules are reviewed, tweaked, and adopted. The core rules and adjustments are written by veterans of legislative service who understand the necessity and wisdom of anticipating the crises likely to develop. Veterans know that when a crisis is in full swing, it is usually too late to begin thinking about adopting new rules.

An experienced presiding officer like Mallory knows how to use the power of the rules to keep order. The presiding officer is granted authority to assign bills to committees, limit debate, declare who wins in a voice vote situation, appoint members to committees, and specify when and where they may meet. These, as well as an unbelievable combination of similar powers, make the presiding officer the unmistakable boss. It is also a truism to say that he who knows the rules, rules. The substance of a proposal is often never even debated because it is defeated or declared a winner by a knowledgeable member using the rules. Every time the legislature meets, there are situations in which the rules arc uscd to win a skirmish or make an important point. One such skirmish was won by a seasoned member of the House when challenged by a newcomer to the legislature.

## Roy vs. Ray

The old saying about the advantage of knowing the rules was proven to be true by Roy Surles, a seasoned and clever representative from Polk County, with the victim being an inexperienced member of the 57 Club, Ray Maddox, also of Polk County. Both were good speakers, but Roy knew the rules.

The rule Roy used is technical, but very important. It states that every bill must be read three times and passed by the House before the rules allow it to go to the Senate. Any attempt to send it to the Senate before three readings is normally ineffective and a waste of time, so no one tries to do it.

When a bill has passed the House after the third reading, it may, with members' consent, be immediately certified to the Senate, which dramatically shortens the time for completing work on the bill and is, therefore, a positive motion. The motion to immediately certify is appropriate only after the bill passes on third reading.

The bill at issue, between Roy and Ray, was only on second reading and the freshman, Ray, had been successful in preventing the more seasoned Roy from damaging his bill by amendment. But Roy was not easily beaten, and he knew the rules. So, when Roy's damaging amendment was defeated, he made a brief speech about how he understood the mood of the House, knew he had been defeated, and thought it a good time for him to quit. Then, with the tone of a good loser, he moved that Ray's bill be immediately certified to the Senate. He spoke in a way that sounded like a good sport trying to be helpful.

The members were either not paying close attention or were unfamiliar with the rules. Perhaps some representatives were even supportive of Roy's actions. In any event, they agreed to the motion. Thus, the freshman's pet bill—which was only on second reading when the motion to certify passed, and so was not eligible for Senate action—went off into oblivion and has never been heard from since.

I often wondered what Ray told his constituents when they asked him what happened to that bill.

### John Crews

It was also during the 1957 session that I first heard the saying, "Even a blind hog roots up an acorn once in a while." I feel certain that I heard it from John Crews of Macclenny in Baker County, one of the brightest members of the House. He used it in good humor when one of his friends was trying to develop support for some new concept, and he used it again when an adversary was a bit angry because he was surprised that John, an experienced representative when we 57 Clubbers were first elected, could be so effective in making a point in debate. It could be said as a truism that he was a positive element in the legislative environment.

John earned a reputation for bravery while serving in the Marine Corps, and he displayed that same bravery whenever needed during his subsequent public service. He received his formal education, including a law degree, at the University of Florida, but often spoke as a less-educated person, thereby saving his real talent and acquired skills for important situations.

Because he came from Macclenny—a small town in a small county, about twenty-five miles west of Jacksonville—John had all the requirements for membership in the Small County Bloc, and he seemed to fit the mold most of the time. Those who watched him learned of his courageous stand against bootleggers in his home county. He took them on with the full knowledge of the physical and political danger involved, and he survived.

Watching John on the floor of the house was quite an experience. He had to be sure that his formal votes were satisfactory to his rural, conservative constituents and the leaders of the Small County Bloc, but he would not violate his conscience by voting for hateful, hurtful, or unconstitutional proposals. A good example of his skill in that regard was the Last Resort Bill, which autho-

John Crews discusses a bill with me. It was a treat to watch him debate an issue.

rized the closing of public facilities, including public schools, as a last resort to avoid racial integration. Most of the supporters were from small counties, and it appeared that all members of the bloc were obliged to conform to the party line which entailed a "yes" vote on that awful bill. John was expected to vote for it, but to his everlasting credit he did not do so.

It was a treat to watch John in debate. His vocabulary was enormous. His preparation was thorough. His memory was unusually good and when all of his talents were at work, he made debates sparkle.

He had also memorized virtually the entire Bible. He could quote chapter and verse, and often used his biblical knowledge to effectively make a point. For instance, when he was involved in a heated debate and a colleague accused him of changing his position on a particular issue, he replied immediately not with the expected denial, but with an appropriate quote found in 1 Corinthians 13:11: "When I was a child, I spoke as a child, I felt as a child, I thought as a child. Now that I have become a man, I have put away childish things."

Those words from the Good Book took the wind out of the sails of his opponent. After leaving his challenger dumbstruck, he continued on in his typical, persuasive style without offering any excuses for having changed his position.

It is fair to say that he conducted himself in a way that earned him the respect of most of his colleagues. John became a circuit judge after his legislative service and earned the reputation of being a good and fair jurist.

## A Few Who Came Later

Then there were those who were elected after the 57 Clubbers. They were ineligible for membership in the Club, but formed meaningful alliances with members and contributed their time and talents to the legislative process. They enriched our experiences.

## Louis de la Parte

One of the finest state legislators of all time was Louis de la Parte of Tampa. His competence was widely recognized in state governmental circles. His achievements are testimony to his talent, knowledge, and skills.

He came upon the legislative scene without fanfare in 1962 and won the minds and hearts of his new colleagues with his easygoing manner and ability to instill confidence in those with whom he had contact.

As a debater he ranked up there with Jack Mathews and John Crews. He prepared well for debates—he did his homework. When handling a complicated bill, he would make it seem simple. His explanations were articulate and logical. He had the courage of Jack Orr and the charm of LeRoy Collins.

Louis served in the House until a seat in the Senate for Hillsborough County came open and he won it. When I was elected to the Senate in 1968, Louis was there to inspire and encourage me. It was good to serve with him once again and to be satisfied that he had not lost his sense of humor.

Louis was passionate about helping the poor and those with physical and mental handicaps. He believed that if the relevant state agencies were properly structured and adequately funded, they could do wonders for those who were his main concern. Thus, he never let up. Their needs were his goals.

He was not one to share intimate details of his thoughts and plans, so I doubt if anyone really knows what force was driving him. Those who knew Louis best and spent a lot of time with him concluded that he was motivated by a genuine empathy for people who were suffering in some way. He was so observant and so knowledgeable concerning his less fortunate friends that

Louis de la Parte (center) and I share a *St. Petersburg Times* award presented by Senate President Jerry Thomas.

one could easily assume that he had been in exactly the same position as the person he was working with, and accordingly, he knew just what to do.

Whatever it was that drove Louis to work so hard, it was an effective propellant. He advocated an increase in the number of state employees tasked to work with his friends in need as well as improved funding for the agencies as he guided his reorganization legislation to passage.

On several occasions, Dempsey Barron, who had also moved to the Senate and become friendly with Louis, opposed some of De la Parte's liberal legislation. During the debate on one such proposal, Dempsey seemed to be getting the better of the argument. At that point, Louis referred to Dempsey as "Red Barron," a reference to the World War I German flying ace who shot down so many American pilots. De la Parte drew a word picture of "Red Barron" lurking in the shadows waiting to ambush a wholesome member of the opposite side and doing a lot of damage.

Dempsey was a fierce competitor, and was on a mission to stop De la Parte and his expensive proposal, but when Louis tagged him as a bully and one who would sneak up on an opponent to gain an advantage through surprise, he caught the attention of the senators. By the time they stopped laughing, Dempsey's attack had lost its steam and went down in flames.

The nickname "Red Barron" stuck and lasted throughout Dempsey's political career.

The good projects that Louis de la Parte proposed and accomplished for the state in social legislation and in such local matters as the "West Coast Water Wars" are well known, and were very beneficial. He was a fine legislator. As should be expected, he is held in high regard by those who worked with him, and of course, by the residents of Tampa and Hillsborough County.

During De la Parte's time in the Senate, Mallory Horne was elected by his fellow senators to be Senate president. At the same time, De la Parte was elected president pro tempore, or second in command. In 1974, Horne decided to be a candidate for the U.S. Senate and resigned from the presidency of the Florida Senate. De la Parte moved up and served out Horne's unexpired term. All who knew him were delighted that he had that honor before succumbing to a debilitating illness.

## Beth Johnson

After the 57 Club had been organized and all the members sworn in, there was a special election in Orange County to fill a vacancy in that county's legislative delegation. It was necessary to have a special election because the Florida Constitution did not permit anyone to appoint a member of the legislature. Every single member of the House and Senate had to be elected to the office.

Orange County, whose principal city is Orlando, was interested in every action of the legislature, and its delegation was an integral part of the governance system. If that vacancy was left unfilled, the entire county could have been damaged by being left out of the process. And so, as soon as the legislative vacancy occurred, the planning for a special election began. The governor ordered the special election, which had to be scheduled far enough in advance to allow the Orange County supervisor of elections to secure all the necessary polling places and retain all the people to operate them. There also had to be sufficient time for the candidates to have a reasonable period to campaign for the office, including time for fundraising.

Beth Johnson qualified as a candidate to fill the Orange County vacancy, and she was successfully elected. She became a state representative later in 1957. She did not qualify for membership in the 57 Club, although she was so close to our own starting time that I believe she most likely would have been

Beth Johnson and I look over a bill. She was the first woman elected to the Florida Senate. (Photo courtesy Florida Archives.)

unanimously approved if there had been a substantial request for a special dispensation.

Beth was not the first woman to be elected to the Florida House of Representatives, but she was still something of a pioneer there and must have been terribly lonely in that male-dominated institution.

We learned that she had lived in Orange County since 1934, was very popular there, and had a history of involvement in good causes. She had the look and demeanor of self confidence. No one doubted her competence. She was not a fierce debater, but she did her homework on any bill she picked to support or oppose. Her primary interest was in education at all levels, with a bit of a preference for college and university education. Her role in securing funding for startup costs and site acquisition for the University of Central Florida was well documented.

Beth's presence as a member of the House changed the dynamics of the body for the better. She was a good legislator and helpful to all those who needed assistance. She served in the House until 1962 and subsequently served in the Senate until 1967. She was the first female elected to the Florida Senate. In 1986, Beth Johnson was inducted into the Florida Women's Hall of Fame.


## Lawton Chiles

After the 57 Club members had a little time in office, along came Lawton Chiles of Polk County. He defeated Roy Surles, a seasoned veteran of legislative battles, for his seat. His David vs. Goliath election attracted attention because the wise and able Mr. Surles was considered invincible to attacks by young, inexperienced, ambitious opponents like Lawton Chiles.

We were curious as to how he did it, and what we learned should have prepared us for the success of his political career, as he went on to eventually become our U.S. senator and then our governor. The way he had taken down the powerful Surles was the old-fashioned way: through hard work and personal contact with the voters. He and his wife, Rhea, had gone from door to door throughout the county, shaking hands and asking individual residents to vote for him. The technique was so straightforward, simple, and effective that Roy Surles was taken by surprise.

It was a strategy that Chiles enlarged upon when he ran for the U.S. Senate, and the one that earned him the nickname "Walkin' Lawton." It was based on his plan to walk from one end of the state to the other. Technically, he walked from Pensacola to Key West. As I understood it, he actually rode when passing through some of the sparsely populated rural areas and when he would move from one side of the state to the other. The fact is that his campaign was successful, and he won a seat in the U.S. Senate. There again he took almost everyone by surprise.

Those of us who knew Chiles quite well and had watched with interest as he developed his political skills were not surprised by his victory. He clearly had the attributes of a successful leader. He was smart, empathetic, personable, and persevering.

I had first-hand knowledge of Chiles's leadership style on my first day in the Florida Senate. I was on my feet all day, speaking from the lectern and reporting to the Senate on seventeen cases of local officials who were suspended by Claude Kirk, who was governor at that time. The cases had been assigned to me by Senate president Jack Mathews immediately after my election. At the end of the day, I was weary but privately pleased. Every single one of my recommendations was adopted by the full Senate, and in the process I suddenly became well known to all members.

Lawton Chiles gained the nickname "Walkin' Lawton" during his Senate campaign. (Photo courtesy Florida Archives.)

As I was returning to my seat after a standing ovation of gratitude for hard work by my committee, a messenger stopped me and handed me a note. It was a thoughtful message from Lawton Chiles, welcoming me to the Senate, congratulating me for a good job, and wishing me well. It was a meaningful gesture. It also told me a lot about the man who was to have an enormous influence on all of Florida.

I followed Lawton's political career quite closely for a number of reasons. First, as a resident of Florida I have always been interested in present and potential leaders. I learned early on how my family, friends, and indeed all citizens are affected in one way or another by the quality of political leadership.

Also, I followed his activities because I was responsible, in a way, for his having the assistance of a person who was a major fundraiser and a reliable advisor to him. Earlier, in the course of my disastrous campaign for governor, I asked a friend, Tom Stead, to help me by being the treasurer of my campaign. He accepted and did a super job. That led to the opportunity to introduce him to Lawton. They liked and had confidence in each other, and, when my campaign was over, Tom and Lawton joined forces. It was an alliance that was mutually beneficial and long lasting. In fact, it lasted all the remaining days of Lawton's life.

The alliance was good for me as well. Our friendship with my former treasurer gave us a common interest and enhanced the bonds of friendship between Lawton and me. Had I needed the help of the senator or the governor-to-be, I had a surefire way to get my message to the man himself.

The other reason I followed Chiles so diligently was that I liked him personally and felt comfortable with his being in high and powerful positions. I wanted him to succeed.

Following the completion of his first four years as governor, he decided to seek reelection. His opponent was Jeb Bush, the son of former President George Bush and brother of Texas governor George W. Bush, who would later become president. Jeb wanted to be the governor and thought he could beat Lawton.

One evening during a debate in Tampa, near the end of the campaign, the pundits were calling it a tight race. Jeb and his followers were overly anxious and thought that because the pollsters indicated that his campaign was gaining on Lawton, he was going to have his wish come true.

Lawton, on the other hand, had never lost a political race and had no intention of allowing this one to be the first. He remembered an old southern hunter's saying about a last-minute surge in any competitive contest. He said that he was confident he would win because "the old he-coon walks before the light of day."

All the interested voters were watching and wondered about the relevance of the saying. It is based on a legendary, big male coon who had learned that feeding opportunities were best and few hunters were in the woods just before dawn. That is when he walked around safely and found plenty of food. The saying caught the attention of people everywhere. The next day it was the subject of conversation all across the state. Most had never heard it before, and they were trying to understand what Chiles was talking about. Those of us who were familiar with the saying enjoyed the opportunities to explain the meaning. It was interesting to watch a simple, folksy saying draw so much attention.

Without a doubt it was the turning point in the campaign. Sure enough, Lawton, like the "He-Coon," walked in at the last minute of the campaign and surged ahead to become the winner.

Lawton served for almost all of his second term. He died of heart trouble on December 12, 1998, just three weeks before his retirement was to begin. Lieutenant Governor Buddy MacKay of Ocala filled the post until the term was over.

## Reubin Askew

When Reubin Askew was first elected to the House of Representatives, he resided in Pensacola, Escambia County, which is in the far western segment of Florida's Panhandle. He was a lawyer in practice with an up-and-coming partner named Fred Levin. Askew came to Tallahassee too late to be a member of the 57 Club, but he was friendly with many of us and fit right in with the legislative culture.

Fred Levin, by the way, concentrated on the law while Reubin and others with like feelings went into politics. He was so successful over the years that he was able to give a substantial gift to his law school. It was so substantial that his name appears prominently on the law school building at the University of Florida in Gainesville.

Askew was soon recognized by his colleagues as someone with high personal standards and sufficient ability and energy to achieve his ambitious political goals. His formal college education was at Florida State University, where he was active in student politics. He was surely good at it, because he was elected president of the student body.

Like so many of the young political leaders of that era, Reubin first ran for and won a seat in the House, then won a seat in the Senate at the earliest opportunity, and stayed there until he ran for governor.

All who are elected to serve in the legislature come to understand that one does not suddenly know everything about all subjects. There is nothing about an election that makes a person all-knowing. Yet he or she is quickly expected to vote intelligently on a broad range of complex questions. It is often said that a legislator knows a little bit about a lot of things, but not much about anything. However, that unwritten rule is modified when an individual takes a strong interest in one or more subjects and does the homework

During his term as governor, Reubin Askew found time to visit me in Tallahassee Memorial Hospital. (Photo courtesy Florida Archives.)

and self-study required to create expertise. That is what Reubin did. He took a special interest in reapportionment and the budgeting process.

With respect to reapportionment, he became an expert. He drafted plan after plan and advocated their adoption. He knew so much about the subject, including the geography and many characteristics of people throughout the state, that it was easy to follow his lead. It was a shame that the lawmakers would not accept any of his plans, but it was also understandable. It is virtually impossible to induce a legislator to vote away all or a large part of his acquired power, and that was what was required to pass a reapportionment plan that would stand a chance of being approved by the federal court. Unhappily, it became necessary for the courts to intervene, and when they did, there was near chaos. As a senator, Askew helped the state through those troublesome times.

Askew gained more respect and enhanced his status through his work on the spending bills. He could grasp the totality of a massive appropriations bill and work with all those who had problems with parts of it as though he had before him a grade school arithmetic problem. He served the state very well.

When he began his campaign to unseat Governor Claude Kirk in the 1970 general election, the pundits didn't think he had much of a chance to win. But Kirk read him properly and predicted that Askew would be the most difficult opponent in the race. Reubin ran a good race and got the job done. He beat Kirk in 1970 with votes to spare.

Following the defeat of Claude Kirk and Askew's election as governor, three situations developed that disclosed much about the man. The first one occurred when I was a patient in Tallahassee Memorial Hospital with a life-threatening condition. Each day, doctors told my wife, Mercedes, that they weren't sure I would make it until nightfall. I was heavily sedated and lucid only in intervals. One day I awoke to see my wife talking to Governor Askew. Frankly, I thought I might be hallucinating. The year was 1975, and Askew was a governor with all the responsibilities a person could tolerate. As it turned out, he really was there. He had come over from the Capitol to visit and pray with me if I was willing. It was a pleasant surprise, and I was willing. It helped.

The second incident involved my experience in attempting to be seated on the Supreme Court of Florida. In 1975, a vacancy opened in the court, and it was the governor's responsibility to fill it by appointing a qualified person. There existed a Supreme Court Nominating Committee, a group duly appointed to screen the applicants and recommend not less than three of them to the governor. The process was designed to minimize political intrusions into the appointment proceedings and provide the committee with the incentives and tools necessary to winnow out candidates unqualified to serve on the court. The governor was obliged to make his appointment from among those who were qualified and recommended by the committee.

The committee took its duty seriously, and after receiving applications from the candidates, scheduled a lengthy interview with each one. Then, after all references had been verified, the committee met to review all material and make its recommendations.

When Governor Askew received the committee's report, he discovered that all who were recommended were his friends. I was one of them, and I thought that because of our relationship in legislative matters I would receive some kind of special consideration. Because of his visit to me in the hospital and other manifestations of our friendship, and, of course, my credentials, I really thought that I would be the one selected.

He did not appoint me, and he offered no excuses or explanations. Joseph Hatchett, an African American who was little known in political circles, was his choice. Although disappointed, my respect for Governor Askew went way up on the measuring stick. I knew him well enough to believe that he had considered all relevant facts, including my illness—which raised serious questions as to my physical ability to serve—as well as the quality of experience each of us had. He did what he thought was right, regardless of friendship or political alliances.

And, finally, the third incident occurred about two years after I was discharged from Tallahassee Memorial Hospital. During that period I became a candidate for the Florida Supreme Court, and I was elected.

At that time all judgeships were elective offices. If a vacancy occurred around midterm by reason of death, disability, or resignation, the governor could appoint someone to fill the vacancy until the next general election. Otherwise, the voters filled the vacancy in a statewide, nonpartisan election.

A justice who was serving on the state's highest court and believed in the election of judges decided to retire. He very carefully calculated when he could step down and be certain that his seat would be filled in an election. When he resigned, I qualified as a candidate to replace him. To my surprise, two others also became candidates. After nearly a year of campaigning, I won. I also became the last elected justice of that court. There was a constitutional amendment on the same ballot I was on that changed the way Supreme Court justices and district court judges were selected.

Askew was still governor, so I requested his presence, and, if possible, his participation in my investiture ceremony. He was present and made a memorable speech about my public service. I took my place on the court with pride.

It happened that the constitution of 1968, which became effective in 1969, required periodical constitutional reviews. The drafters of the constitution very thoughtfully included that provision to facilitate the discovery and correction of mistakes and omissions, and to pick up any needed additions that appeared after the final draft of the constitution had been approved. However, those drafters had not been very careful when they crafted it. It was open to two different interpretations as to when the review group could be appointed.

Governor Askew construed it as giving him the right to impanel the group and receive its report before his term was over. The other interpretation would leave it for his successor. He asked the court to give him an advisory opinion for his guidance. I knew that he would want to appoint the reviewers, but I felt certain that those who wrote the constitution intended to have the state operate under their product for the full term of years mentioned in their provision, which would give the responsibility to his successor. Therefore, I drafted a proposed opinion for the court's consideration and circulated it.

I admit that I had some qualms about writing an opinion contrary to what my friend the governor wanted so badly. He had been so concerned about me that he had visited me in the hospital, and as mentioned, he participated in my investiture ceremony when I took the oath of office to become a justice. I valued his friendship. However, I was so sure I was right that I could do nothing else. I knew how he must have felt when he passed me over for the appointment to the court.

At the end of the day, I was in the minority, and what I wrote became the dissenting opinion. Although he had never been critical of an opinion of mine, I thought I might hear about the published dissent from his staff, but I didn't. The truth is that he was too ethical to attempt to intrude on the court even in that minor way, and for that and other reasons I respect him.

# 3   *The Home of the Capitol* ————————————

Following the general election of 1956, the Florida Legislature—including the thirty-nine members of the 57 Club—met in the state Capitol in Tallahassee to take the oath of office and organize both houses. Unlike the House of Representatives, only half the members of the Senate had to take the oath because senators were elected for four-year terms and their terms were staggered. Therefore, half of them ran in a general election and the other half ran two years later. Stated in the vernacular of a legislature that met every other year, the senators were elected for two sessions, while the House members were elected for only one.

The oath was taken by House members in small groups and was administered by a member of the Florida Supreme Court. The swearing-in ceremony was short, but meaningful. It was, in a sense, our initiation. In just a few minutes we were enrolled in a fairly exclusive fraternity and vested with an enormous storehouse of power. Until the next general election, we were quite free to exercise our best judgment. We were also expected to treat the power granted to us as a trust, which was supposed to guide our conduct and inhibit wrongdoing.

Any newcomer witnessing this ceremony—or any other state governmental meeting—might wonder how the seat of power for the State of Florida came to reside in a small city in north Florida. First of all, the terrain is more like that found in Georgia or Alabama than in central or southern Florida. And the location certainly is not close to today's population centers of Orlando, Tampa, West Palm Beach, Fort Lauderdale, or Miami.

Two questions often asked are: How did Tallahassee come to be the capital city, and why did it continue in that capacity through the tenure of the 57 Club until the present when the major population concentration was south of central Florida?

The second question has a short and simple answer, which is that the less-populated counties—commonly referred to as small counties—were in control of the legislature. Many of them were in north Florida, and all of their representatives were courted by the public officials and leaders of Tallahassee. They liked having the capital city close by, and they were prepared to fight anyone who suggested moving it to another location.

The question of how it became the capital city in the first place has many answers, but one stood out for me. I heard it in a welcome speech given by Tallahassee's mayor at that time. It went something like this:

Chief Justice Roberts administers the oath of office for the new legislative term, which included many members of the 57 Club. (Photo courtesy Florida Archives.)

There was a time not so long ago when there were but two principal cities in Florida: St. Augustine and Pensacola. Almost exactly halfway between the two cities was a spot on the gulf coast known today as St. Marks, located just at the end of a river that made its way to the Gulf of Mexico. In due time it seemed logical for the state capital to be located in the vicinity of St. Marks, and a committee with members from each city set out for that location.

Upon arrival at that spot, however, the residents told the group about a place to the north that would be even better suited. They described its small-though-majestic hills, the trees, and the flowers. So persuasive were their descriptions that the committee decided to have a look.

They were not disappointed. They made the twenty-five-mile trip while admiring the landscape and the wild animals there. Then they came to the hills—those beautiful hills. They learned that the hills were not only picturesque, but served to provide a generous supply of high, dry land for future homes, churches, and businesses.

It was springtime, and the azaleas and dogwood were in bloom everywhere. The committee members thought they were in a giant flower garden, and they were sure it was a bit of the Creator's Heaven. The whole area was at peace, and the peacefulness permeated every square inch of the soil that was about to become the capital of Florida.

The committee reported these attributes, so the story concludes, and the capital was established where the members recommended. Today, Tallahassee still has much of its original charm.

Tallahassee is the only municipality in Leon County. The boundaries of the city are not the same as those of the county, so each has its own government. Historically, this system of governance worked well. Also, the city has operated an electric utility for many years, which tends to hold down the need for property taxes and which the homeowners find desirable.

Among the points of interest in 1957 Tallahassee were the steak houses, where legislators ate many of their evening meals as guests of lobbyists. Several restaurants were known for serving excellent food. But serving alcoholic beverages was another matter. At that time in its history, Florida had what was called "local option" as to the sale of liquor. That is to say, a county could decide to be "wet," which permitted the sale and possession of alcohol; or it could go "dry," which was Prohibition reincarnated.

Leon County, which included Tallahassee, was dry. It was said that this status was perpetuated by an unlikely coalition of preachers and bootleggers, with financial support from liquor sellers in adjoining counties. It doesn't take a genius to recognize the potential conflict of interest built into that situation. How could the sheriff enforce the law that prohibits the possession, sale, and use of liquor without an alliance with those who were operating their businesses in violation of the law?

However, one of the most popular Tallahassee restaurants, the Silver Slipper, did not allow the dry status to interfere with its very successful food service business. For starters, its customers were allowed to bring their own bottles and drink before, during, and after eating. The Slipper made its profit on the food and setups for the drinks.

## Silver Slipper Caters to Legislators

The Silver Slipper was located south of town on Monroe Street, near the fairgrounds. The entrance was attractive and well decorated, with an oversized aquarium and an open glass counter where the finest steaks were displayed. One could select a steak on the way in and have it cooked to order and served with a crisp salad topped with their famous "Kumbak" dressing.

I welcomed well-known Tallahassee restaurateur Jim Kalfas to my district, Volusia County.

The Kalfas family had long owned the business and catered to legislators in various ways. One such method was collecting and displaying pictures of prominent House and Senate members along with those of governors, U.S. senators, and congressmen. A legislator had arrived when his picture showed up on the wall of the Silver Slipper.

Another way was old-fashioned friendliness. The family made it a point to know their customers and to speak to them by name. They had relatives in Volusia County who were friends of mine, so I knew the Tallahassee branch of the large Greek family before I was elected. Chris Kalfas, son of the owner of the establishment, was a sports fisherman and took me to the Gulf of Mexico to catch trout a few times, and he did the same for others. It all paid off in business. The place was crowded every night when the legislature was in session.

The main dining room was modest in size because most patrons opted to dine in one of the many private rooms that were separated by curtains. Privacy was the key. If one felt like greeting people coming and going, he simply opened the curtain. However, if some measure of privacy was desired, the curtain could be closed. Every private room had a call button to summon one of the well-trained waiters. A few of the rooms even had doors to the outside which permitted customers to arrive, have dinner, and leave without going into the entrance area or being seen.

Lobbyists generally invited a group for dinner each evening; hence, almost every night during the session the place would be full of legislators and lobbyists. It was probably a truism when it was said that a great many legislative issues were resolved at the Slipper.

## Joe's Spaghetti House

Tallahassee boasted another restaurant which was similar to the Silver Slipper. It was Joe's Spaghetti House on East Tennessee Street. It, too, had private rooms, setups for those who brought bottles, and wonderful steaks. There were subtle differences between the two prominent places, and it was not uncommon for legislators to express their preference for one or the other.

After a few years in the legislature listening to one's colleagues and being just plain observant, it was fairly easy to know where the prominent political figures could be found on any given evening. Thus, I came to believe that Jack Mathews expressed a preference for Joe's, and it was generally known that he could found there. By the same token, Dempsey Barron preferred the Silver Slipper.

## The Talquin Inn

A third popular eating establishment, the Talquin Inn, was west of town. It was smaller and somewhat more family-oriented than the big two, but it had great service, wonderful steaks, and its specialty—shrimp wrapped in bacon—was known far and wide. Other restaurants tried to emulate the Talquin's specialty, but could never match the recipe. There was some secret as to how the bacon and the shrimp were first cooked separately. To my knowledge no other restaurant in the state ever discovered or successfully duplicated that entree.

Not only was that shrimp dish a very popular treat, but the name was once the code word for a major legislative bill. When the 57 Club was still in its infancy, a lobbyist for one of the race tracks joined the fray. He was a very personable man, and predictably, he became popular with the members. He stayed in the lobby force for many years and entertained Club members and others, of course, when we were senators.

His specialty was taking legislators to dinner at the Talquin Inn for shrimp followed by steak. That habit of his was well known, and his invitations were seldom refused. He never asked for a favor in return, although everyone who knew him and knew of his client had no illusions about what was coming. As sure as the world is round, it was said, the day will come when all of his friends will have to do as he asks or become former friends.

The popular Talquin Inn on West Tennessee in Tallahassee.

The day did arrive, but there were those who did not realize it at first. The bill the lobbyist wanted was innocuous, but important to him and hard to identify. Then one of the senators was recognized to speak. His speech was brief but well understood. He said, "This is the Shrimp Wrapped in Bacon Bill." It passed.

The Talquin Inn had another very valuable asset—a tall, thin waitress. I never knew her real name, nor did I ever hear her called or addressed as anything other than "Olive Oyl," as in the Popeye comic strip, and she looked the part of her namesake. She greeted guests, called them by name, and provided prompt, courteous service.

## A Festive Atmosphere

It has been said that a legislative session is like a convention that lasts sixty days. That certainly was true. Everyone was away from home, and they often seemed to be in a festive mood. There was hard work and fierce competition all day long, but when it was time to take a meal or attend a party, the mood changed and the partying began. Rules by which people played in their hometowns were sometimes suspended in Tallahassee.

Temptations were a part of the scene, and history tells us that a few legislators tended to give into them. And, of course, a great deal of alcohol was consumed. That does not mean that everyone was corrupt or that all legislators left their morals behind in 1957, for that was not the case. There was, however, a general loosening of the usual restraints, and even those who did not get into any mischief—and I believe that to be the majority—participated in the festivities. This was one of the reasons that steak houses like the Silver Slipper, Joe's, and the Talquin Inn were so successful.

## Capital City Hotels and Motels

In preparing for my first legislative session in 1957, I rented a small house on one of the perimeter roads, the one closest to downtown. I had no need to check out the hotel situation, or so I thought. I soon learned that a good legislator made it his business to know all about them. Hardly a day passed during the sessions without some need to know the address or location, the quality of accommodations and food, and all sorts of other information relating to each hotel. Constituents, relatives, and friends visited regularly. They somehow developed the notion that their state representative who worked in the capital part time was all-knowing when it came to hotels, and that he or she could hardly wait to participate in the decisions of the visitors about where to stay.

I was confronted by a typical problem having to do with my staff. Actually, the staff consisted of one secretary, and her name was Betty Carter. She applied for a job with my law firm a month or so before the 1957 session. She had a remarkable record of stability in her previous jobs. She was also above average in her skills in transcribing dictation and in producing quality typewritten documents.

Betty was really qualified, so the firm hired her to be my secretary. I promptly talked to her about going to Tallahassee for the session, and she was duly skeptical. I told her that I would have my family with me and that she would be welcome at the house at any time. I admitted that I knew little about the city or places to stay, but that I had heard of the Cherokee Hotel, which was the most popular downtown facility. I assured her that the per diem to be paid would cover her expenses while there. Finally she agreed to go.

I felt like celebrating because there was a dearth of good secretarial help in the capital, and working for a freshman member of the House was not a prestigious occupation. I was lucky to have such a qualified person as my staff. She made arrangements to stay at the Cherokee, sight unseen, by telephone and confirmed by mail. I prepared for my first session thinking that she was well cared for. Then she went to Tallahassee and checked in—and my life took a turn for the worse.

The hotel appeared to be fairly nice for a small town facility so long as one was in the lobby or the dining room; otherwise it was very old and looked its age. The room in which they put her was the size of a closet, and her description of it reminded me of an expression used by my brother when referring to anything equally small. He said, "It was so small, I had to go outside to change my mind." It was not only small, she told me, but it looked old and dirty and was not soundproof. Worse still, there were plenty of roaches. However, she stayed there for sixty days, and although she was a relatively good sport and tried to make the best of a terrible situation, she

Betty Carter put on a brave face while staying at an old hotel in Tallahassee.

detested the place and didn't hold back on her complaints when talking to me. After fifty years, I still remember well those daily conversations about the hotel that I had recommended, and I still feel guilty for having allowed that to happen to her.

I feel certain that there were several other hotels in Tallahassee at the time, but I didn't know about any of them except the one named the Floridan Hotel on Monroe Street. It was a couple of blocks closer to the Capitol than the Cherokee, but from what I heard, proximity was the only advantage. By any other test, I understood, the Floridan came in second.

As time went on, I heard several unsavory stories about the Floridan, and I was able to respond to my secretary's complaints about the Cherokee Hotel by saying that she should feel lucky that I hadn't recommended the Floridan.

In spite of the negative rumors about the Floridan, several powerful senators stayed there during the sessions and, during my first session, a few receptions were held at that hotel.

Before long, the Duval Hotel was opened for business and soon became the first choice of legislators and people who regularly watched them. It was several blocks north of the Floridan on Monroe Street. When members of the legislature congregated at a given hotel, it soon filled up with lobbyists and others who had business with the members. Thus, the Duval was a huge success in its early days. It was no great facility when compared to hotels in larger cities, but compared to the Cherokee and the Floridan, it was a palace.

One of the defects of the Duval was its paper-thin walls. On one of my visits to the hotel, I was annoyed by loud voices in the room next to mine until I began listening to them. I came to understand that it was a meeting of officials from road building companies, and it was the night before the sealed bids of those competitors would be submitted and opened by the Florida Road Department. The contracts, which involved millions of dollars, would be awarded by that department based on those bids. Unfortunately, I had to leave just after I began paying attention, because based upon the little I heard, I believe I might have learned how they could be conspiring to divide among themselves the jobs that were to be contracted the next day. I guess I told that story in the wrong places, for I never heard of such a meeting again.

For a few years the Duval was the place to be, and then the competition began to increase with a vengeance. Holiday Inn, Quality Courts, Sheraton, and several non-chain facilities opened and prospered, but Tallahassee remained that quaint little town that was selected to be the capital of Florida.

## Beaches, Lakes, and Ponds

Those of us who grew up in coastal towns like Daytona Beach, Fort Lauderdale, or St. Petersburg missed being in close proximity to the Atlantic Ocean or the Gulf of Mexico when we were in the capital. St. Marks is twenty-five miles south of Tallahassee, and is the closest access to the gulf. To make up for that perceived shortcoming, residents as well as visitors spent time on the many ponds and lakes throughout Leon County and a few of the neighboring counties.

One such lake is in Liberty County, near the town of Bristol. I single this one out because it is unique and has a colorful history. The name is Lake Mystic, which is an appropriate title. It is quite deep, around twenty feet near the edges and eighty to 100 feet in the center or in the little cove. The lake is spring-fed, but mysteriously not as cold as most spring water. Near the surface it is just the right temperature for swimming. The water is absolutely beautiful. It is clear and a gorgeous shade of aqua, about the same color as the water around the Bahamas in the Caribbean.

The lake is located about forty miles west of downtown Tallahassee, so a good many residents of the capital—and some legislators—had second homes there. These legislators were all quite well known, but one stands out: Fred O. (Bud) Dickinson.

Dickinson was addicted to politics. After WWII he attended Stetson University, where he was deeply involved in campus politics. While a student he was the campus leader for one of the candidates for governor. Shortly after graduating, he went to Palm Beach County to practice law, and like many of us jumped right into politics. Dickinson was a state representative, and at the first opportunity he ran for and won a seat in the Florida Senate before the 57 Club members were elected to office. Twice he ran unsuccessfully for governor and ended his political career as state comptroller, one of the cabinet offices.

Dickinson also loved Lake Mystic. His home away from home was very nice, and he and his family spent many happy hours in that lakeside residence. At the height of his political activities he had access to a small seaplane, and he often had the pilot fly him to the lake to meet his family. He would call ahead, of course, and then come in for a landing. It was an exciting procedure to watch, what with the beautiful water and the plane approaching the lake into the wind and then gracefully touching down on the pontoon-like landing gear that was installed to take the place of wheels. The few natives of Liberty County complained privately about Bud's arrogance in having the lake cleared of fishermen and recreational boaters so the plane could land and take off safely, but since the other residents around the lake did not complain, nothing was ever done about it.

Over time there had been two different public entertainment facilities at the lake, and both were remembered fondly. Based on the folk tales, I understood that the first was on the western edge of the lake at a place referred to as the Cove. Actually, it looked as though it was a manmade cut in the western shoreline to accommodate a bathhouse-type operation. The water was deep right up to the dock of the facility. There had been a diving tower and a springboard in addition to the other water recreation facilities.

The second public facility was on the eastern shore and was the place where those seeking a small nightclub-style ambience assembled. Here again, the residents expressed concerns about what went on there and what it did to the image of the lake as a family swimming paradise. The rumors were plentiful, rich in exciting details, and reputedly enjoyed by all—including the complainers—but I saw no proof of unlawful or immoral conduct. Many of the rumors originated during the war, when Lake Mystic was popular with soldiers and sailors who were stationed nearby. The facilities at the lake were among their favorite places to spend the rare hours when they weren't training for combat.

I was never there during those days, but years later when I purchased a summer place on Lake Mystic, all I cared about was the present use of the lake. If there had been mischief in days gone by as was alleged, it was nonexistent by the time I became aware of the lake's beauty and charm.

A few days after my wife and I purchased a small place on the south side of the lake, I was puttering around in our yard when an elderly man rode up on his bicycle and greeted me. I noticed that he had a small plant in his hand, and he almost immediately asked if he could plant it in our yard. I had no objection, so after we agreed on where it should be planted, he dug a hole and put the plant in with a bit of fertilizer and a lot of water. Then we sat on the porch watching the lake and getting acquainted. He was an old timer. He knew "where all the bones were buried," so to speak. He loved to share the stories of the lake with me.

The best story was about him. It seems that when he was a young man he started the custom of planting something in newcomers' yards. He explained to me with pride that something from his yard was growing in every yard around the lake.

What he had planted in my yard, as it turned out, was a gardenia bush. It grew and grew, and when it bloomed it proudly displayed hundreds of those beautiful white flowers with an aroma that filled the air with a scent that brought back memories of the pre-war days when I would send my prom date—and other special dates—a gardenia corsage.

Liberty County, where Lake Mystic is located, is large in land size but small in population. Much of the land in the county is within the Federal Land Preserve, so it may never be developed or support growth in population. There were only about 3,000 people living there in the '50s, but the county enjoyed a full range of public officials.

There is a Board of County Commissioners as well as all the constitutional officers that the big counties have: the sheriff, clerk of circuit court, tax collector, property appraiser, and supervisor of elections. The local government also includes a county judge, a school board, and a school superintendent. However, the way they conducted business was sometimes different from the larger counties, as I was soon to discover.

As we were getting settled in our place, I found that I needed a well and some sort of driveway from the road to the house. I made inquiries about such things and learned more than I had bargained for.

First, there were no land use regulations or zoning ordinances. I found that strange, so I asked how it worked. I was told that the folks protected their property and its value by themselves. If I intended to do anything significant on the property, I should talk to the neighbors.

The illustration used was a story of a man who bought a tract of land fronting on Lake Mystic and subdivided it. All the deeds from him to the buyers described the lots by archaic metes and bounds, and very carefully left out a strip of property lying between the lake and the property being conveyed by the seller. The buyers thought that they had purchased lakefront property, but they had not. All the land bordering on the lake was still the property of the person who had subdivided it and sold the lots.

One day, so the story goes, the seller wrote to each lot owner telling them the bad news: that if they wanted access to the lake they would have to buy it from him. An informal committee soon called upon the seller and explained how things worked in Liberty County. Without delay or charge he deeded the strip on the lakefront to the lot owners. I never learned what was said to that seller, but obviously it was said with feeling because it was effective.

The other thing I learned about Liberty County was that people did business with county government the old-fashioned way. I was informed that I should buy the fill dirt I needed for my driveway from the county. I contacted the county commissioner for that district and confirmed that it was available. We agreed that he would have the dirt delivered to the right of way in front of my property so I could easily move it onto my land and spread it the way I wanted.

I went away for about a week, and when I returned the dirt had been delivered. However, the delivery was not as we had agreed. It was not left on the edge of the right of way near my land, but rather on my land and, what's more, it was spread just where I had staked out the driveway. When I inquired about it, I was told that it must have been a mistake. Then I tried to get a bill for the dirt and labor involved in the spreading. However, it was delayed so long that there seemed to be no record of the project and it took forever to get all that straightened out. I wasn't used to that method of doing business.

## Attempts to Move the Capital

Meanwhile, the City of Tallahassee, with its everlasting charm, continued to be the capital. Every attempt to designate some other city was fought off successfully.

The committee originally charged with finding a suitable site for the capital city had no way to know just how the state's population pattern would develop, but as millions of people moved into the state—and in spite of the beauty of Tallahassee—there was increasing talk about how ridiculous it was to have our state government centered in Tallahassee. Most of the people lived in south Florida, and central Florida was growing rapidly as well. Somewhere near Orlando seemed to be the logical location for conducting state business.

However, none of that logic really mattered. The powerful leadership of the Small County Bloc in the House and the Pork Chop Gang of the Senate were in favor of the status quo, and that settled the issue. Nevertheless, from time-to-time, someone would introduce a bill just to keep the issue alive. Customarily, there would be little or no debate. One of the small county legislators would simply ask to be recognized and would then explain how foolish it would be to move the capital when the state had such an enormous investment in the buildings of Tallahassee. He would then spend a few minutes explaining the political peril one would place himself in should he be bold enough to support the move. When the vote was taken, the proposal would be soundly defeated and the issue would be shelved once more.

One day we were all surprised when my colleague, Jim Sweeny of Volusia County, was recognized to speak in favor of the proposal to make Orlando the capital city. He was closely aligned with the Small County Bloc, so everyone wondered what he was up to.

Jim Sweeny (front row center) spoke in favor of moving the capital to Orlando, but members soon realized his remarks were all in fun.

Jim's speech was well done and deserves a special place in the history of the Florida Legislature. He first explained that he had decided to join those advocating the move because of the logic of doing so. Then he addressed the issue of the expensive buildings. They would not be wasted, he explained, because there were alternative uses for them.

He used the historic, domed Capitol as an example. It could, he said, house the medical school that Florida State University so desperately wanted at that time. It would be perfect for that use because the House chambers, where he was speaking, would be used as the operating theater. Medical students would sit in the gallery where the visitors were sitting, and they would have a perfect view of the operations of the teaching surgeons. Very few renovations would be needed because it would be a continuation of substantially the same activity; that is, a group of people watching operators perform on the floor of the House.

And, he went on to explain, the chamber of the Senate at the other end of the building would be the perfect place to store the cadavers used by the medical school, because it could hold nearly forty of them and nobody would notice that lifeless bodies had been substituted for the senators.

His timing was so good and his speaking techniques so effective that he kept us mesmerized. At first everyone thought he was serious, but we soon realized that it was a tongue-in-cheek speech, and we began to appreciate his humor and showmanship. It was a good speech.

## Attributes of Tallahassee

Those who fought for the right to make Tallahassee their temporary home when the legislature was in session developed an affinity for the city, and no wonder. There were so many things to see and do that no matter the taste or preference, something appropriate could be found. One example was the festive occasion known as Springtime Tallahassee. The permanent residents celebrated the glorious springtime, virtually worshipping the azaleas, dogwoods, and other blossoms and blooms. The parade was always well attended and appreciated because it was really good. So were the social events, where everyone donned costumes and put on the very best manners for the ball. And the so-called Old Tallahasseeans occasionally reached out to visiting legislators and included them in select events.

Anyone who wanted to attend a house of worship in Tallahassee found that there was every kind of religious structure and denomination. Some of the buildings—and for that matter, the beliefs—were old and quaint, while others were modern. Again, there was something for everyone.

Tallahassee was also the home of Florida State University and Florida Agriculture and Mechanical University. The system of community colleges came into being soon after the arrival of the 57 Club, and Leon County was promptly named as a site for one of them. Interestingly, when the community college program was adopted and given authority to site schools and start developing the system, there were to be two physical systems—one for "white" and one for "colored." The wasteful plan of building a "separate but equal" community college for blacks wherever the "white" school was located was deemed to be necessary. It was politically correct, given the then-prevailing legislative attitude toward integration. Pragmatically, it is fair to say that it was the proper way to go if there was to be any hope of securing funding for the system.

Each educational institution in Tallahassee was outstanding in its own way and fulfilled a legitimate educational purpose. The administrators, professors, and graduate students made up an identifiable part of the population of Tallahassee. However, while they joined with the old-time residents and the political community for certain functions or purposes, they maintained their autonomy just as other groups did, and each segment traveled its own path. In a sense, Tallahassee was four separate but compatible communities: educational, political, old or long-time residents of Tallahassee, and African Americans.

Florida State University was a dominant part of the city and a fine institution. When originally founded, it was a college for women and operated under the name Florida State College for Women. Parenthetically, at the same time the University of Florida in Gainesville admitted only male students. I was a freshman student at UF in 1942 before joining the Army. While the two schools were some 150 miles apart—and that was a long way to travel in '42—there was an awful lot of visiting between the students. The roads were narrow and generally not heavily traveled, but on weekends or other special days, students going from one school to the other in search of companionship kept the pavement warm.

One of the many attributes of FSU enjoyed by legislators was the circus staged by students. When legislators were meeting, there would always be a special performance for them. It was an unusually good show, even though the performers were students and, therefore, amateurs. The show was made up of traditional circus acts such as high-flying trapeze and high wire performances. Clowns were everywhere and very skillful. Even the master of ceremonies looked and sounded as though he came straight from Barnum & Bailey. The only things missing were the animals that were a part of the professional big top productions.

As each special show concluded, legislators and their families looked forward to the next presentation. It was always well done and on a high professional level. The great mystery was how ordinary college students could be so well trained and induced to perform those dangerous, death-defying circus acts. The other mystery, for some of us, was why the news media seemed to make so little of the existence of the circus. We thought it was underexposed and deserved more coverage.

Florida State University also operated a model grade school on its campus, and legislators who had children could bring them to Tallahassee during the session and enroll them for two months in the special school. The teaching staff was carefully selected, and all personnel connected with the school were well paid. It was a demonstration of what public education could be if we were willing to find enough money to adequately finance it. The quality of the education experience for the youngsters was very good. It also impressed the parents.

## Tallahassee Golf and Country Club

There were other noteworthy places to congregate, not the least of which was the picturesque and well-kept Tallahassee Golf and Country Club. It was a source of pride for the city. The golf course was challenging, and the views from key places would take your breath away. The clubhouse was large, well planned, and suitable for the fanciest balls. The parties given by the Speaker of the House and the President of the Senate were black tie affairs, and such formal balls just didn't get any better than the ones held there.

Then, as the integration movement began to accelerate, the city fathers decided that they should privatize the entire facility rather than admit African Americans. The title was transferred to a nonprofit corporation, and the public ownership was eliminated. The club meant so much to the community that its privatization was a major occurrence, and it caused quite a stir. The plan was successful for a while, but ultimately everything there was integrated.

## The Old Capitol

Situated on the top of a small hill near the intersection of Apalachee Parkway and Monroe Street in Tallahassee was the Capitol. Today we refer to it as the Old Capitol, because a new building to house the legislature and a part of the executive branch of Florida's government was constructed during the 1960s.

As one approached downtown Tallahassee from the east, she or he would be treated to a beautiful sight. It was rolling terrain, and the Parkway rose to the top of one of the hills about a mile from the intersection and then took a long dip before rising again to the Old Capitol. During the day the vista was impressive from that distance, and when the azaleas and other flowers were in bloom, it was picture-quality beauty. After dark the Capitol was illuminated with enough bright lights to attract attention to it, and the lighting accentuated its structural beauty. Many a night I arrived after dark and experienced a moment of genuine pride in our government as I came to the crest of the hill and could see that old building atop its own hill, looking back at me as if it understood my awe.

Working in the building was different than seeing it from the roadway. The workplace is a part of the legislative environment, and the Old Capitol was where the legislature met during the '50s and early '70s. The ambience was a part of the culture, and it was quite interesting. It also provided color in the legislative environment.

The Old State Capitol in its glory days.

Every senator and a few representatives had brass spittoons on the floor next to their desks. The surprise was that the members actually used them for their original purpose. Boiled peanuts were sold throughout the Capitol by local children, and their business was good. No one knows how many little brown bags filled with boiled peanuts were sold, but it was a big number. Other local children made a few extra dollars shining shoes in the hallways.

Then there were pages and messengers who served the coffee, delivered their messages, and otherwise contributed to the notion that legislators were important. It was a wonderful experience for youngsters. They were a part of the ambience. A few of them returned in later years as legislators or other officials.

In some ways, the Old Capitol was a source of embarrassment. Today it has been beautifully restored, but in 1957 the building was badly abused and neglected. Moreover, there had been additions on both the north and south ends to provide space for the House and Senate. They were poorly constructed, as anyone could see while walking in the basement, as the floors were at different levels.

I often spoke at committee meetings, which were held in crowded and sparsely decorated rooms in the Old Capitol.

## Jim Takes a Fall

Further evidence of the deplorable condition of the Old Capitol was the area directly beneath the dome of the building. It had been divided into rooms for offices, and at one point my offices were there. We were ever fearful of being trapped in a fire, and the dust was a respiratory menace. One day my son Jim, who was in middle school at the time, came for a visit and fell through one of the rotten areas of the floor down into the office below. Fortunately, only his pride was hurt.

However, as one might imagine, there was a lot of sentiment associated with the building, and most of us were glad it was saved and restored when the new Capitol was built.

# 4  *A Citizen Legislature* ————————————————

In 1957, the burden of solving all the major issues in Florida was placed on the shoulders of its citizen legislators, a group of part-time public servants with low pay and infrequent sessions. We met for sixty days every two years. It was often said that the state would be better off if the legislature met for two days every sixty years. Representatives were paid a mere $100 a month whether they earned it or not, plus $25 a day while in session. It was definitely a part-time job.

Legislators did not have private offices, there were no dictating or transcribing machines, secretaries worked in a common room, and all dictation took place at the members' desks on the floor of the House. Conferences with visiting constituents and lobbyists were also held at the members' desks.

Those desks were used so much, and for such a variety of tasks, that they occupied a special place in our hearts. Some members began to feel like they owned their desks while others, after sitting there for so many hours, felt a comfortable attachment to the old things. When the new Capitol was ready for occupancy, members were offered the opportunity to buy their desks. They sold out in a hurry. Mine was refinished by my son, Rick, and is currently used by his daughter to help facilitate her college studies.

It wasn't all that easy to keep abreast of what was going on when the House was in session. Bills were typed on a manual typewriter, reviewed by clerks, and delivered to the clerk of the House to be read for the first time and re-

Since there were no private offices, our conferences were held on the floor of the legislature. I'm on the left, speaking with Jim Russell of Pinellas County, Jim Sweeny of Volusia County, and Woodie Liles of Hillsborough County.

ferred to one or more committees. Eventually they were printed so that each member could have a copy, but quite often we would have to work with the only original copy, which was kept at a desk in the front of the chambers or, on occasion, a mimeographed copy. That was a complicated and inefficient procedure, especially when several people wanted to read a document at the same time.

Similarly, amendments were handwritten or typed on a form provided by the clerk. It was virtually impossible to have easy access to the content of an amendment under consideration by the House. The situation was uncomfortable for the members and, as I said before, terribly inefficient. Representatives frequently voted for or against a bill or amendment without the slightest hint as to what the written document contained.

Shortly after I left the House, a member representing Volusia County was asked by a constituent what happened to a local bill that the constituent and his organization were interested in defeating. The representative told the organization all about how the bill had been kept on the calendar until the end of the session and that it had died there. He was surprised and horrified shortly thereafter to learn that the bill had not died an ignominious death as he reported, but was instead passed and on its way to becoming a law.

Such political goofs were commonplace and caused untold embarrassment. The system was not entirely to blame, because representatives could familiarize themselves with the contents of bills if they were willing to spend time and energy on research. Nevertheless, we had to live with the system as it was. Much to our amazement, we were told that the system had been drastically improved in recent times and that we should be elated that we didn't have to work under the old procedure.

Serving in the Florida Legislature in the late 1950s and early 1960s was quite costly and ethically challenging. When I was first elected, all three partners in my law firm agreed on a plan that would guide us ethically and financially through the upcoming issues when questions and conflicts surfaced during my term of office.

We decided to open a new checking account, into which I would deposit every legislative salary check, every per diem check, and all expense reimbursement checks. Every expense involved in my legislative service for housing, food, transportation, and the like was paid from that account. By establishing this procedure, we could prove that the firm did not receive any of the funds paid to me by the state and that I did not receive any unauthorized income. After eight years in the House, that checking account was almost exactly $4,000 short of having enough money to pay all my expenses. That amount today would be two to four times the 1964 amount.

It should also come as no surprise that the members of the citizen legislature had more conflicts of interest than did the members of a more professional body. Back then there was no effective code of ethics. Each member pretty well set his own ethics agenda and—quite on his own—maintained his personal, moral, and ethical standards. Moreover, whatever rules or codes might have been adopted for the purpose of improving legislative conduct, enforcement of those rules would still have been a problem.

Public support is critical in order to compel adherence to a code of ethics, and the public was less concerned with potential conflicts of interest at that time. Voters did not demand a higher standard of conduct, and everyone understood that legislators could not live on the compensation paid in 1957. Representatives had to have a way to earn a living, which normally meant a full-time job or some other professional commitment. Those jobs, no matter how carefully screened, usually involved some sort of conflict with the public interest.

For example, I had clients in my law firm who moved furniture from state to state and from county to county. Their trade association often had an interest in certain bills pending before the legislature. They probably counted themselves lucky to have their lawyer on the inside of an organization that would be making decisions important to them. I had to inform my clients that if their legislation came before me, I would be obliged to recuse myself and not vote. They were disappointed, but agreed that I had an ethical obligation to remove myself from votes on issues that might be in conflict with the greater good of the public.

There were several other clients, such as banks, insurance companies, car dealerships, and also restaurants with liquor licenses that always had to be considered when legislation was moving across my desk. My observation was that almost every member had the same kind of conflicts I did. However, if I was not conscientious about the conflicts, there was no one whose job it was to remind me.

Unless an adversary or some other interested person made an issue about it, no one would even be aware of potential conflict. I tried to be especially careful because I was so concerned about building an image of integrity. I also had a senior partner who was overly sensitive about this subject and put it on the agenda of firm meetings on a regular basis. I observed that not all my legislative colleagues were that careful, and I'll wager there was a good bit of ethical mischief over this point.

Contrast the operational handicaps and ethical issues of the '57 legislature with what one sees in Tallahassee today and one can easily realize what changes have occurred over time. For instance, immediately west of the Old Capitol that was in use when the 57 Club was formed is the new Capitol. Even though it appears to have been modeled on the male genitalia and has also been the continuing butt of jokes that compare it to the finger symbol given by many irate drivers, the new Capitol is massive and functional.

The amenities of the House and Senate in the new Capitol are relatively modern. Voting machines instantly flash each member's vote, giant screens provide information such as the numbers and titles of bills under consideration, and electronic communication and information systems are available at each member's desk.

In the late '60s, legislative pay was increased from $100 to $1,000 a month over the objection of then-governor Claude Kirk. The pay, as well as the per diem payments, have been increased periodically ever since.

Today, legislators have good help from staffers and are provided small but adequate private office spaces equipped with modern electronic aids. There can hardly be any excuse for a member not knowing what is going on with legislative issues under consideration.

### An Often Told Story

As one might imagine, with all legislators being elected and, therefore, somewhat outgoing, there were jokes and folk stories exchanged throughout
the session. One story I heard at that time, and have frequently used in my
speeches, involved a young preacher who was called to a church in a rural
north Florida community.

The church had the reputation of being awfully hard on preachers, and it
was known that the congregation changed preachers frequently. So, as the
story goes, the young preacher worked very hard and prayed fervently for
success. After a year he stopped one of the older members of the church and
said, "Please tell me what is going on. I'm still here, but nobody says anything
to me about how I'm doing."

The old man replied, "All right young man, I'll tell you. You are doing a
good job, because if you weren't we would have asked you to leave. But don't
get the wrong idea, because the truth is, the people in this community don't
want any preacher at all, and you are about as close as we've ever come."

### Old Timers

As noted earlier, when the thirty-nine freshmen representatives arrived Tallahassee in April 1957, there were fifty-six House members already there and,
to some degree, they were experienced in the legislative process. Some had
survived at least one reelection campaign, but others had been in office long
enough to be called veteran lawmakers.

For the most part they were friendly, courteous, and helpful to the newcomers. There were opportunities to get acquainted with them, and it's fair
to say they were good mentors. It seemed that each newly elected legislator
gravitated toward those who paid attention to him or had some special quality
that was interesting to him individually. That was certainly applicable in my
case.

### Tom Beasley

Even though I did not vote for Tom Beasley to be our speaker, he didn't hold it
against me. We developed a casual friendship, and he treated me fairly during
the time he held that powerful office. He appointed me to the Appropriations
Committee, and toward the end of the session, when it was time to merge the

House and Senate budget bills into one so both houses could adopt it, he appointed me to the Conference Committee that authored the joint bill—a great honor for a young legislator. However, I'm afraid that I made his life miserable while I served on that committee.

On the day of my appointment, Tom asked me into his office and said that he was considering making me a conferee, but he wanted to know whether I would be a strong advocate for the House's position on the spending bill. I assured him that I could be as strong and tenacious as I needed to be and would not give in to the Senate members. As a matter of fact, I liked the spending bill we had worked out in the House, particularly the parts for funding public schools. I had worked hard throughout the session to win some favorable appropriations and wanted to keep them in the legislation.

The Senate conferees were seasoned members of the leadership, including Wilson Caraway of Tallahassee, who took LeRoy Collins' seat when Collins became governor; John Rawls of Marianna; and Tom Adams of Clay County. They came to the table prepared to dominate the proceedings and began by announcing that Wilson would be the chairman of the Conference Committee.

I considered objecting, but refrained from doing so after I was cautioned that it was the custom for the senator who chaired the Senate committee to assume the role of chairman of the joint committee. However, when Wilson began announcing what decisions he would be making for the group, I objected, and things suddenly turned ugly.

The senators were in a hurry and thought they knew what was best. It was obvious that they had no time for the likes of me. But I remembered my pledge to the speaker and told all members of the committee that I felt bound to fight for the more liberal provisions in the House bill and, therefore, could not condone the allocations announced by Senator Caraway.

Heated words flowed freely, and Tom Adams was assigned the job of taking me to another room and explaining the procedure. Tom was a leader in the Senate at that time and in later years became Secretary of State. He also ran with Reubin Askew as Askew's lieutenant governor. They served together for four years. Adams was without a doubt the political strongman on the Senate committee at that time. Senator Rawls—who was no softie either—and I also faced one another and had a few tests of wills. I stubbornly continued to explain my obligation and my unwillingness to give in.

Then came the climax. The heat was so intense that I wasn't sure how much more of my behavior Rawls would tolerate before he really lost his temper. He was a bull of a man, and I wasn't anxious to test his strength in a one-on-one physical confrontation. Adams and the others also lost patience with me, and even my fellow House members were chagrined. I asked for a recess and went to the floor of the House where there was a session in progress. I asked to be allowed to speak to the assembled body of legislators and was granted the privilege of using the lectern.

I quickly explained my position on the Conference Committee. I told my House colleagues about how I had derailed the train that was fired up and on track to give the Senate conferees what they wanted. I told them how much pressure had been focused on me—and that I was willing to take the heat—but needed to know I was doing what they expected of me. They gave me a resounding vote of confidence.

Speaker Tom Beasley was a bit shaken, but stood by me. Then he privately advised me that I wouldn't have to fight every issue that way, and he would be quite satisfied if most of the House positions were adopted, but he did not insist on all or nothing. So I went back to the committee, and we wrote a spending bill that both Houses accepted.

I was treated differently after that showdown. As a matter of fact, Speaker Beasley became quite friendly and helped me a lot as long as he served in the House. He eventually became a circuit judge. As for the other members of that Conference Committee, I worked closely with Senator Caraway for years in connection with the Southern Regional Education Board (SREB). He was also on that body's legislative advisory committee, and we attended meetings together regularly. We made one SREB trip to New Orleans. Senator Rawls became a judge on the District Court of Appeal, and we were together from time to time while I was on the Florida Supreme Court. Senator Adams urged me to run for Secretary of State and agreed to help in the campaign. I was certainly tempted, but felt that the time wasn't right.

Every two years a new Speaker of the House is installed with a fair amount of pomp and ceremony. When Tom Beasley was invested, his formal remarks were preceded by a few stories, one of which was about his early years in the world. He explained how important it is for a politician to have a humble beginning: "Being born in a log cabin is an excellent credential," he said. "I was not born in a log cabin, I'm sorry to say, but we did move into one as soon as my folks could afford it."

## Verle Pope

One of the most interesting senators we met at the St. Augustine Caucus in 1956 was Verle Pope. He was an old timer when the 57 Clubbers assembled in Tallahassee, and he had firmly established his niche in the legislative structure.

He represented St. Johns County and lived in St. Augustine, which should have aligned him with the senators from the small counties popularly known as the Pork Chop Gang. However, he did not follow any traditional logic or rule about such things. His role was that of a maverick.

Verle was a powerful speaker with the delivery of an evangelical preacher. He regularly spoke against special interest bills or amendments, and his verbal attacks were searing. Newspaper reporters liked him and were generous in the media space they gave him. His nickname was appropriately the "Lion of St. Johns."

None of the awards or attention he received affected him. He was seemingly unaffected by his stature in the Senate, and he was always courteous and helpful. His hobby was fishing for largemouth bass in the lakes and ponds around Tallahassee. He was a good fisherman and frequently invited me to accompany him on his outings.

The first few years I knew him, our relationship was relatively casual. I pretty much admired him from a distance, except when we were on a pond catching some of those bass. There we were competitors, with each of us trying to catch more or larger fish than the other.

When I reached the Senate, I was seated next to him. That was truly an experience. By that time, his hearing was beginning to fade, and he depended on me to tell him what was happening during debates. I would listen intently to my colleagues speak, trying my best to follow and evaluate the various arguments while Verle seemed to be nodding off or on a mental visit to another place, when all of a sudden he would ask me what was before the Senate. Because of his hearing problem, it was hard for me to quietly tell him what he wanted to know without interrupting the rest of the Senate, but I would always try.

As soon as I finished my explanation—or sometimes before I finished—Verle would be on his feet seeking recognition and permission to speak.

I've seen him begin an effusive oratory with only a vague idea of the specific point being debated and then proceed to make the most understandable and effective speech of the day. He always spoke extemporaneously—I don't remember Verle ever using notes. A legislator could feel good about the outcome of a debate if he was on the same side as the Lion of St. Johns.

I've also seen Verle's not-so-civil side. Picture this: Governor Claude Kirk is up on the rostrum in the chambers of the House of Representatives delivering his State of the State message to a joint session of the House and Senate. All the justices of the Florida Supreme Court, the elected cabinet officers, and hundreds of people are present to hear the significant words of wisdom from

Verle Pope seems to be dozing while I speak on the floor of the Senate. Dempsey Barron is on the right. (Photo courtesy Florida Archives.)

our state CEO, and there in the front row is Senator Pope with his legs crossed reading the morning newspaper. He even loudly turned the pages a few times. Everyone knew that it was payback time for some unkind thing the governor had said about the senator or, worse still, one of his pieces of legislation.

That was quite a sight. Not only did Verle make distracting noises with his newspaper, he stole the show from the governor. The reporters and cameramen instantly became more interested in what Verle was doing than in what the governor was saying—and Claude Kirk was a good speaker.

I introduce New York Mayor John Lindsay to Verle Pope in 1972, when Mayor Lindsay addressed both the Florida House and Senate.

## Movement Toward Professionalism

Throughout my years in the House, the issue about the value and effectiveness of a citizen legislature was always around. Being in the House was both a privilege and a tremendous responsibility. It was an important office with unlimited opportunities to make significant changes in state government. However, those opportunities were hard to develop because being a House member was only a part-time job and there was no professional staff to assist representatives working on major projects. When select committees were established for some special purpose (the vigilante-like Johns Committee, for instance), they were routinely authorized to hire staffing personnel. That offered some degree of help, but for all practical purposes the legislature was dependent upon the executive branch for its technical advice and clerical help.

There was a good bit of support for a more professional legislature. It was made up of those who thought the state would be better served if legislators were paid enough to justify annual sessions and something more than a biennial look at the business of the state by the legislative branch.

Also in that corner were those who were resentful of the executive branch and the control it exercised when the legislature was not meeting. And, of course, there were those who just thought it would be nice if their pay was increased.

On the other side were the young business and professional people who did not want a full-time political job and could not live on the amount of compensation being discussed, usually about $10,000 to $12,000 per year. However, the strongest arguments came from people like Senators Lawton Chiles and Louis de la Parte, who felt that until legislators had sufficient support for quality research and other assistance that freed up the member's time from the landslide of minutiae, nothing of any real importance could be accomplished by the legislature.

Lawton and Louis were right, of course. I was appointed vice chair of the Education Committee in my second session. Later, I became chairman in my third and fourth sessions, and I learned well how impotent a committee could be without research and clerical support.

My Education Committee made some wonderful improvements. We secured decent appropriations and helped establish the kindergarten and community college programs. We used flexibility in the Minimum Foundation Plan, which dealt with the financing of public education, to give some relief to the fastest growing counties while at the same time providing creditable support for the smaller and less-affluent counties. But, important as these victories were (and notwithstanding that they earned me the honor of being awarded the coveted School Bell Award), they did not represent the degree of catch-up that was necessary at the time. There was so much more that needed attention and that could have been accomplished if we had the proper support.

Sadly, it was not until the 1968 constitution was adopted that many of the needed changes were made. Once we started annual sessions and provided professional staffing for the committees and their key members, things began to change in a hurry. The sessions of the early '70s were perhaps the most productive and invigorating in the history of Florida. The changes brought about by the code of ethics and the sunshine laws were truly significant.

When the state abandoned the citizen legislature and adopted a professional approach with higher compensation, adequate staffing, single-member districts, and term limitations, the tone and core attitudes changed. Whether it is better or worse than what the 57 Clubbers knew is a question for the historians. However, as a member of the 57 Club, I have no hesitation about declaring that the modern legislature is more effective and technically qualified than ours was. Nevertheless, I am also obliged to say that we did some wonderful things and moved the state forward even in the face of tremendous opposition. Those were the good old days and the stuff from which we fashioned precious memories.

# 5 *The Social Calendar* ——————————————

In addition to the entertainment opportunities described previously, there was a lot going on that could not in good conscience have been considered work.

From the time of their election, 57 Club members received invitations to events around the state. Those parties and trips were so much fun and so beneficial that they were highlights of our legislative service, and we soon began regarding them as entitlements. A few events were regular, periodic affairs while others were one-time only events.

## The Daytona Speedway

The Daytona Speedway opened in the 1950s, and the Daytona Beach Chamber of Commerce, along with others, put on a wonderful party at the speedway honoring Representative Mallory Horne of Leon County. Mallory was not a member of the 57 Club, but he was always friendly to its members. Shortly after the speakership for the 1959 session was settled, we voted to make Mallory the speaker for 1961 so, at that weekend party, he was honored as the speaker-designate. His outstanding achievements in the legislature also included his later service as the President of the Senate.

During the party, members were introduced to Bill France, the man responsible for the huge speedway that is now known worldwide and attracts more than 200,000 fans for the annual Daytona 500. His engaging personality made everyone he met automatically like him. He was such an interesting man and his Horatio Alger story so exciting that all of us were fascinated and wanted to learn more.

Before France settled in Daytona Beach, he had been working as a mechanic and opened his own garage near Washington, D.C. In his free time, he raced on the local dirt-track circuit. Then, in 1934, he moved his family to Florida. According to stories at the time, he intended to move to Miami, but his car broke down in Daytona Beach. He liked the area, so he decided to stay there. He operated a small Amoco gas station on Main Street, trying to earn a living for his family by selling gasoline at around 20 cents a gallon.

At that time Daytona Beach was a mecca for land speed record attempts along its beach. However, the larger and safer Bonneville Salt Flats in Utah had just opened, and Daytona was losing much of its speed record appeal.

When France arrived in Daytona, there was a different kind of racing along the beach. The cars were "stock cars," very much the same as one could buy at an automobile dealer's showroom. Half of the race course was on the road and the other on the beach. The road portion was narrow and bumpy, and the beach portion was wide at low tide, but narrow when the Atlantic Ocean tide was high. At either end of the course there were turns where the drivers moved from the beach to the road at the north end and from the road back to the beach at the south end. Those turns were hard to navigate and became worse after every lap. Racing on such a track was much more that just driving a fast car. It was a test of skill and innovation as the drivers developed new techniques of driving in shallow water on the beach to try to cool the engines, and learning to put the cars into a broad slide on the beach as they approached the north turn. Bill France became interested in beach/road racing and was soon driving a car at awesome speeds on that race course.

Before long Bill became a racing promoter instead of a driver. Then it became apparent that the beach/road course was not going to work much longer because the weather and beach conditions were too unstable and difficult to predict. Also, crowds were difficult to control and the attendance capacity was limited. At the same time, the public's interest was growing in that rough-and-tumble sport. Having known Bill France, I always believed that he knew how popular stock car racing could become if properly promoted. At any rate, he decided to build a track with a new concept, and formed the National Association of Stock Car Auto Racing (NASCAR). Under that umbrella, he began sanctioning races in the South. He found a way to herd the drivers into NASCAR—no easy task, I'll wager.

The Daytona Speedway was a separate enterprise but, at the same time, it was related to NASCAR. Bill France went to the Florida Legislature shortly before the birth of the 57 Club and created a separate local authority that successfully negotiated a long-term lease on city property and adjacent privately owned land and also helped secure tax-exempt financing for a track to be operated by a corporation owned and controlled by France and his family.

The leasehold agreement with the city was an interesting and critical milestone in the development of the Daytona International Speedway, home of the Daytona 500. The land was very valuable, so it was a significant asset of the city. It was the ideal location for the speedway, and the only parcel of land in that vicinity with enough acreage to accommodate the proposed race track. Consequently, use of the city land was an absolute necessity for the project. Negotiations were confidential (the sunshine laws were not yet on the books) but filled with tension.

One issue illustrates the way in which the parties behaved. There was a profit-sharing provision advocated by those concerned with protecting the public's interest. This provision was opposed by France and his associates. After a lot of give and take, a watered-down alternative was agreed upon in which there would be no obligation for France to share profits with the city until the profits reached a threshold, after which the city would receive a modest percentage of the bottom-line profits.

Needless to say, the profit threshold was so high that no one thought it would produce very much for the city or be very meaningful to the financial operations of the speedway. Nevertheless, it was a part of the package that went to the city commission for approval. On the evening when the lease was to be considered, and at an appropriate time, one of the commissioners moved that the lease be amended by striking from the lease the paragraph containing the profit-sharing provision. However, his motion only referred to the paragraph to be stricken by its number, leaving everyone in the dark as to what was in that paragraph—except, of course, those who knew the motion was coming. Those individuals knew what they were doing.

Without explanation or debate, the motion was passed and the profit-sharing provision went off into the obscure place where discarded provisions go to die.

History tells us that the speedway and other elements of France's enterprises have been good for the city of Daytona Beach. Whether the profit-sharing provision would have produced revenue for the city has become a moot issue. No one seems to begrudge the speedway's enormous success, all of which began with that lease of city land.

The speedway was also the place where the party for Mallory Horne was held and where legislators experienced high-speed rides around the banked, tri-oval track and saw a NASCAR race; they also met a few of the then-famous drivers; plus they were treated to the customary food and drink for lawmakers—all that near the "World's Most Famous Beach."

## Culture in Sarasota

At the other end of the entertainment spectrum, the City of Sarasota hosted a fine party every other year that featured a touch of culture at the Ringling Art Museum, located in a large building on very valuable land in Sarasota. The museum contains some of the world's art treasures, and it all belongs to the state. Legislators were treated to a fine meal catered at the museum and accompanied by lovely music, although it was not live. Next was a guided tour of the paintings and the building. Then we would hear about the need for a new roof or a new air-conditioning unit to save the works of art. The rest of the weekend was spent on the water or on the golf course, and the food and accommodations were very good. As at other such parties, we were treated as though we were important dignitaries.

## Miami's Social Affairs

Parties in Miami were always favorites with legislators because they were so well done. There was also a wide variety of things to do and places to visit. But back at the Capitol following one of those annual outings, Representative Mack Cleveland of Sanford asked for permission to speak on a point of personal privilege about his experience at the weekend affair. Mack, like Mallory Horne, was not a 57 Club member. He had been elected in Seminole County two years before, but I had known him much longer and held him in high regard. His county was one of those that had two representatives, and Mack was fortunate to have Gordon V. Frederick as a colleague. Gordon was a member of the 57 Club, and

Mack Cleveland's address to the House on a point of personal privilege was ill-considered. (Photo courtesy Florida Archives.)

a good one. He and Mack complemented each other, and there was a good bit of synergism when they teamed up on a project. They worked well together and represented their county with considerable skill.

Since speaking on a point of personal privilege was reserved for sensitive issues like an alleged unfair attack on a member by the press or a colleague, everyone suddenly began to pay attention to Mack. Most members even put down their newspapers and interrupted their eating of boiled peanuts. It was a dramatic moment. When all members were attentive, Mack began, and his speech went something like this:

> Mr. Speaker, members of the House, members of the press, and fellow Floridians, I rise to speak to you today on a point of personal privilege because of the seriousness of what happened in Miami. First, I want you to know that I am a bachelor, a single man. I have never been married and I have no present intention of marrying. I want all of you to know that because I don't want a repeat of what happened in Miami recently.

> I'm sure you remember that when we were in Miami for that legislative weekend, one of the prominent department stores gave each of us a credit card. When I opened my envelope, I found a card in the name of Mrs. Mack Cleveland. Again, there is no Mrs. Cleveland.

Just then a representative from Miami was recognized to ask a question. He said, "Mr. Cleveland, would you believe me if I told you that we made the list for the credit cards from the hotel registry?"

Mack took his seat mumbling something about not knowing how to keep his mouth shut. Gordon said nothing.


## Official Functions

There were formal parties, most of which were official functions. The governor held a reception at the official residence shortly after the convening of each biennial session. He was there in the capacity of host. Other guests included the justices of the Florida Supreme Court, cabinet members, and always a few special friends.

Legislators were guests of honor and made to feel honored, which reminded me of the old corporate practice of giving subordinates something for the ego to keep them happy in lieu of pay raises. In any event, they were nice affairs. Men wore their tuxedos, women wore long gowns, and everyone was on his/her best behavior.

As I was dressing for one of those parties, I thought I must really be somebody, all dressed up and going to an affair with the governor and the leaders of the legislative and judicial branches of government. But, as I came into the room where my children were waiting to say goodbye, my little girl, Cynthia, brought me back to reality by saying, "Oh Daddy, you look so nice. You look just like a waiter."

## Private Homes

Then there were the parties in private homes. They ranged from small receptions to elaborate, catered theme parties. Two of the more fancy ones come quickly to my mind.

The first was an especially elaborate party at the home of the owner of Rose Printing Company. The company had a lucrative contract to print the legislative calendars and journals. A yacht owned by the company was always standing by for fishing trips in the gulf, and the home of the owner was large and beautiful.

As the guests arrived for this particular affair, the men were furnished with denim overalls and the women were given denim skirts which were to be worn over their clothing. These outfits made us appear as though we were all farmers. The theme of the party was the musical *Oklahoma*, and it was carried out in great detail. Costumed Florida State University students served drinks, professional waiters served the well-prepared food on pewter plates, and FSU music students performed skits from the play. Needless to say, no one dared tamper with the Rose printing contract.

The other party is remembered for a humorous incident. It was one of those affairs where the representatives, their families, and their staffers were invited. The home was beautiful and the party was held on the deck around a huge swimming pool. Representative Baldy Strickland, a commercial mullet fisherman from Citrus County on the west coast, was in attendance, and it was he who made the evening absolutely unforgettable. As he arrived all dressed up and a bit uncomfortable in a suit and tie, he began making his rounds and greeting the other guests. As he approached where I was standing he spotted Betty Carter, an aide in my office he had come to know. For some reason, he picked her up and walked to the edge of the pool as though to throw her in, but at the last second he stopped and backed away.

I knew and liked Baldy, so I joined with the others in being amused at his bit of nonsense. Only I went a step further and asked, "What's the matter Baldy, no guts?" Whereupon, he returned to the pool and with the lady in his arms stepped off the edge and into the deep end. The two of them—he in his good suit and she with her pretty dress and fresh hair-do—went in over their heads.

For my part in the fiasco, I paid for a new hair-do, the cleaning of the dress, and the repair to her wristwatch that also took a dunking. It was a dumb thing for me to do, and an even dumber thing for Baldy. I hope we have both since been forgiven. I'm absolutely certain that Baldy was because he was so likeable.

Baldy supported himself by catching and selling mullet. It is fair to say that in those days a commercial mullet fisherman did not earn a lot of money, in spite of the fact that the mullet was a unique fish. For one thing, mullet are not caught with a hook and line. If one is to catch mullet, there must be a net of some sort; either a cast net that requires strength and skill, or a commercial net that is set with the use of a boat, unless the mullet being chased are in shallow water where the net may be set by waders.

Whether mullet are good to eat is a controversial question. There are a lot of bones and the meat is heavy and oily. Most of the southern people I know developed a taste for smoked mullet, but it is seldom featured on a restaurant menu.

Baldy Strickland was a mullet fisherman when not serving in the Florida House. (Photo courtesy Florida Archives.)

When I first met Baldy, I was aware of his commercial mullet fishing business, so I asked him if he had heard the story of Tampa attorney Pat Whitaker and his famous defense of fishermen accused of violating state fishing laws. Whitaker had won the case by asserting that mullet are not really fish because they have bird-like gizzards rather than stomachs. Therefore, he maintained, his clients could not be guilty of violating a fishing law. Baldy knew of the story, but firmly believed that mullet were fish, not fowl, regardless of their digestive system or the brilliant defense of attorney Whitaker.

## Notable Homes and Estates

There were historically significant private homes and other properties to be seen and appreciated, and the Parade of Homes always included a few that were the most modern and luxurious of them all. However, there were two multi-acre properties that were the most interesting and best known among legislators. Moreover, they were as much a part of the political scene as the legislative halls in the Capitol where the state's business was conducted.

The first one was the Piney Z Farm, located east of town on Highway 27, also known as Apalachee Parkway. At the time of the 57 Club, the farm was owned by Senator Pete Gibson of Perry. It had been in the Gibson family for a very long time, and the family members had resisted developers' desires to put improvements on it. There was a large home, acres and acres of fertile farm land, and a good-sized lake. The lake was, in a sense, man-made by Pete's father when he dammed up a large stream that ran through the farm. He did that and changed the course and flow of the stream before there were significant controls on such alterations to the environment. Apparently there were no successful challenges once it was done.

Pete Gibson was a bright, successful young man who won a seat in the Florida Senate. He regularly entertained his Senate friends at the farm and allowed all of his friends and their families to enjoy activities such as picking ripe berries and ears of corn, fishing in the lake, shooting skeet, and swimming in the pool. It was a treat for those fortunate enough to be invited. The Piney Z Farm was privately owned, but was enjoyed by so many who were politically involved that it took on a semi-official role in all important political events. An invitation to visit or participate in something being held at the Piney Z was tantamount to being an integral part of the legislative process. Consequently, most representatives coveted their inclusion in this private legislative club.

Pete died an untimely death, but his widow Grace (now Grace Dansby) carried on with Pete's tradition and Piney Z Farm remains the basis for fond memories of those days when southern hospitality at the farm rivaled that of any similar facility.

The other noteworthy estate was known as the "Slew." It was located north of town, and was reached by traveling north on Meridian Road. The name of the road is appropriate because it follows the Tallahassee Meridian, an imaginary line known to all surveyors and land title attorneys as the place where all property descriptions in Florida originate.

At some point in time, said to be during the '50s, the Slew was acquired by Mallory Horne, an attorney and state representative from Leon County. The property soon developed the reputation of being something like an annex of the Capitol. The main building was a large, lodge-like facility. There were sleeping rooms, a master dining room, and a large room suitable for entertaining or just lounging. There were also plenty of bathrooms and outbuildings.

As mentioned previously, Mallory was a master host. He seemed to enjoy every minute of his time in that role, whether he was entertaining a small group of special friends or the entire Florida Senate. He made the Slew available for special events such as informal caucuses and gatherings sponsored by lobbyists where privacy was a key factor. Individuals often arranged to stay there from time to time.

Incidentally, when the Slew was at the peak of its popularity, "Government in the Sunshine" laws did not exist, so individuals and official groups could meet there privately with impunity. And, like Las Vegas, "What went on at the Slew, stayed at the Slew."

The outdoors were as impressive as the indoors. There was a large lake with boats for fishing and airboats for sightseeing and other thrills at high speed. The wooded areas were pretty much in their natural state—rugged beauty.

Like the Piney Z, it truly was a branch of the Capitol. I would venture to say that there was almost as much state legislative business transacted at the Slew as at the Capitol.


## Informal Gatherings

There were other forms of entertainment that were less formal, but just as much a part of the legislative culture. Included in this category were hospitality rooms at local hotels, hunting and fishing trips, and important sports events. One trip in that category was a weekend fishing trip to a spot in Jefferson County.

It was a special weekend at Nutall Rise, to which I was invited by Representative George Anderson. George and I were friends from our early days as legislators. The invitation was informal and nonspecific. The date was about the only thing he told me about the trip at that point. I liked to fish, and I was always up for a trip so long as there were no strings attached. George assured me that it was not a legislative affair, only a gathering of some friends who liked to fish.

George and I learned much about one another during that long weekend of fishing with his friends from Monticello. I also learned his friends were real and true. They genuinely liked George. They enjoyed his company, and during the weekend everyone managed to talk with me one-on-one and tell me of George's attributes. He could do no wrong in their eyes.

At Nutall Rise, one of the poker players used the expression made famous by Lawton Chiles near the close of his campaign with Jeb Bush: "the old he-coon walks before the light of day." The poker player was bluffing. For him, unlike Lawton, it was wishful thinking.

George Anderson's friend, Tippy Shuman, was the organizer, chief cook, and fishing guide for the weekend. He did a great job, and we kept in touch for several years thereafter. There were three or four other friends and they were all male, of course, and all great hosts. One was a dentist who seemed to own the house in which we stayed at Nutall Rise. Importantly, there were no other legislators nor any lobbyists invited. Everyone—particularly George—avoided talk of legislative issues and interests. It was a purely social and recreational event for me.

As I said earlier, Nutall Rise is in Jefferson County, which adjoins Leon County, the home of Tallahassee. So we were never more than about an hour from the capital. We did not take time away from fishing for lectures on geology or geography or names of landmarks. However, the first time we left the house in the boat, someone pointed out the "rise," or spring, where water comes up to the surface from underground and runs off to the Aucilla River and ultimately to the Gulf of Mexico.

Years after the fishing trip I learned that the Aucilla River actually goes underground at two or more locations and then rises to the surface and flows as an ordinary river. Since those places where it comes up to the surface are somewhat different from the typical spring, the term "rise" makes sense. Incidentally, the Aucilla River and Nutall Rise are valuable sites to those who gather and study artifacts and other evidence of prehistoric people and animals.

I am still not certain why the word Nutall precedes Rise, but I have been told that there was a Nutall family that was influential since Civil War days. The family lived nearby and owned much of the land around the rise. I'll probably never know whether that story was true, but I'll never forget the fish we caught, cooked, and ate, or the other things that occurred there. Those fish were thoroughly cleaned by Tippy and cooked to perfection in a batter that had as its moisture a quality beer. A dinner like that must be preceded by a bit of beer directly into the diners. We followed that rule.

## An Obstacle Course

Another telling example of the quality of the experience of fishing near Nutall Rise was the thrill of getting to and from the fishing spots. Along the way, the river picks up water from drainage sites and small springs or "rises." Some of those tributaries are good for fishing, but getting to them is difficult. In fact, getting down the river safely required a navigator skilled in avoiding the hidden rocks. In parts of the river, there is no marked channel and the rocks are huge. A boater's worst nightmare is hitting a large, submerged rock at high speed.

Notwithstanding the obstacles and fearsome rocks, it was thrilling to go speeding down that river, believing the pilot knew where each rock was located and praying that he didn't forget a single one. And, of course, catching fish until we were tired of pulling them in made it a happy holiday.

# PART 2

*The Issues*

# 6  *Segregation* ─────────────────────────────

It should not have been a surprise to any member of the 57 Club that serious racial issues confronted them at the 1957 session of the legislature. After all, every one was a resident of Florida, and it would not have been possible for a person to live in the state and be unaware of the racial segregation that existed everywhere.

Neither could a person have been through a political campaign for any public office—and particularly for the legislature—and not know that there was agitation for change, and that change would bring controversy. However, the specifics of segregation and the intensity of demand for change varied from county to county. That could account for some of the differences that existed among state legislators concerning this sensitive subject.

Obviously, the greater reason for the differences of opinion stemmed from individual experience. Since every person is the sum of his or her past, if we could trace each life through the growing process we might better understand what moves people to behave as they do. While time and space prohibit such a study here, we should briefly and informally review what occurred in Florida in terms of racial segregation leading up to the first session of the 57 Club.

Although Florida was, in 1957, a tourist-oriented state in which there were pockets of cosmopolitan populations, it was situated in the Deep South and in many ways resembled its sister states in the southeastern portion of the country. It had been a part of the Confederacy, and its soldiers fought the

Army of the United States in the Civil War for the right to secede from the Union. Florida fared no better than the other Confederate states in the Reconstruction of the South, and that unhappy experience intensified the bitterness generated during the war.

We must remember that the culture of the South was based on slavery. No matter how much we deplore what was done to the African Americans who were brought here by unsavory slave traders, we must concede that slavery was the way of life for those who lived here. Although they were misguided and cruel in the way they engaged in commerce and relied on slave labor, white Floridians, for the most part, treasured the material things the prosperity brought them and were extremely resentful when, as a part of Reconstruction, their way of life was taken away and a whole new system installed, with former slaves involved in the governance process.

Predictably, the bitterness did not subside quickly. There are people today who still detest an entire race of human beings based upon the resentment generated in the last half of the 1800s and passed down from generation to generation. That anger was at least partially responsible for the formation of the Ku Klux Klan and undoubtedly served as justification for the atrocities committed in the name of vigilante justice.

Although each community throughout the state has its own history, all the tales of prejudice are pretty much the same. Wherever there was hatred and wherever one race of humans detested another, there were deliberate acts that caused humiliation, hurt feelings, and damage to persons and property. Since there was some measure of anger and bitterness in every community in Florida, it follows that there were hurtful and damaging actions in every community. The perpetrators of violence picked the time and place for their acts of terrorism, and for the most part they chose wisely, because it was a rare happening when the government punished one of them for their hurtful actions.

## Rosewood

One place where racial hatred turned regular people into a vicious mob was in Levy County of northwest Florida, where the small town of Rosewood was located near Cedar Key. Rosewood, whose name came from the red cedar trees that grew wild around there, had only black residents, and not many of them. It is said that the total population at the time of the tragic incident was less than 400. The brief history of what happened was told by Daryl L. Jones on June 11, 1999, in a speech in Washington, D.C. The substance of what he reported is summarized here:

On New Year's Day in 1923 a young white woman, who lived in a nearby town where quite a few men of Rosewood were employed, asserted she had been attacked in her own home by a black man. An escaped convict was in the vicinity, and for various reasons he was assumed to be the perpetrator of the alleged crime. A manhunt followed, and vigilantes participated. Tension mounted, and it was thought the convict was hiding in Rosewood.

After at least one act of violence by the hunters, the people of Rosewood gathered in specific houses and tried to prepare for the worst. One of the houses was used as a shelter for the children, and several armed citizens were there to protect them. That house was approached by a team of vigilantes, a pet was shot and forcible entry was attempted. Then a fire fight broke out where the children were hiding and two vigilantes were killed early on.

The reaction was swift and with equal violence. Rifles and shotguns were fired from the outside, killing more people. The battle continued to escalate, and there were additional casualties on both sides as well as extensive property damage. As a matter of fact, it was reported that by Sunday morning only twelve houses were standing in the little town, and soon they were all burned to the ground.

## Martin Luther King Jr. Visits St. Augustine

More than four decades after the violence in Rosewood, the hatred remained. It manifested itself again in 1964, when Dr. Martin Luther King Jr. appeared on the Florida scene. He targeted the historically important city of St. Augustine to break down old prejudices and discrimination in the state. His followers went to the motels en masse and dared to jump into the swimming pools. They were arrested, and many were locked in jail under deplorable conditions.

## A Lawyer Named Toby Simon

During this tense time, a matter that gave me an opportunity to help a friend and bring about a happy outcome related to a lawyer named Toby Simon. Toby was never a legislator; however, he lived at the same time as we who were members of the 57 Club. Moreover, he was a fighter for fairness in racial matters, even as we were fighting to keep our public schools open. Toby and

I came to know one another because we were both interested in what was happening in our state and active in the efforts to shape the future. Our paths were bound to cross.

Toby Simon was practicing law in Miami when he heard what was happening in St. Augustine. At his own expense and at considerable risk to his personal and professional well being, he went to the troubled city and began assisting the protesters with their legal problems. He worked hard to get several out of jail.

Not everyone appreciated his intervention. The St. Johns County Bar Association soon notified Toby that it would be instituting proceedings against him in response to a complaint that he was soliciting legal business, a grievous sin of ethics. Because of the intense feelings, his right to practice law was in danger. Toby was worried.

He asked me to help him, but prefaced the request with assurance that he would understand if I declined. He knew how bitterly controversial his case would be and how serious the legal and political fallout could become. He also asked activist attorney Cody Fowler of Tampa, a senior partner in Fowler White, one of Florida's leading law firms, to assist him. Both of us agreed without hesitation to try to save his license. Toby was grateful until the day he died, and Cody Fowler and I were proud that he turned to us.

Our victorious strategy was to spread a little sunshine on what was happening in St. Augustine because we believed that the Bar committee would not continue with the persecution of Toby if it occurred where everyone could watch it. We filed a motion in the Florida Supreme Court asking for a totally open proceeding and attached a copy of the notice that Toby had received. (See the Florida Bar, Complainant, v Tobias Simon, Respondent, Supreme Court of Florida, 171 So. 2nd 372, December 17, 1964, for a summary of the formal proceedings. A copy is in the Appendix.)

While the petition was being processed, my responsibility was to establish contact with the local Bar Association and make ready to defend Toby in that venue. Although our request in the Supreme Court

Toby Simon put his license to practice law on the line when he assisted followers of Dr. Martin Luther King Jr. in St. Augustine.

for an open process was denied, the opinion and media interest it stirred helped to accomplish our goal. The needed sunshine was there. The rest was confidential.

Eventually the whole matter was dropped, but Toby's courageous service during those dark days continues to be commemorated. Each year, the Florida Bar selects a lawyer who has provided important legal services without charging for doing so and designates that person to receive a very prestigious award. It was appropriate for the Bar to honor Toby by naming the award the Tobias Simon Pro Bono Award and relating it to the kind of services he was providing when he was threatened with punishment for doing so.

## Daytona Beach

I was born in Daytona Beach, located on the eastern coast of Florida, in 1924, and I grew up there. Generally, it was a relatively progressive city. The daily newspaper, the *Daytona Beach News Journal*, was an opinion maker. It was owned and operated by the Davidson family, who were bona fide social liberals and who dedicated their time and a generous portion of their newspaper capacity to exposing injustice and discriminatory practices. They advocated tolerance and empathy as opposed to a desire to keep African Americans in a subordinate role.

Notwithstanding those and other efforts to promote good will and peaceful coexistence in Daytona, I saw things in my early years that are hard to believe today.

There were, of course, the separate public restrooms and drinking fountains for "white" and "colored." The signs posted were neither discrete nor subdued. They were posted in plain sight in all the places where prospective users could see them. The message was perfectly clear—people of color were not allowed to use the facilities designated for white people.

Segregation was also practiced in hospitals, doctors' offices, law firms, and almost every place else. The public schools were said to be separate but equal. They were certainly separate, but they were anything but equal. Segregation meant that, insofar as race was concerned, whites were superior to blacks, and that was a terrible and direct insult. It was demeaning and demoralizing to all who were black, and it also perpetuated racial hatred and bitterness.

Segregation had led to an outrageous practice common in coastal cities such as Daytona Beach, where there was an inland waterway that separated those who could afford to live near the ocean from the others. There was a rule that no black person could be on the beach side after dark unless working for a white resident, and he/she was required to carry a note from the employer. One incident I remember well occurred just after sundown, when a black man was reported to be violating the rule. All four draw bridges were raised to prevent him from crossing to the mainland, and he was hunted down. He was caught and arrested after he jumped in the river and attempted to swim back to where it was legal for him to be out on a public street.

Another typical story involved a neighbor of ours when I was eight-to-ten years old. The neighbor had been a "Rum Runner" in the days of Prohibition. He would pick up a load of intoxicating liquor at Ponce Inlet, south of Daytona, and, using back roads, drive it north to some staging area in Georgia, North Carolina, or Tennessee. He was a fearless driver, and his cars had been modified to carry heavy loads and travel at high speed.

I overheard him tell my father about his ability to outrun state and federal officers who were trying to catch him. He eventually was caught, spent a year in jail, paid fines, and suffered humiliation, but was always proud of the driving skills he acquired and the large amount of money he earned and saved. He drove in several of the Beach/Road stock car races.

Early one fall morning, my father and that neighbor were going quail hunting. Shortly after reaching the open highway, they came upon an old car being slowly driven by an elderly black man. Over my father's objections, the neighbor drove right up to the rear of the other car, maneuvered so as to place his front bumper against the rear bumper of the man's car, and speeded up to more than sixty miles per hour. He pushed the other car at that speed over a narrow, bumpy road for ten miles or so. While being so pushed, the driver fought to retain control of his car as it weaved back and forth, nearly leaving the road several times.

My father never hunted with him nor did he ever ride with him again. However, it didn't bother the neighbor one bit. Soon he was telling others how he terrified a black man by pushing him at high speed. It was considered a funny story by most of those who listened, even though it was terribly dangerous and not a bit funny to the victim. Had the other driver actually lost control, there would have been at least one fatality.

In that same time period in Daytona, there was a gruesome accident in which a taxi driver, who happened to be an African American, ran over and killed a three-year-old white girl from a fairly large family. He was arrested and arraigned before a justice of the peace, but there was no testimony about how the accident happened. Did the child run into the path of the car?

Did the driver have any way to avoid the accident? Was the driver guilty of negligence?

The justice of the peace routinely ordered the taxi driver transported to the county seat, some twenty miles to the west, for the purpose of booking following his arrest. As the constable was driving, the prisoner was locked in the rear seat of the squad car. About halfway to the county seat, the constable said, two men stopped him, took his prisoner, and shot him. There were no witnesses except the constable, who said that he was unable to identify the killers. It was rumored that the older brothers of the little girl were responsible for the crime, but there was never an arrest or trial, and life went on as before.

## My Thinking Changes

Then came World War II, where I had a little taste of what segregation was like, although it was nothing as compared to the separation of the races.

As a private in the Army, I was turned away from the officers' club, the officers' mess hall, and their restrooms by stark signs that read: "For Officers Only." When I was first confronted with that, it provoked in me feelings of being unclean and unworthy. It even made me question my relevance as a human being. Those feelings helped me to realize that the system of segregation I had grown up with—and continued to live with—was an indefensible atrocity perpetrated on the black race. More important, the experience enhanced my empathy for others. Within six months I became an officer, and I got over the hurt of those days, but I never forgot the sting of segregation or the effect it had on me.

## A Surprise in England

There were other experiences during my days in the Army while the war was raging that had an effect on my attitude related to the subject of race relations. One such example occurred while I was in England recovering from wounds I received in Europe. It came to my attention that a large number of young British women, who happened to be white, were hosting integrated dances for American soldiers. Biracial social functions—particularly dances—were just not done where I had grown up. It was the type of activity that the strongest supporters of segregation feared and abhorred.

When first confronted with this in England, I was still under the influence of my racial socialization of prewar days in Daytona Beach, and I couldn't

An integrated social gathering in 1945 England—an event unheard of in the southeastern United States at that time.

believe it was happening. As I pondered the social event, I soon realized that my reaction of astonishment was unjustified and that my viewpoint was beginning to change.

At about the same time, I was experiencing further personal changes in my thinking as I prepared to go back to my tank platoon near the Rhine River in time for the planned crossing and movement toward Berlin. Given the combat experiences I had already been through, and the dark cloud of depression hanging over me because of what I knew was awaiting me on the other side of the English Channel, I realized that I was not the teenage boy who left Daytona Beach such a short time before. I needed to allow my conscience and beliefs to mature and catch up with my general maturity.

Thoughts that challenged my moderate, learned attitude toward segregation flooded my mind and a battle of sorts raged within me. One part of me was clinging to the old way. The rest of me was coming to the realization that segregation was wrong and that it had to change. That inner conflict provided respite from anticipatory thoughts of the coming battle, but it nagged me for reconciliation. When I finally arrived back in my hometown after the war, I could not understand why there were still so many people lacking in empathy who were determined to preserve the traditional practices of segregation.

## Mary McLeod Bethune Intervenes

In Daytona Beach in the early 1940s, black people were not allowed on the beach or in that part of the Atlantic Ocean. There were no demonstrations or protests. That was the law, and it was enforced by city police and sheriff's deputies. It finally took the efforts of Mary McLeod Bethune, founder of Bethune-Cookman College, to acquire a swimming facility for blacks.

Bethune-Cookman College was located on West Second Avenue in the part of town where most black people lived, and Mrs. Bethune spent most of her time there. She and her staff were moderates. That is to say, they advocated change and kept the pressure on, but there was no inflammatory rhetoric, no threats of violence, and all participants conducted themselves in an orderly manner.

Mrs. Bethune led a drive to raise enough money to buy a tract of beachfront property in Volusia County, south of New Smyrna Beach, where she and others established a swimming facility named Bethune Volusia Beach. It was more than an hour's drive from the campus, but it provided a place where African Americans could enjoy the ocean and sunshine without risking arrest, or worse.

## Military Intervention

World War II saw great changes in the state, including in my hometown. The Army took over hotels and other facilities for use by trainees, including members of the Women's Army Corps (WACS). Airports were taken from the cities and counties, and new ones were built to accommodate the training of fledgling Navy and Army Air Force pilots. By and large, the men and women training in Florida were white. But, as time went on, the gradual integration of the Armed Forces became more than rumor and black troops appeared.

I don't know about the rest of Florida, but in the Daytona Beach area the integration movement provoked some hard feelings and required a bit of discretion. The first time in my life I ever saw African Americans playing on the beach and swimming in the ocean was when I was home on leave from my duties in the Army. While riding in a car on the "World's Most Famous Beach," I came upon a section of the beach that was roped off and closed to vehicular traffic. Within the enclosure were the military people, including African Americans. I learned that it had become a common practice to set aside areas of the beach in that way, and that protests from local folks fell on deaf ears.

One would think that the locals would have grown used to the changes the war brought to communities, and I feel that most did. My own attitude certainly grew even more empathic toward minorities as a result of my service in the Army. The military never became fully integrated until Harry S. Truman was president, but in Europe, and in the military facilities in America, there was growing evidence that integration was coming and that people could adjust to it.

But, for the record, I can testify that the wartime experiences did not extinguish all of those old feelings and attitudes in many people from all walks of life.

## The Judge Declares an Emergency

At least twelve years after the war, when I had been elected to the House of Representatives and was a member of the 57 Club, there was an incident which demonstrated that old feeling do not easily disappear.

One bright morning after I had been elected to the House, a municipal judge burst into my office in Daytona Beach. He looked as though he was going to have a heart attack. He had been driving along the beach and had seen a small group of African Americans (only that wasn't the way he described them) enjoying a morning dip in the Atlantic Ocean—something that was not done at that time. He was furious and objected to their presence on the beach. He wanted to know what I, as his state representative, was going to do about that "emergency."

I had never seen him so excited or so demanding, and he wasn't easily calmed. I assumed that I lost his future political support for my failure to prevent token racial integration of the Atlantic Ocean.

## Racial Prejudice Remained Alive and Well

Moreover, when I was a candidate for election to the House, I discovered how alive and vibrant the racial issue was. I found it to be something that was on the mind of most every voter at the time. It would come up in almost every conversation in some way. Sometimes I would be asked forthrightly about my views on integrating the schools or some other venue that had been in the news, such as lunch counters, beaches, or movies. Some would let me know that they had come to a rally to hear what each candidate had to say about integration. Others were indirect. They would tell me their views and then await my response. It was on everyone's mind—including my barber's.

I had a favorite barber on Main Street in Daytona who had cut my hair ever since I delivered newspapers in that neighborhood while I was still in high school. He was an outspoken segregationist who would talk into his customers' ears as he worked on their hair. The "N" word was used regularly without shame or embarrassment, even when the young black man who swept the floors could hear him. Otherwise, he was a fine barber and a decent person.

When I qualified as a candidate, he readily put one of my signs in his front window and spent time talking into the ears of his customers about me. There were two strange things about that situation. First, he did those things knowing I was starting as the underdog, and that the odds of my winning made me the long shot, yet he campaigned for me as though I was the favorite. No one was happier than my barber when I won.

The second and most important oddity was that he never talked to me about segregation. I suppose he assumed that since I had been in his shop so many times I surely knew his views, and he was right. But interestingly, he never questioned me about my views nor did he ask me to vote in a way he wanted me to on any issue. Political help like that was a rarity.

## The Black Vote

In each community there was the black vote that every candidate wanted. If there was to be any hope of success, the campaign had to find a way to win a fair share of those votes. When I started my campaign, I knew practically nothing about how to campaign for the African American votes. I had some vague idea about what the residents from the black section of Daytona Beach wanted from the government, but the logistics of an organized effort to get the voters to the polling places and induce them to vote for me were still a mystery. Moreover, I learned early on that debating the issues, promising better roads, or paying more attention to their announced needs did not have much to do with how many votes I would get. Much of what I learned came as a shock to me, and the wonder was that my inexperience didn't wipe me out.

My first move was a visit to Bethune-Cookman College. Many alumni stayed in the Daytona area following graduation, and they tended to maintain contact with the school. The combination of their presence and the community leadership role played by the college created a logical presumption that those who were leaders in the school were also leaders in the African-American community. It followed, I assumed, that if I could induce the executives of the college to support me, I would have it made. And, because during her life, my mother was a friend of Mrs. Bethune, it was convenient and easy to believe that I would be welcome at the college and that they would actively work to have me elected. I was partially right.

I was welcomed with open arms to the campus. The group of faculty and alumni treated me with respect and made several thoughtful gestures to make me feel at home. Eventually we got around to the subject of my campaign. They explained about how they deplored the history of the way a handful of black men in the community conspired to deliver the black vote for a fee, and the way politicians encouraged them in such corruption by paying them their asking price.

They further explained how there were several echelons or variations of that insidious practice, including those in the community who did no more than drive voters to the polls. In the process, they convinced me that their long-range goal was to change the black community's attitudes and practices so that in the future politicians would court the black voters by discussing their qualifications and the issues important to African Americans. They believed that the time had come to make fundamental changes in the political environment, and they wanted my commitment that I would support such a movement. I agreed it was a good plan and that I would do what I could to help them execute it.

Next, they explained what they would do to help me win my race. First and foremost, I should understand that they did not want me to pay them anything. They would use workers who understood their goals and approved of them. Those workers would line up support for me and keep a record of what they had done and the people they had recruited. Those same workers, and others of like mind, would be available to drive voters to the polling places on election day. They would use volunteers whenever possible, but if any payment was necessary for gasoline or a worker's time, they would fund it.

The group was candid enough to tell me that they would have a slate of candidates, but they would be the exclusive decision makers. I would have no role in making up the slate. All they asked of me was good, honest government and a willingness to hear their position on important issues.

I was elated when I left that meeting. It was a good beginning of my quest for support in the black community. I had assumed that Tom Cobb, the state representative whose place I was trying to take (and who was general counsel of the college and a member of their board of trustees), would have them committed to support one of my opponents whom he favored. But it appeared that he had not asked them to help his hand-picked successor—or that they had rejected his request in spite of his connections. I never learned with any degree of certainty why they opted to support me rather than Tom's man. I just took the support and was grateful for it.

Soon after the meeting I told my small group of advisers about the dramatic happening, but they cautioned me not to get carried away by it. They reminded me that at best the college would influence only a small portion of the African American voters in and around Daytona, and it was unlikely that they would help me in DeLand, the county seat, or in New Smyrna Beach in the south end of the county.

In the course of the campaign I was approached by several men who offered to help me on election day. One by one they told me substantially the same story. The only way I could win, they said, was to hire them to get out the votes. They claimed to have encouraged a large group to register to vote and those folks were willing to follow their suggestions as to how they should cast their votes. They suggested to me that on the day of the election they would be busy all day picking up people, driving them to the polls, and giving them a printed slip with the list of candidates they favored on it.

Voting machines at that time were mechanical, with a numbered lever for each candidate. A couple of those soliciting my business assured me that their slips had the lever numbers printed on them so that those who couldn't read or did not want to be bothered reading names could simply vote the numbers. Each one of those political experts asked for money for their help.

## A Screening Committee

On a somewhat higher plane, about a dozen African American business and professional men formed a group that followed all the campaigns, interviewed all the candidates on their qualifications and positions on the relevant issues, and distributed their conclusions to a large group of voters who followed their recommendations in each election.

In 1956, my first election experience, I didn't do very well with that group of black leaders. I explained how I thought I had the right attitude about the segregation issues and that I was sure they would approve of my voting record when I became a member of the legislature. I also told them of my mother's relationship with Mrs. Bethune.

The group was interested in my military experiences vis-à-vis racial matters, and questioned how I felt when required to salute an officer who outranked me and was black. They also seemed interested to learn that I had a cousin who was on the U.S. Supreme Court and had authored opinions on civil rights and antilynching legislation.

My cousin, Frank Murphy, was appointed to the U.S Supreme Court by President Franklin D. Roosevelt in 1940. A lawyer by education, his prior political career included serving as the Mayor of Detroit, Governor of Michigan, Governor-general of the Philippines, and U.S. Attorney General, where he established the first civil rights unit in the Justice Department. During his tenure on the court, Murphy's support of African Americans, aliens, dissenters, Jehovah's Witnesses, Native Americans, women, workers, and other outsiders evoked a pun: "tempering justice with Murphy." Aiding the poor and promoting industrial peace during the Great Depression were major achievements, and knowing him helped inspire me to be on the Supreme Court.

Despite their interest in my cousin, I lost the group when I attempted to explain that I didn't think they should keep moving so fast, and that it would be better to take a more moderate approach similar to that advocated by the Supreme Court. I wasn't speaking against their movement or in any way opposing the progress they were making. I just wanted them to be aware that if they moved too fast they might put the whole package of hard-won successes in jeopardy. One or two of the group called on me and tried to rehabilitate me with the African American organization, but it didn't work. I had spoken my mind and I was unwilling to reverse my position, and they could not accept it.

Interestingly, LeRoy Collins was running for governor at the same time and his position had been about the same as mine, yet he was not criticized by black leaders as I was. I concluded that this was because he was so much better known than I and that they had seen him in many more situations in which his racial beliefs were projected. Therefore, they could better judge how he was likely to perform in the future. Also, I speculated, perhaps their knowledge of him gave them comfort that he would continue to act reasonably. I further concluded that before the campaign was over, they would be able to do the same with me and, for that reason and the fact that my attitude was more progressive than either of my opponents, I would be all right on the issue of integration.

Meanwhile, a good many white people had come to the realization that Collins was more liberal than they had thought, and a substantial number of Floridians were critical of him. Although our respective philosophies were similar, I was not seen as being as liberal at that juncture. I was a supporter of Collins and was developing a friendship with him, but feelings were running so high over segregation that it was hard to be his friend on the campaign trail. I wanted to be his friend and did not deny it or shy away from it. We both won. Over the years we became quite good friends and the perceived differences between us vanished.

During the same time frame, as we made ready to attend the special session and the 1957 regular session, we became acutely aware of the status of integration right there in the capital city. We knew segregation was practiced throughout Leon County and that those who practiced it had no intention of changing their behavior voluntarily or without a fight. It was almost as though segregation was an essential element of patriotism. That is to say, anyone who favored integration—and therefore was willing to change the southern way of life—couldn't be a good and true American.

Some of us had personal friends living in Tallahassee and as one might expect, we made a special effort to see them and induce them to guide us into the best known and most friendly civic and social groups. The friends were not interested in being subtle about the subject of racial equality. They told it just the way it was. Their consensus was that the people of north Florida were deadly serious about maintaining the status quo in racial matters and would not take kindly to strangers who were only here for sixty days every other year trying to change the social environment. "Don't be radical dumb asses," was one piece of advice often given.

Their evaluation of the situation was accurate. The level of tension was high, and the residents of Tallahassee, being the hosts with full measures of southern hospitality, proved to be quite anxious for us to be respectful of their culture while we were their guests.

## Tallahassee in Transition

When members of the freshman legislative class of 1957 took their seats, Tallahassee was in transition with respect to racial matters. There were still separate restrooms for "white" and "colored" in public buildings. Theaters either did not admit blacks or required them to sit in the balcony or some other segregated place. Similarly, local bus service was still segregated, as were lunch counters and all other eating establishments.

For all practical purposes the churches were segregated, although a few of them had begun the process of accepting the inevitable and allowed African Americans to attend various services. There was in Tallahassee and elsewhere an ever increasing demand that the traditional barriers be dismantled and the communities fully integrated. The pressure was felt at every level of government.

Tallahassee was the capital city of Florida, and the place where the thirty-nine members of the 57 Club engaged in their legislative labors from the spring of 1957 until Dempsey Barron, the longest serving member, completed his tenure. Just like the rest of the state, Tallahassee went through every phase of the turmoil that entailed integration. Feelings were intense—probably a bit more intense than in other parts of the state because, at that time in the history of Florida, everything that happened in the capital was affected and colored by the threat of integration.

Tallahassee was the battlefield for the movement to integrate all aspects of government, business, transportation, and recreation. The ugliness of the struggle sometimes affected the beauty and natural tranquility of the city, but the damage was temporary. When the crisis passed and everything began to settle down once again, the charm of the city with the hills that were covered with azaleas and dogwood manifested such peace and brotherhood that there was no room for internal strife, and Tallahassee reverted back to its charming old self.

# 7 *Racial Issues* •————————————————

The 1957 session of the Florida Legislature may not have been ranked as the most racially charged session in the history of the state, but it certainly was one of the top few. Tension still hung in the air from the special session convened in the summer of 1956, and Representative Jack Orr's speech was widely discussed. A preoccupation with racial issues did not develop out of boredom or just happen to flow in to fill the few vacant time slots. Those issues were created in reaction to the events of the time.

The country seemed focused on racial matters. All southern states were under pressure to integrate schools, public institutions, food and entertainment facilities, and transportation systems. Each state reacted in its own way, and within the states forces were at work trying to find ways to accommodate the emotion-driven demands of the citizens and still keep the peace.

We had our share of racial issues in Florida, and many of them were laid on the legislature's doorstep. Most were delivered by people who were unhappy about the decision of the U.S. Supreme Court in the case of *Brown v. Board of Education*. They were not content to wait and see how the products of the special session would work. They wanted to take the initiative and stop the movement toward integration.

Legislators were busy, and because of the added load and the importance of the racial issues, they were obliged to put in long hours at grueling speed just to get through all the important proposals served up.

In 1957, Florida was at the threshold of dramatic growth and major changes, including changes in the political environment. No shortage existed of relevant issues in addition to those involving segregation, and they helped set the direction and pace for what was to come. These issues helped shape the political environment.

Florida's education system was in need of attention. No public kindergarten system was in place at that time. Also, the legislature's tightfisted policies over the years, when combined with the antics of the infamous Johns Committee—formed in 1956 to investigate communism and homosexuality at state colleges—had badly damaged the state's higher education system. Every educational program from kindergarten to graduate school was struggling to make a respectable showing in the face of imminent growth, and God knew what else the desegregation order would bring.

Florida didn't even have a free textbook program, and teachers complained about the difficulties of teaching a class when some of the students had textbooks (but not all the same version) and others had none. The system desperately needed attention, but attention was hard to come by because fear and anger at the prospect of integration had the people divided. What made the situation even worse was that lobbyists for those who didn't want to be taxed or have their taxes increased used the specter of school integration to fight appropriations for things like textbooks. If the attempt to garner more money for such purposes could be stopped in the appropriations bill, there would be no need for taxation to pay for them.

Rather than wait and see what the legislature would do in the spending bill, and then choose sides and fight one another about where a necessary new tax would be levied, key business lobbyists joined hands early in the process and jointly fought additional appropriations for education. Thus, there would be no new tax law for them to try to deflect away from their individual clients. Raising tax money for schools was not a piece of cake. Legislators who advocated increased spending for schools—even for such obvious needs as textbooks—were promptly labeled as liberals and rumored to be friendly with African Americans. There was even an abrasive term for those legislators. They were called "N——— Lovers" in the hallways and at evening entertainment events, but seldom in more public settings.

Meanwhile, population growth was forcing legislators to take a serious look at other urgent needs, such as whether law enforcement funding was adequate to protect the public, and how the need for improved state highways, bridges, and other infrastructure could be met. All of these emerging issues called into question the tax structure.

In addition, there was a perceived need for openness or transparency in government and, therefore, vigorous agitation in favor of laws requiring our state to operate in the sunshine—a very controversial subject. As if that wasn't a plate full, the court system needed major reform, a hot button issue for incumbent judges and other regular participants in the justice system.

Gambling was yet another issue. Horse racing tracks, dog racing tracks, and jai-alai frontons were very profitable, but their owners regularly approached the legislature with their problems or internal disputes. Insurance companies and agents were also a major source of legislative business, as were health-care providers, mobile home builders and sellers, small loan companies, and a plethora of other private sector interests.

With so much to do, many issues challenged our intelligence, political philosophy, and courage.

Within the broad definition of racial bills, more than enough action was present to keep us from being bored.

In fact, so much activity related to racial matters in the legislature that one needed a program to attempt to keep abreast of what was happening. One major undertaking that eventually turned out to be a positive move was the formation of the Southern Regional Education Board (SREB).

## Southern Regional Education Board

The thought of black and white children in school together triggered all sorts of action. Fearful that African American youngsters who wanted to study medicine might actually win the fight to enroll in their all-white universities, southern states banded together to form the Southern Regional Education Board. There certainly were other motivating factors. For instance, it was said that one such motive was to provide black doctors to treat black patients so white doctors would not have to do so. Conversely, some folks were not so concerned about segregation and supported the plan because they simply wanted to expand every opportunity for qualified students to learn.

At any rate, a multistate compact was formed that allowed each state to enroll and subsidize a specified number of African American students in Meharry Medical College located in Nashville, Tennessee. It was part of a black university and was in need of paying students. The plan worked in that racial barriers were preserved for a time, the college was energized, and many black students received affordable medical training.

On a personal level, my family also found that the plan worked. I knew a young African American man who wanted to be a doctor and was having a hard time financing his education. I had money problems of my own, but I found ways to help him a bit, mostly through advice and recommendations. I was really pleased when I heard that he had received his medical degree with the help of the SREB program.

It was not long after that my eldest son, Rick, accidentally cut his foot. Because the wound looked deep and serious, I took him to the emergency room of a local hospital. I was surprised and pleased to find my young doctor friend on duty there. My son's wound involved a severed ligament which if not properly diagnosed and treated would have condemned him to a lifetime handicap. He received proper treatment from the doctor, and both my son and I have been grateful ever since that such a smart, talented, and conscientious person had the opportunity to attend medical school and become a doctor.

By the time the 57 Club came upon the scene, the SREB had been expanded and its mission broadened to include goals unrelated to racial considerations. Each state opened the doors to some or all of its graduate programs by setting aside a given number of student places for residents of its sister southern states. Thus, a person living in Florida who wanted to study dentistry and had to go out of state because Florida had no college of dentistry could, if approved, enroll in a school in one of the SREB states. The tuition would be equal to that charged by Florida schools to residents of Florida. In turn, Florida set aside places in its colleges that the other states did not have. Our forestry school at the University of Florida, for example, was popular in the SREB program.

**Legislative Advisory Committee**

Oversight of the program was provided by a board made up of the governors of the member states. A legislative advisory committee was active and supportive. It met regularly to consider substantive educational issues as well as structural and financial issues. Management was under a CEO. Governor Collins appointed me to the Legislative Advisory Committee during my second term in the House, and I remained a member until 1962. In all the years I was active in SREB, legislative financial appropriations never generated significant controversy. The expenditure of every other tax dollar fostered competition and conflict, but not so for SREB. The money we contributed pursuant to the interstate compact was appropriated without serious complaint.

The complicated financial scheme actually helped bring equality and fairness to the plan. So, although it became a commendable, cost-saving project that was open to all students, SREB was rooted in racial segregation and remained a tool for the prevention of integration.

## George Anderson's Local Bill

On a totally different platform, George Anderson, a member of the 57 Club and the state representative from Jefferson County, played out an anti-integration scenario that was largely symbolic but nevertheless attracted attention and provoked a bit of heartache and emotional turmoil.

George was not a liberal. Rather, he was closer to the conservative end of the political spectrum. But notwithstanding legislation about racial matters, he was, in my judgment, one of the good guys.

He was something of a protégé of the respected and influential Senator Dill Clark, who was almost always cited as the senator with the most outrageous example of a mal-apportioned district. I believe it was Senator Clark who was fighting a reapportion proposal that combined his district with the very small Liberty County, which was known for its tightly controlled political activity and other distinctive characteristics. After explaining his reasons for not wanting to represent that county, he made a dramatic plea by saying: "If you give me 'Liberty,' you give me death."

Being linked with Senator Clark gave George a special status. However, he was unaffected by his vicarious power and certainly did not abuse it in any way. His home was in Monticello, the principal city in Jefferson County. He was a graduate of Florida State University and earned his living as an insurance agent for State Farm Insurance Company. Somehow he preserved his image as something of a redneck. He and I met in St. Augustine at the Democratic Party Caucus held in the summer of 1956. We were about the same age, but we had very little else in common. George was a southerner and a bona fide "good old boy." He had a quick wit and a likeable sense of humor.

He also had the reputation of being loyal to the Small County Bloc and of being a solid citizen who was as good as his word. He earned that reputation by the way he spoke and otherwise conducted himself. True, he introduced a far out, racially motivated local bill and voted for some other terrible bills, but he was not a mean-spirited person, nor did he allow his votes on racial issues to permeate other issues like those dealing with economic matters.

George Anderson and I had little in common, but we were friends. (Photo courtesy Florida Archives.)

I had quite a different set of credentials; nevertheless, we struck up a friendly relationship. There was an unspoken understanding that he was closer to my philosophy than he seemed to be. By that I mean he had a good attitude about adequately funding education and social programs, and he was always ready to support tax bills that were fair to all taxpayers.

Also, George was very devoted to his family and felt empathy for dysfunctional, poor, and neglected families. In his day-to-day, one-on-one personal relationships, he was as kind, considerate, and sympathetic as a person could be. Unlike many others, George was not critical in private conversations of members of a different race or of people who had a different sexual orientation.

We had a litany of activities we both enjoyed and principles to which we steadfastly adhered. Both of us liked to fish, and we were super protective of the trees, bushes, and wild things living among us. Our legislative duties kept us in touch, and we spent some recreational time together at social events and on the water.

George and I regularly found ourselves on opposite sides of an issue, and each of us had associates whom the other could not tolerate. However, this did not prevent us from being friendly toward each other. We recognized early on that we could spend time together and even fish together despite the differences we had.

Toward the end of a regular session, George came to my desk to tell me that I would probably want to change my vote on his local bill that had just passed.

By way of explanation, a local bill applies to one county or a limited geographic area, so it is generally of interest only to a representative whose county is touched by it in some way. However, such a bill might be of interest to a broader group if the subject affects other geographic areas or is in some way offensive.

There were many local bills introduced every session, and each one had to be approved by both houses. In fact, there were so many that if processed and considered the same as general bills, they could potentially clog the entire system. Therefore, local bills were handled differently.

From time to time, all pending local bills were checked by a committee appointed for that purpose to be sure they were local bills and not general bills disguised as local bills to take advantage of the procedure. Then the bills were gathered up and put before the legislature together. Without explanation or debate, members cast one vote for the entire collection of proposed bills. However, when the Journal was prepared, it was made to appear as though each bill was considered separately. Should a member want to vote "no" on any particular bill, he could do so by informing the clerk of the House, and the Journal would be made to show the negative vote.

George's bill was a multipurpose bill, and I still don't know how it survived the scrutiny of the committee system. Part of the bill made it a felony for anyone in Jefferson County to sponsor, coach, participate in, or attend a racially integrated sports event—and I had voted for it along with all the other local bills on the calendar that day.

I asked George if he had lost his mind. He explained that the bill was just a gesture. The people in his county were so bitter about the possibility of their schools being racially integrated that they demanded their representative speak out against integration in every way and in every forum. Refusal to introduce that bill would have been political suicide. George introduced it knowing that it could never survive a test of its constitutionality.

I hated to see George pandering to his friends and supporters, but being aware of the intensity of feelings about integration, I understood his need to align his record with his constituents' attitude. For technical reasons I was not able to have the record show my negative vote, but I notified the Governor's Office of the status of the bill in case they were not aware that it had passed the House. Governor Collins promptly vetoed it, and George let it die. He never tried to override the veto, for which I was thankful, because given the emotional environment it probably would have passed, the veto of the governor notwithstanding.

After our time together in the legislature, George and I began to lose contact as the gap in our interests widened. We corresponded irregularly for a while, and then we neglected to write at all. However, I learned that George gave up his business, enrolled in seminary, became a Methodist minister, and was sent to a small congregation in Tennessee where he remained until his death.

### The Last Resort Bill

One of the most dangerous bills introduced in reaction to the U.S. Supreme Court's decision in the *Brown* case was the Last Resort Bill. The bill's title came from its principal purpose, which was to close a public facility—such as a school—if all the delaying tactics failed and integration was inevitable. Of all the bills offered up to try to halt integration, this bill posed the greatest threat. It had widespread support and considerable momentum.

The bill was very popular in the Capitol. That was no surprise because everyone knew the legislature was not fairly apportioned and that the small county representatives were in charge of that branch of government. Most of the people who worked in and around the Capitol were residents of Tallahassee or one of the small counties in close proximity to it. By and large, a majority of the people in the small counties favored segregation, and they elected state representatives of like mind. The resulting political climate created the impression that the whole world shared their views.

The one island of reason in Tallahassee was the Governor's Office, then occupied by LeRoy Collins. Like so many Floridians, Collins experienced a metamorphosis with respect to racial integration. Howard Troxler, a well-known and respected columnist for the *St. Petersburg Times*, once gave an insightful evaluation of Collins. He wrote:

> Collins led Florida on a path of moderation during the troubled years of desegregation and the civil rights movement. His greatest success is what did not happen in Florida—no Little Rock showdowns, no George Wallace standing in the schoolhouse door.

"In his gentle way, he helped make racial prejudice unacceptable in the modern South," Troxler wrote, but then added:

make no mistake—by modern standards Collins was part of the Old South. He has been and still is criticized for holding back. At first he decried the U.S. Supreme Court's rulings on desegregation and paid lip service to protecting 'our state's customs and traditions.' He criticized the early lunch-counter and civil rights protestors as lawbreakers.

But his heart was not in it. Before his term was up, Collins was encouraging Floridians to accept the Supreme Court rulings as the law of the land and to treat all people equally in public accommodations. Even if segregation might be argued in court to be legally permissible, he said it was morally wrong. For a lot of his contemporary critics, Collins might as well have declared himself to be a Communist.

The conflict between the strident advocates of segregation in the legislature and the voice of moderation in the Governor's Office erupted over the Last Resort Bill. Those who had the strongest objections to school integration felt that the schools should be closed rather than allowing black children to learn in them. The bill they offered was described as a school-closing measure, but it was much broader than that. It had the potential of closing not only schools, but any public facility.

The Last Resort Bill actually passed both houses and was sent to the gover-

Attorney General Richard Ervin (second from right), talks with me and other House members regarding one of the many bills filed in an effort to prevent or slow integration.

nor. When Collins received the bill he had three choices: sign it into law; hold it and allow it to become law without his signature; or exercise his constitutional veto power. The procedure was straightforward. If he planned a veto, then within the time specified in the Florida Constitution he had to prepare a written message addressed to the legislative body where the bill originated, informing that House of his reason for withholding his approval and then deliver the message with a copy of the bill to that House.

In this case it was a House bill, so the message was addressed to the speaker. Normally such a message would be dispassionate and confined to the technical defects in the bill. Here, however, the bill was so important and so infused with emotion that Governor Collins felt the need to use both approaches. He began the letter by identifying the bill; then he discussed the technical defects—principally the scope of power granted by it to close not only schools as was indicated by the supporters, but every public facility and institution in the jurisdiction involved. Then he built up to a crescendo of condemnation that was as emotional and inflammatory as one could make it. He wrote:

> This measure ignores a workable approach to vexing problems and encourages the substitution of a chaotic abandonment of reason.
>
> It pours across the face of a great State the highly combustible fuel of racial hatred and beckons to firebrands and the irresponsible to come and ignite the

flames. When men harbor hatred in their hearts for their fellowmen, it is a regrettable thing. But when government is used as an instrument for translating racial hatred into a force to destroy the very institutions which nurture and sustain it, then such is an even more serious wrong, and I condemn it.

There was no hope of upholding the veto in the Senate. If the veto was to be sustained, it would have to be in the House. It took a vote of two thirds of the members voting in both the House and the Senate to pass a bill over a veto.

The Speaker of the House, through his Rules Committee, had control of the veto message and could bring it on for consideration when he was ready. When a speaker was anxious to pass a bill over a veto, he could be a valuable asset. He could give the proponents advance notice of when it would be debated so as to give them adequate preparation time. He could let it come up only when he felt that he had the votes to pass it. It was hard to beat the speaker at this type of debate and, presumably, he used all his power to override the veto.

The bill with the governor's veto message came roaring toward the House like a summer thunderstorm. The message was strong and condemned the bill with specificity. Needless to say, it energized the bill's advocates. (Because of its importance, Collins' entire veto message is reproduced in the Appendix.)

Collins' prompt veto infuriated the proponents of the Last Resort Bill. They wanted to pass their piece of dangerous legislation the first time around. They were impatient to get on with the procedure that required a two-thirds vote to pass the bill over the veto; or, to put it in the vernacular of the legislature to pass the bill, the veto of the governor notwithstanding.

But we were not just sitting around wringing our hands and wondering what we would do when our schools were closed. No, we were active and effective. We polled House members and found that the vote would be very close. Although the usual controls were in place, we had a chance to stop the bill—and every vote would be critical.

Our job was cut out for us. First, we had to contend with our own constituents back home. By the time the bill came on for debate, every member's district had some support for the bill, and we were getting calls and letters urging (sometimes demanding) that we vote for it. Then we had to be sure we could get the votes to stop it. A few of our friends went home, but we found them and lobbied them by phone. We not only needed to get their commitment to vote our way, we had to try to get them committed to being present to cast their votes.

We worked frantically around the clock, soliciting votes and holding the hands of those already committed so they didn't change their minds. There were some disappointments and a few surprises. One pleasant surprise was Dempsey Barron, who was considered to be a member of the Small County Bloc. He had promised to vote to sustain the veto. Everyone recognized that he had a tough decision, and we knew he was under awesome pressure from his colleagues and friends. All things considered, he probably had the hardest time of all with the decision.

When all was said and done, we sustained the veto and that snake of a bill was dead. Dempsey survived the next election, although the margin of victory was small. He felt threatened enough to call some of us to come help him. He asked me to visit with the teachers of Bay County and to be sure they knew how he had helped to keep the schools open.

## Ben Hill Griffin Jr. and the Last Resort Bill

A flurry of activity swirled around the Last Resort Bill from the moment it was introduced, and most of us were involved with it in one way or another. One of the members of the 57 Club who was troubled by the Last Resort Bill happened to be the wealthiest member of the legislature, Ben Hill Griffin Jr.

Ben Hill's prime legislative interest was in bills affecting the citrus industry, where his family had amassed most of its wealth. He worked hard on them. He would brief us on proposals and explain his position on each one. At that time, I owned a twenty-acre grove in west Volusia County, but those bills were so far removed from the operations of a small grove that they made no sense to me. So I listened and listened . . . and listened some more. I learned more about the business of citrus than I ever wanted to know.

Ben Hill Griffin Jr., the wealthiest member of the 57 Club. (Photo courtesy Florida Archives.)

As the House first began debating the Last Resort Bill, we counted on Ben Hill to oppose it. But as the time for voting approached, he came to me and explained that he couldn't go with us and would have to vote for it. He said that he had too many friends and supporters who favored the bill for him to vote "no" on final passage.

It was a message I didn't want to hear, and I said so. However, I understood what he was going through, so I didn't condemn him. I was really disappointed and said that also. Sure enough, when the vote was taken, he voted for the bill.

I am happy to say that after the veto, Ben Hill had a change of heart. He stiffened his back, voted to sustain the veto, and helped to finally kill the infamous Last Resort Bill. It must have been very difficult for him to take the position he did on the veto. He faced enormous pressure when the bill was first brought before the House, and he gave in to it. That only made it harder to reverse his position after the veto.

One important lesson the 57 Clubbers learned early in their public service was that one should not lose confidence in a colleague who votes differently. Neither should one nullify a friendship over any one issue or vote. We were told to always keep in mind that there would be another day or another issue, and that a person who disappoints you one day may be the deciding vote in your favor on another day. That advice proved to be very sound many times. It was appropriate in the case of Ben Hill Griffin Jr. and the Last Resort Bill. Frankly, it would have been easy to be critical of him when he voted for the bill. Happily, we waited and did not put him down, and sure enough, he more than made up for it when his vote was so badly needed to sustain the veto.

**One of the Good Guys**

When I first met Ben Hill, I was comfortable with him. It wasn't just his obvious wealth that made him impressive. He had an engaging, outgoing personality and a pleasant but aggressive way. In retrospect, I can report that I liked him, and to this day I believe he was one of the good guys.

However, it was difficult to overlook his wealth and his family's prominence when we gathered in Tallahassee. People knew him and deferred to him. The temporary housing he arranged was obviously expensive, and his demeanor and appearance spoke of his affluence, although I hasten to add that he did not flaunt it or use it in any inappropriate way.

During the sessions at the Capitol, representatives made their own living arrangements. The Tallahassee Chamber of Commerce, realizing the value of the legislative sessions, set up directories of available residential facilities to assist us. There were all kinds of choices. Single members were the easiest to accommodate. They mostly stayed in motels, hotels, and private homes where boarders were welcome.

I was fortunate to find a small private residence southeast of town on Magnolia Avenue that was large enough to accommodate my family while not being too expensive.

Ben Hill, on the other hand, rented a large elegant house that was rumored to cost about five times what I paid. As the session progressed, I learned why he wanted the size and quality of house he had selected. He entertained constantly. Early in the session he had receptions or mixers. Later on, he added lunches and other affairs.

Early in the 1957 session, I was appointed to serve on an important select committee, and Ben Hill was also a member. He invited all members of the group to his "home away from home" for a meal that featured fried quail. Although my father and I had hunted quail for years—and I had cleaned them in preparation for roasting by my mother—I had never tasted fried quail, nor had we ever bagged enough to share with others. So I was quite surprised to see so many quail in one place. And what's more, they were delicious and served by a professional waiting staff, which was something I had never experienced in my own home.

Wealth aside, how a person conducts himself vis-à-vis an important piece of legislation is a window to the qualities of that person. Thus, the way Ben Hill reacted to the Last Resort Bill tells us much about him. A group of House members and, of course, Governor Collins, saw the danger of the legislation and were violently opposed to it. For various reasons, it was assumed that Ben Hill would be a part of the group led by the governor. I wasn't surprised when he voted the other way because, as mentioned earlier, he told me what he intended to do and why he felt he had to vote that way.

Ben Hill also has the distinction of being the only member of the 57 Club who gave millions of dollars to the University of Florida and had the honor of having the football stadium named for him.

Those 57 Clubbers whom I was friendly with fully expected Ben Hill to seek higher office. Members counted on supporting and/or serving with him in either the Governor's Office or the U.S. Senate. But for reasons I never fully understood there was never to be such an opportunity. Ben Hill stayed in the House until 1965, then ran for and was elected to a seat in the Florida Senate, where he stayed through the special session of 1968. He died in 1990 at the age of seventy-six.

## The Shame Avoided

Without belaboring the point further, I am pleased that we mustered enough votes to sustain the veto, thereby killing the Last Resort Bill and sparing the state the shame of having it on the books.

It was a mean, tough fight filled with bitterness, and each member of the legislature had his own reason for voting as he did. The Last Resort Bill was a really bad bill by any test. Today there is a different mood in the Capitol and the passage of such a bill would be unthinkable. It could not cause the grief that it brought us in the '50s.

## Exciting Fallout

It was also around that time that I was taught just how tension-filled the dispute regarding the Last Resort Bill could be. I was at home in Daytona Beach after the debate on whether to sustain or override the governor's veto. Late one day a couple of young teenagers who lived in the same neighborhood were in the back yard of a neighbor's property. They were close to my property because the back yard lot lines of both houses were contiguous. I doubt that anyone in the neighborhood—other than the two boys—knew they were playing with a small pile of gunpowder.

Suddenly the peace of the area was breeched by a loud explosion. All who heard it wondered what was going on, and the most paranoid of the group quickly put the worst possible face on it and assumed it was some kind of attack. I dare say everyone around there felt that something untoward was happening. Interestingly, most of those who went outside to try to find out what happened came to my house. At first I was pleased so many of our friends were concerned about us. But upon reflection I realized they came because they knew of the racial tension generated in Tallahassee and my part in the scenario, and assumed I was reaping the consequences of my actions. It was an eye opener. Fortunately it was nothing more than an accident, and no one was seriously hurt by the explosion.

The Last Resort Bill was not the only anti-integration legislation considered. One bill was the forerunner of the voucher law we know today. It would have allowed students to attend private schools and also provided their parents with financial assistance through tax credits or cash grants.

The Johns Committee—the infamous group that almost destroyed our university system through its hunt for communists and homosexuals—recommended another package of bills to forestall integration, and, as noted earlier, Representative George Anderson's local bill sought to prohibit interracial sports events. Then there were numerous other attempts to slow down or thwart integration. Being a legislator in 1957 was not all fun.

# 8 *The Johns Committee* ————————————————

The infamous Florida Legislative Investigation Committee was born in 1956. Senator Charley E. Johns was named its chairman and the committee quickly acquired a nickname: the Johns Committee.

As strange as it may seem today, the legislature created the committee, provided adequate funding for it, and every two years named senators and representatives to serve on it even though it was engaged in questionable conduct. There was no organized effort to stop Senator Johns or withhold funding. In many ways it was analogous to U.S. Senator Joe McCarthy's handiwork in Washington, D.C.

Charley Johns was elected to the Senate in 1947 to represent a district well known as the location of the state's penitentiary. The district included Bradford County, represented by Doyle Conner, the Speaker of the House. Johns was a member of the Pork Chop Gang. The gang was given its name by a reporter who observed that about sixteen senators effectively ran the Senate and that their interests were self-serving.

Johns worked as a railroad conductor and later as an insurance agent. He never earned a college degree. Johns was a dynamic speaker—articulate, animated, and able to stir his audience. Listening to him make a point that was important to him was like being in a country church and hearing an energized preacher denounce the devil and all he stands for.

Johns was elected by his fellow senators to be the President of the Senate and was serving in that capacity when Governor Daniel T. McCarty died in office shortly after his inauguration. At that time, Florida had no lieutenant governor, so the Senate president served as acting governor until the next general election.

Thus, Johns entered the Governor's Office. He served less than two years—from September 1953 to January 1955—because at the next general election in 1954, State Senator LeRoy Collins defeated him. Johns was legally able to return to the Senate as a rank and file senator, and he did so. Shortly after his return to the Senate, the U.S. Supreme Court outlawed segregation in schools and Johns thrust himself into the ensuing turmoil and bitterness as public pressure for integration escalated.

At that time, some of the demagogues in the South equated civil rights activists with communists. America in the era of the Johns Committee was fighting a Cold War against Communism, as well as a few

Charley Johns served as acting governor and chairman of the infamous Johns Committee. (Photo courtesy Florida Archives.)

wars that were not so cold. With that environment, Johns and his committee traveled around the state seeking out communists and homosexuals. The rest of their work was more subtle. It had to do with undermining the work of civil rights advocates and organizations that were set on doing away with segregation in the schools.

One target—the National Association for the Advancement of Colored People—became well-known because the ensuing battle went all the way to the U.S. Supreme Court. The Court ruled in favor of the NAACP and against the Johns Committee, which wanted access to membership records, and stated:

> In a Florida State Court, petitioner, who was president of the Miami Branch of the National Association for the Advancement of Colored People, was adjudged in contempt and sentenced to fine and imprisonment for refusing to divulge contents of the membership records of that Branch to a committee created by the Florida Legislature, which was investigating the infiltration of Communists into various organizations. There was no suggestion that the

Association or its Miami Branch was a subversive organization or that either was Communist- dominated or influenced. The purpose of the questions asked petitioner was to ascertain whether 14 persons previously identified as Communists were members of the Miami Branch of the Association. The principal evidence relied upon to show any relationship between the Association and subversive or Communist activities was indirect, ambiguous, and mostly hearsay testimony by two witnesses that, in years past, those 14 persons had attended occasional meetings of the Miami Branch of the Association 'and/or' were members of that Branch, which had about 1,000 members.

Held: On the record in this case, petitioner's conviction of contempt for refusal to divulge information contained in the membership lists of the Association violated rights of association protected by the First and Fourteenth Amendments. Pp. 540–558.

Among the committee's favorite hunting grounds were college and university campuses. The targeted institutions were made to suffer. The damage inflicted on individuals and the state education system was significant and widespread.

All of that activity was particularly hurtful to the University of South Florida in Hillsborough County, which was just coming into being. Because it was so young, there was not a potent alumni association to defend the faculty or otherwise offer protection from Johns' abusive treatment. The newly appointed president of the university, John Allen, was tormented, and the morale of all those involved hit an all-time low. The damage done by the committee was said to be a near-fatal wound. Somehow, USF survived and is a successful and thriving institution today, but there are those who still remember well the dark days of the Johns Committee.

### An "Inexperienced" Committee Is Tested

One of the first tests for a few of us who were freshmen began in the normal course of legislative business when the Speaker of the House established a small committee and appointed several newcomers as members, including Buck Vocelle and me. I never knew why that committee existed, but one reason might have been to allow the speaker to give every member two or more committee assignments.

When a committee is made up almost entirely of inexperienced members, there is no way to predict with accuracy how they will perform, so normally they are given a minimum amount of work—and nothing that could seriously affect the leader's programs. For those reasons, I always believed that our little committee was designed to keep a group of us busy and out of trouble.

However, things did not work out that way.

An early product of the Johns Committee was a group of bills with the transparent purpose of tormenting the NAACP. One in particular was offensive not only to the NAACP, but also to every church, lodge, or club in the state.

It granted the Florida Attorney General the authority to inspect the records of most organizations in Florida. That would mean all membership, financial, and policy records would be open for the curious, the mischievous, and the hateful to see.

That was a bad bill, but so were all the other bills in the package proposed by the Johns Committee. The bills were based on the old common law offenses known as champerty and maintenance. Those two terms referred to the frowned-upon practice of encouraging another person to start a lawsuit or help said person maintain the suit. In this situation the bills were designed to stop the NAACP from setting up, encouraging, or financing test cases in court.

The legislation was dangerous because the bills were so broad. For example, people who innocently advised a friend to get out of a bad marriage would be in violation of one of the Johns Committee's bills and subject to severe penalty.

In any event, the entire package was sent to our committee for review in 1957. I feel certain that we were expected to approve the bills without delay, and that's how it started. Someone moved that the first bill be reported favorably, and with a minimum of discussion the vote was taken. It passed with only one negative vote. That lone vote was mine.

Suddenly I was standing alone just as Jack Orr had when he cast the sole negative vote on the Fabisinski report, a measure designed to slow integration.

However, when the next bill was up for consideration the situation changed. Buck Vocelle of Indian River County, Ralph Blank of Palm Beach County, and a few others spoke out and voted "no." When the committee adjourned, only one bill was reported favorably, and that was the first one up and passed, with me casting the only "no" vote. The others were either reported unfavorably or postponed to avoid sudden death. The rules provided that a bill would be considered dead if a committee voted against it, unless the full House, by a two-thirds vote, brought it back.

Then the outside world began to react.

I received many calls from constituents. Two stand out because the callers were from my home district and were so important to me. One call was from my senior law partner, Paul Raymond, and the other from Francis Whitehair of DeLand, a strong political leader. Both asked me to vote for the one bill that came out of the committee and to help get the other Johns Committee bills out alive. I declined, and to Paul's credit, he heard my argument, agreed that it was a bad bill, and encouraged me to stand firm. Whitehair was not so amenable, and he never forgave me. I'm certain that other committee members received similar calls. However, the most severe reaction occurred in the State Capitol.

I received a notice placed on my desk informing me that I had been made an honorary member of the NAACP—definitely not a popular award at the time, even if it had been bona fide.

Also, I was told that Buck Vocelle got into a fistfight at the Silver Slipper Restaurant over his vote. Indeed, those were times when tempers were short and emotions were strong.

## A Look at Representative Government

In the midst of the turmoil we created, Jack Orr, the courageous member who stood so tall in the summer special session, came by my desk and brought me a quotation on representative government written by British statesman and philosopher Edmund Burke. Jack knew of our experience in the committee and came to commend and encourage me. His gesture was appreciated and the Burke quotation was relevant. It spoke to the question of whether a representative should vote the way his own conscience dictated or the way his constituents ask him to vote. Burke wrote:

> Certainly, gentlemen, it ought to be the happiness and glory of a representative to live in the strictest union, the closest correspondence, and the most unreserved communication with his constituents. Their wishes ought to have great weight with him; their opinion, high respect; their business, unremitted attention.
>
> It is his duty to sacrifice his repose, his pleasures, his satisfactions, to theirs; and above all, ever, and in all cases, to prefer their interest to his own.
>
> But his unbiased opinion, his mature judgment, his enlightened conscience, he ought not to sacrifice to you, to any man, or to any set of men living. These he does not derive from your pleasure; no, nor from the law and the Constitution. They are a trust from Providence, for the abuse of which he is deeply answerable.
>
> Your representative owes you, not his industry only, but his judgment; and he betrays, instead of serving you, if he sacrifices it to your opinion.

Eventually, all the bills died, but the Johns Committee did not die so easily.

## Buck Vocelle Takes a Stand

Buck Vocelle's stand against the Johns Committee bills was indicative of his honesty and courage. His home was in Vero Beach and he represented Indian River County as a legislator from 1956–1962.

I did not know Buck before we met as newly elected state representatives and we were never close friends. However, during 1957 we shared a couple of legislative skirmishes where our respective reserves of political courage were tested, and we learned that we were quite close in our political standards and beliefs. He earned my respect and I have always remembered him as a decent human being.

When Buck came to Tallahassee as a freshman legislator and a member of the 57 Club, he had an advantage over the rest of us who were also beginning our careers in public service. His father, James Vocelle, had been a state official and had served honorably and competently. Before coming to Florida the senior Vocelle served in the Georgia Legislature. Soon after moving to Florida he was appointed chairman of the Florida Industrial Commission by Governor Dan McCarty. That was the commission that served as the first echelon of the appellate system for Workers Compensation cases, and it set the tone for the entire system. Parenthetically, the system was then officially entitled "Workman's Compensation." Jim, Buck's father, was the chairman through three governors. All who knew Jim respected him, and he knew a lot of people in state government.

Although Buck benefited from his father's good work, he was his own person and had won his seat in the legislature fair and square. However, because his father was so well respected, he didn't have to spend time telling people who he was, where he came from, or what he believed. Rightly or wrongly, many folks made assumptions about such things based on the reputation of his father.

After his legislative experience, Buck was appointed to the circuit court in Indian River County by Governor Bob Graham and dedicated the remainder of his professional life to the judiciary. He died of cancer in 1996 at seventy years of age.

Buck Vocelle was involved in a number of skirmishes where his political standards were tested. (Photo courtesy Florida Archives.)

While serving as a medium tank platoon leader during World War II, I came to fully understand how important it was for those around me in combat to stand firm. If anyone in a tank weakened or gave up, the entire crew was in jeopardy. On that basis, I have said before and proudly repeat here that I would be comfortable taking a tank full of Buck Vocelles into any battle.

## The Johns Committee's Wrath

An example of what we believed to be the handiwork of the Johns Committee can be seen in the saga of a well-known reporter for the *Orlando Sentinel*. A great many people read and liked what he wrote and he was very popular. He was also very critical of Charley Johns and his committee.

One evening, the reporter was at a bowling alley in Tallahassee and struck up an acquaintance with a young and beautiful woman. Eventually, they checked into a motel. While they were at the motel, a photographer accompanied by witnesses burst into their room and took pictures of the reporter and the woman engaged in an act that was outlawed by statute in Florida at that time.

The reporter asserted that the young woman and the photographer were working for the staff of the Johns Committee and that he had been set up. Of course, he was dumb to let himself be put in that position, and the scandal exposed by the staff of the Johns Committee ruined him, as he was caught committing an "unnatural act" as defined and condemned in Florida law.

## The "Purple Pamphlet"

Finally, in 1964, the committee went out of business. The demise is said to have been connected to the committee's publication of a report published in 1964 that became known as the "Purple Pamphlet." I'm certain that the pamphlet was a factor, but it is hard to know the actual reason for termination. There was a backlash of sorts to the situation with the reporter from the *Orlando Sentinel*, and there was a clear feeling that the public had endured enough of the committee's investigations. University supporters and press people were anxious to be rid of the troublesome group. I believe it was simply time for the curtain to come down, and the Purple Pamphlet served as a trigger device.

It wasn't that the pamphlet lacked a symbolic offensive odor. Some folks said outright that it stunk. However, there was so much already wrong with the legislative agenda and actions of the committee that it is difficult to identify one particular incident as pivotal in its dissolution.

The photos in the Johns Committee report were indicative of its racy content.

Whether the pamphlet caused the demise of the committee is not the basis for judging its handiwork. One has only to look through the booklet and the essence of the committee comes to light. It contains explicit photographs of homosexual activities. There is a full page of pictures of young men and boys with a caption reading: "These photographs are from the catalogue of a supplier of homosexual erotica. Five by seven inch prints of each pose were offered at a dollar each. The youth of the model is indicative of the frequent homosexual fixation on youth."

The text also contained statements and conclusions that smacked of anti-gay propaganda. The pamphlet's appendix included an extensive list of Florida statutes that defined proscriptive laws and disclosed the penalties. Then there was a glossary of homosexual terms and deviant acts, as well as a list of psychopathic sex crimes, sexual nuisances, and sexual obscenities. Finally, there was a bibliography on sexual deviations. It was quite a report. Some critics labeled it pornography.

The preface recites some of the history and direction of the committee:

The 1963 Florida Legislature created the Legislative Investigation Committee, a continuation of similar interim committees active on behalf of the state since 1955. Included in the committee's mandate from the legislature was the direction to investigate and report on 'the extent of infiltration into agencies supported by state funds by practicing homosexuals, the effect thereof on said agencies and the public, and the policies of various state agencies in dealing therewith.'

To understand and effectively deal with the growing problem of homosexuality, an understanding of its nature and manifestations is essential; and it is for that reason that the committee has sought in this report to preface its recommendations for special studies leading to legislation with a review of the scope and nature of homosexuality.

Although this report has been prepared, in keeping with the committee mandate, primarily for the benefit of state administrators and personnel officers, it can be of value to all citizens; for every parent and every individual concerned with the moral climate of the state, should be aware of the rise in homosexual activity noted here, and be possessed of the basic knowledge set forth.

The following excerpts also gave the reader the flavor of the report:

Many homosexuals, and the majority of those apprehended by law enforcement authorities, take their sex where they find it, be it in a restroom of a park or other public place; a car, be it moving or parked; a residence or a hotel room.

And this generalization on love is revealing:

One flaw in this thesis is that the sort of love relationships lyrically described are notoriously few and far between among male homosexuals. Fleeting relationships are the order of the day in a great many cases, and multiple sex acts with a procession of partners who are often strangers known only by a first name or nickname frequently occur within the space of one evening.

Another example of generalization and subjectivity:

Homosexuals are generally outwardly gregarious people, free with gifts and money for those they like or are currently enmeshed with. Many find association with extreme youth a solace for their anxiety over aging, just as some aging 'straights' seek out the companionship of youthful members of the opposite sex.

The appeals to youth by homosexuals are manifold. They are masters of flattery, playing up to the teenager's desire for recognition and equal status in an adult world. They will provide the youth with opportunity to attain goals made attractive by adult practitioners—a car to drive, cigarettes to smoke, liquor to drink. Frequently, pornographic materials of a heterosexual nature are used. One strip of photos we have seen starts off depicting in detail and clarity a male-female sexual relationship; and as the ensuing photos unfold, the man leaves the woman and joins another man in a series of poses leading up to vivid homosexual erotica.

Then a discussion of teachers:

The same legislative session revised the Statutes relating to the revocation of teaching certificates to make more certain the withdrawal of teaching privileges from those against whom homosexual charges have been verified. From 1959 through January 1, 1964, a total of 64 Florida teachers have had certificates revoked by the State Board of Education; and, of these, 54 were on morals charges. An additional 83 cases are now pending before the Board. While this is a relatively low number in the light of Florida's more than 40,000 certified teachers, it is ample to warrant concern by educators and parents.

## A Committee Advisor Speaks

Inclusion of the following statement from an investigator of homosexual activities who was in consultation with the committee has the effect of making his statement the words of the committee:

There are those who feel that this particular type of investigation—against homosexuals—is just too touchy to fool with. But it must be done. It must be done.

The homosexual groups, Homosexuals Anonymous, the Homophile Institute, the Mattachine Society and others, are now coming out in the open in our larger cities like New York and Washington, trying to gain social acceptance in publications. Late last fall, they actually sought a permit to solicit on the streets of Washington.

Since the homosexual has seen fit to come out into the open and try to get himself accepted by society, I think it is about time the thinking members of society, the persons in positions of responsibility, get up off their duffs and realize that if we don't stand up and start fighting, we are going to lose these battles in a very real war of morality.

The homosexuals are organized. The persons whose responsibility it is to protect the public, and especially our kids, are not organized in the direction of combating homosexual recruiting of youth.

The problem is so little understood by lay people that the homosexuals will win every battle that is fought unless we band together to educate ourselves. There is only one thing that the homosexual fears as far as straight persons are concerned, and that is a straight person who knows him and the gay crowd for what they are.

The conclusion contains this recommendation to the state legislature:

We believe that a law embodying elements such as these would serve to radically reduce the number of homosexuals preying upon the youth of Florida, would stiffen the state's hand in dealing with those homosexuals apprehended and would provide an element of protection for those homosexuals whose first public venture is relatively mild and whose ability to earn a living or provide for a family would be destroyed by exposure.

It behooves us all to come to know the nature of the homosexual, for he is with us in every area of the state. It behooves us, too, to define for him, and for ourselves, the conditions which govern his presence.

## No Joking Matter

Predictably, there were jokes about it, but in 1964 the Purple Pamphlet was no joking matter. Without a doubt, it contributed to the prevailing antigay attitude and robbed the committee of any semblance of legitimacy.

By the time of its termination the membership had changed. Senator Johns was no longer chairman. The report includes a list of the 1964 members:

*Members from the House*
Leo C. Jones, Panama City
Richard O. Mitchell, Tallahassee
William E. Owens, Stuart
George B. Stallings Jr., Jacksonville

*Members from the Senate*
Charley E. Johns, Starke
Robert Williams, Graceville
C. W.(Bill) Young, St. Petersburg

The last group of committee members is evidence that the philosophical direction of the committee never changed from the time of its creation until its demise. The House members were known to be staunchly in favor of segregation. Senator Johns was still a member, and the presence of Senator Bill

Young—one of the rare Republican legislators at the time—suggested widespread continuing support for the committee.

The very fact that such a committee could be created by the legislature and funded in each biennial budget until 1964, as it was roaming through the state promoting fear and confusion on college campuses, is testimony to the prevailing legislative attitude of that time.

# 9  *Reapportionment* ————————————

The constitution or charter of any governmental entity should contain a description of the power granted to the organization and how the power is distributed. However, there does not seem to be any common formula for apportioning that power.

The Constitution of the United States, for example, currently provides for the legislative branch to consist of the Senate and the House of Representatives. All members of the legislative branch are elected by the voters. Each state in the Union has two U.S. senators regardless of the number of people residing in the state. The House of Representatives, on the other hand, is designed to be representative of the number of people residing in each state. The rationale for the makeup of the Senate is that when the Union was being formed it was necessary to compromise with states that had small populations in order to induce them to join, so the concept of one-man, one-vote was abandoned for the upper chamber. There was nothing new in such a concept. It was probably an adaptation of the British system in which there was a House of Lords comparable to the Senate and a House of Commons in which power is dispersed on the basis of population.

## A Wide Variety of Plans

As each state joined the Union, it chartered its own constitution—including its method of apportioning legislative power. The rule is that the terms of each state's constitution are valid and enforceable unless they conflict with the U.S. Constitution. Thus, over the years, there have been a wide variety of plans for the distribution of state legislative power. Every concept imaginable has been tried in some venue. Even the one-house legislature—the unicameral system—has been given its place in the sun.

When the 57 Clubbers went to Tallahassee for the first time, Florida was under the constitution of 1885, as amended. As has been noted, it provided for a two-house legislature, with thirty-six senators in the upper body and ninety-five members in the House of Representatives. There was no requirement that the Senate districts be single-member districts, but it was required that each district be as near to equal in population as practicable. The 1885 constitution was replaced by the constitution of 1968.

Reapportionment sounds like a snoozer, and many people find it uninteresting or worse, which is too bad because it is so important. The Florida Legislature is required to address the subject every ten years following the completion of the census. Every time it comes up, several issues are raised without any hesitation. First is the selfish interest of every one of the legislators. They are all thinking of the next time they will have to run for re-election, and they are looking for ways to make their districts as friendly to them as possible. If there was a way to make the incumbent an absolute winner, they would opt for it. They have to be heard and satisfied if possible.

## House and Senate Leaders Have Say

Legislators get involved early in the process. They do their own analyses or conspire with the staff to design districts that satisfy the selfish desire for political survival. They lobby their colleagues, enlist the help of their favorite lobbyists, and arrange their schedules so they can attend as many of the reapportionment meetings as possible. Reapportionment is serious business to them. More recently, after single-member districts and term limitations became mandatory, this first issue became less frantic. However, it was around that time when Florida became a two-party state and the political parties took a hand in the process. They had a lot to say about what was going to happen.

The next issue is one that has not really changed over the years. The presiding officers of the two houses seem to have to prove to the world that they are in charge. They have a strong desire to write a proposal in their respective committees that they can support. They don't want it said that they couldn't get it done, even if the goal is the status quo or something close to it. Neither do they want the governor criticizing them and their committees for inaction or for doing a sorry job. Consequently, they find their key appointee among the leaders and tap him after charging the designee as to what is expected. The chairman of the Reapportionment Committee has a moment in the spotlight while preparing for the hearings, and even during the hearings he is in the forefront of legislative activity.

Then comes reality, when passage of the bill without amendments becomes an almost life or death affair. If it passes in the house of origin, the lobbying and negotiation with the other house begins in earnest. Normally what happens next is that each house passes its own bill and a Conference Committee is appointed to attempt to develop a bill that can pass both the House and Senate. Conference committees usually have an equal number of members from each house, with the chairman appointed from the delegation of the house where the bill originated. There is enormous pressure right down to the day when the final proposal is handed down by the Conference Committee and debated in both houses.

The next issue for consideration by the legislature when it was involved in reapportionment was the underlying legal mandate to fairly reapportion the legislative power. Before the courts stepped in the constitutional mandate existed, but it was toothless. It was strong enough to cause the legislature to dedicate much time and energy to it, but there was no guarantee of success. If the Conference Committee could not or would not offer up a bill in keeping with the Florida Constitution, they made the effort and went home. History tells us that later on, after the U.S. Supreme Court ordered the one-man, one-vote rule, any reapportionment bill that didn't pass muster was voided and the legislature was ordered to get back to work.

In the early '60s a plan was adopted and a full legislature elected pursuant to it. A suit was brought alleging noncompliance with the mandate of the court, and the court decreed that the plaintiff was correct. The plan was stricken and a new plan submitted. Legislators who were elected under the invalid proposal had their terms shortened by the court and had to run again if they wanted to keep the office.

## Fair Reapportionment Is Important

Why is fair apportionment so important? The answer is that it is critical to the control of the legislature. If the one-man, one-vote rule is in effect, the big counties—counties with the most people—would be in control rather than the small counties that traditionally held the power. And the reason why control is so important, among other reasons, is the tax distribution system.

Back in the days when there was no gambling in Florida and the big counties on the lower east coast wanted to install dog tracks and perhaps other forms of gambling, a deal was made with the small counties. Gambling facilities would be confined to the lower east coast, but the tax collected on those facilities would be distributed to all sixty-seven counties, with each county receiving the same amount. Thus, little Liberty County with 3,000 people and Jefferson County with 9,000 would each receive the same amount as Dade County—which at that time had 900,000 residents. There is no way such gross inequity could be perpetuated unless those small counties remained in control.

An interesting fact about that situation was that it was not just the legislators who were concerned about maintaining control. The rank-and-file citizens cared a lot about it, as did the lobbyists in Tallahassee. I learned about the citizens in 1964 when I was a candidate for governor and went to Brooksville in Hernando County for a campaign speech.

It was my practice to say the same things in all my speeches regardless of where I was speaking. That day I was in front of the picturesque old courthouse with a few curious citizens who wanted to see what I looked like. I told them I was for fair apportionment and recited some evidence of how unfair it was. If I had any support there it vanished as I spoke. I didn't receive enough votes to put in my hat, as the saying goes.

## A Reapportionment Battle

In 1957, when members of the 57 Club first went to the legislature, those legislators and lobbyists in the know—and a few others—were just beginning to get ready for the reapportionment battles that would follow the 1960 decennial census. At the same time, they were weary from the continuing obligation to fairly apportion representation following the 1950 census, as Governor Collins kept the legislature in special session regarding reapportionment from the adjournment of the 1955 session until sometime late in 1956.

It was a tough assignment for citizen legislators who had to earn a living and could not stand to lose a year's income while cooling their heels in Tallahassee. And the hardship was exacerbated by the racial controversy which permeated everything and the large number of other bills that were crying for attention in our fast growing state.

# 10 *Other Issues and Episodes* •———————

A great deal of activity always swirls around the legislature. It is where the action is. As a matter of fact, that is one of the strongest attractions to service in the legislative branch of Florida's state government. Somehow, the era around 1957 was just a bit different from most other time segments. The two main issues—racial integration of the public schools and reapportionment—were standouts. Had there been nothing else, those issues would have been a gracious plenty. But there was much more. It seems that there were more unusual happenings during those times, and that they generated more intense emotional reactions than was generally the case.

Consider a representative sample of those events to which some or all of those elected to serve for the first time in 1957 were exposed at some time during their service.

## The State Budget

In 1957 the state was still quite small in population, control of tax funds had for many years been in the hands of those with a conservative philosophy, and the constitutional prohibition of the state's doing business on credit had been carefully followed. Consequently, taxes were low and the state's financial status was strong. However, pressure to appropriate more money for education and social services was intense, and competition for tax dollars was fierce.

The House Committee on Appropriations was charged with crafting a bill that could become the budget for the ensuing two years. Accordingly, the committee had a lot to say about how many dollars were needed and how they would be spent. Of course, the Senate had a similar committee and, ultimately, the two versions of the budget would have to be reconciled by a conference committee made up of members of both houses.

The really important money issues were settled there, and in the '50s the meetings were held behind closed doors with little or no input from other legislators or members of the public. The lobbyists, however, could and did get word to the House and Senate members.

## A Learning Experience

A few of us in the 57 Club were favored with appointments to that Appropriations Committee in our early years, and it was a magnificent learning experience. The leaders believed in hands-on legislative oversight, so they managed to obtain the use of buses, airplanes, and other vehicles which enabled committee members to visit all of the institutions that were funded with tax revenue.

We visited every prison, every facility for delinquent youth, all state hospitals—which included several tuberculosis hospitals that were still in operation—and every other facility owned and operated by the state. We saw things that made us proud and things that made us ashamed. We were in new community colleges that were being authorized and made operational at an unbelievable rate, and we sat in "Old Sparky," Florida's infamous electric chair.

The mental hospital at Macclenny, about twenty-five miles west of Jacksonville, was a state-of-the-art facility and a source of pride. However, the hospital at Chattahoochee in northwest Florida was still using buildings constructed during World War I. It was a disgrace.

We saw it all and we heard it all from department heads. We learned about the legislative environment directly from those who were in charge of it. One thing we learned well was how resourceful the experienced officials could be. For example, the Beverage Department requested an airplane to be used in searches for illegal distilleries. State-owned airplanes were developing in popularity, and state officials coveted them. Some were needed while others were simply wanted. We considered the Beverage Department's request to be the latter. Consequently, our committee rejected their request.

The next year it was discovered—and too late to change—that the department had a line item in its budget for replacement of an obsolete plane. When we got to the bottom of the situation, we discovered that the department had accepted a gift of a surplus military airplane and finessed an appropriation to replace it as though it had previously been in their service. In spite of the committee's wishes, the airplane fleet was born, and I'll wager it is still growing.

## Sunshine Was Creeping In

Florida did not yet have "Government-in-the-Sunshine" laws. There was talk of such laws, and they were badly needed, but they were not to become a reality until the 1968 constitution was adopted by the people. So, at the time of the 57 Club, the Senate would regularly close its doors to the public and the press and actually make decisions about public issues in secret.

The Senate committees also allowed voting by proxy, and confusion was sometimes the result. A representative from north Florida once appeared before a Senate committee to speak for his bill. The trouble was that only one senator, the chairman, showed up. "Don't worry," said the chairman, "I have enough proxies to make a quorum." He then told the representative to proceed with his explanation of the bill and confided that he liked it.

Following the presentation, the chairman announced his vote in favor of the bill, but then cast five proxy votes against it. The bill died there. The House member was astonished, and then the committee voted by proxy to adjourn the meeting.

The House was a bit more careful in that regard, but its committees could meet without giving notice to the public, and meetings were held in places not accessible by the public. Unfortunately, the example set in Tallahassee was emulated by local governments throughout the state.

One House member in favor of government transparency was Emory "Red" Cross (who, by the way, was not called Red Cross because of his association with the well-known charitable organization of the same name but because of his reddish hair). He was a colorful character from Gainesville who always wore a white suit. Emory was a strong advocate of open government and, in my estimation, had the right idea, but he was ahead of his time. There's no denying that his crusade kept the issue on the front burner and his perseverance finally got results. Openness in government—the notion that public business IS the public's business—eventually came to Florida and, when it came, it certainly altered the political environment.

## Home Rule Became a Reality

Similarly, Home Rule was coming to the forefront. It is the concept that local government entities can decide local issues just as well as state legislators and that, in the name of efficiency, they ought to be empowered to do so. In 1957, as the members of the 57 Club took their seats, cities which had been created by the legislature had each been given a charter that included a grant of Home Rule powers in some form, depending on the language of the charter. However, counties were still considered to be extensions of the legislature. Consequently, they were practically impotent as to governance and remained so until they were given those powers in the 1968 constitution. Oh, it was talked about a lot prior to 1957, but when the 57 Club members had their first legislative experiences, the local government situation was still confusing.

As I said, counties did not have charters. Their power was limited and they had to go to the legislature for authority to set salaries, name a street or a building, or do any of the things that constituted local government. Every two years, as the biennial legislative session was approaching, each county's legislative delegation would receive a group of requests from county commissioners and other county officials asking for the power to take various actions and/or confirm some action already taken which was subject to confirmation by the legislature.

## A Local Government Fiasco

Another interesting horror story about local government mischief involved the City of Daytona Beach in Volusia County. Prior to World War II, Francis Whitehair—a lawyer and political insider whose office was in DeLand, the county seat—had a serious disagreement with the city commissioners and mayor of Daytona Beach. Whitehair was so influential with the legislative delegation that he was able to induce them to introduce a bill abolishing the City of Daytona Beach and transferring all of the assets to a newly created city, also named Daytona Beach. There would be a new city commission appointed by the governor, who was also a political friend of Whitehair.

That mess was eventually straightened out, but only after the incumbents barricaded themselves in City Hall and the National Guard was called up to restore peace by threatening the use of brute force. In the elections of 1956, voters remembered that fiasco and were still angry about what had happened. They demanded a commitment from all candidates that such a political embarrassment would never happen again and that the public's business would thereafter be in the open. They also extracted a promise that if a local measure was controversial, the people could make the final decision in a referendum.

The grant of Home Rule powers to the counties in 1968 changed local governments for the better and relieved legislators of an aggravating element of their duties, but it also diminished their power.

## An Unexpected Interruption

It was during Bill Chapell's term as Speaker of the House that we experienced a most interesting and important happening. There was no warning. One minute all was normal, and the next minute we were involved in an intriguing situation that called into play the unique leadership skills of 57 Clubber Bill O'Neill.

The House was in session and everything seemed to be normal when business was interrupted by the speaker, who announced the appointment of a select committee with O'Neill as chairman. The speaker did not share with us the mission of the committee, saying only who would be serving on it. Naturally, everyone was curious about what was going on. The interruption was a serious distraction from the work in progress for every representative seated in the chamber. Then, following the announcement of the select committee, its members were excused from the session and told to notify the speaker when they were ready to make their report.

Bill O'Neill's report caused a stir in the House chambers.

As one might imagine, we were all uneasy, given the way the appointments had been handled, and that was added to all the usual tensions of a session. Predictably, rumors began circulating and because of the nature of them, they interfered with the work of the House. However, there was no official explanation.

## The O'Neill Report

Within a few hours, Bill O'Neill was recognized to make his committee's report. With measured tones and in discrete language calculated to avoid hurting any innocent person, he reported an incident in which an offensive note—the specifics of which were never revealed—had been passed to a preteen, female page who was the daughter of one of the representatives. The note was written by Bert Riddle, one of the representatives from north Florida.

O'Neill said the committee had interviewed the author of the note, and the offense was not denied. After suggesting that the conduct was unacceptable and reminding us that constitutionally each house of the legislature is the sole judge of the qualifications of its member, Bill moved that the House expel Riddle. There was a deathly silence.

The speaker then asked the offending legislator (who was present in the chambers) if he wished to say anything or make any statement in his defense. He answered, "No." The vote was called for and we expelled Riddle there and then.

While most of us sat there in shock, the speaker ordered the sergeant at arms to remove the expelled member from the chambers. He was immediately led from his desk to the front door of the chambers and out into the hall where the lobbyists normally wait to speak to legislators as they pass by.

Then, as if there hadn't already been enough drama, the sergeant at arms returned to Riddle's desk, dumped the contents of the disgraced legislator's drawers into a waste basket, and took it out into the hall.

The speaker, realizing that the House was in no mood to do business as usual, ended the legislative day by declaring the House adjourned. There was no objection.

Bill O'Neill was an able legislator. He was smart, hard working, and knowledgeable. He served in the House of Representatives through every general and special session beginning in 1957 and ending with a special session in 1966. Because he was so competent and so qualified, he was given many important assignments throughout his legislative tenure.

I was impressed by him and thought of him as a solid citizen who did his work effectively and on time. Accordingly, I watched him rather closely in an effort to learn from him. Based on my observations, I concluded that he did a good job overall and did everything expected of him and then some on every one of his special assignments. I was also convinced that both his county and the state benefited from his service.

After four terms in the House, Bill returned to the full-time practice of law in Ocala. Even a casual observer would conclude that he was a fine lawyer. I certainly did. One of my lasting resolutions from my 57 Club days was that if I ever needed a lawyer for an important and complex case, I would try to induce Bill O'Neill to handle it.

Sergeant At Arms Amos Davis escorts Bert Riddle from the House chambers. (Photo courtesy Florida Archives.)

## Articles of Impeachment

We have seen that the Florida Constitution provides that each house of the legislature is the sole judge of the qualifications of its members. That means representatives may vote to remove a member who misbehaves. However, the other two branches of Florida's government are treated differently. The leaders of the executive branch are subject to impeachment, as are all justices and judges above the rank of county judge. Impeachment is only one of the procedures available to rid the system of corruption, but it is an important one.

The legislature participates in almost every aspect of the impeachment process. The House initiates the proceedings by voting for Articles of Impeachment, which is the accusatory document similar to a grand jury's indictment. The Senate is the adjudicator, with the House presenting and advocating approval of its articles very much like a prosecutor in a criminal proceeding. The chief justice of the Florida Supreme Court presides over the Senate when it is convened for an impeachment trial and is the only non-legislative state official who plays a major part in the impeachment proceedings.

The process is slow, cumbersome, expensive, and totally political. Yet it was retained in every one of our constitutions, including the one adopted in 1968. Moreover, it is used once in a while. To paraphrase a quote by the famous Benjamin Franklin: Impeachment is the civilized alternative to assassination.

Given the laissez faire political environment of the 1950s, it is not surprising that the legislature seldom used the awesome power of impeachment. However, it was placed in motion at one point, and the members of the 57 Club were there.

## Two Circuit Judges

A circuit judge in Miami was accused of various acts which constituted conduct unbecoming a member of the judiciary. The allegations also qualified as constitutional grounds for impeachment. A House committee investigated and recommended that the House adopt Articles of Impeachment. The recommendations of the committee were followed, and the case was presented to the Senate for adjudication.

In the meantime, there was a movement by citizens of Dade County to defend the judge. One of the defense strategies was the representation that another well-known circuit judge was guilty of similar conduct and, therefore, should also be impeached. Confusion and concern for the judiciary was rampant. Pending a trial of the first case, the House considered the second one and refused to adopt the Articles of Impeachment. However, a motion to reconsider the vote was left pending. That maneuver, because of the rules, kept the issue alive.

In due course, the Senate conducted the trial of the first judge and failed to find him guilty by the required number of votes. As soon as the action of the Senate was official, he was cleared to go back to work in the courtroom. His case was over, as was the case of the second judge, whose charges had been dropped.

We had witnessed the whole process run its course, including the lobbying and public debate of the fundamental issue of probable cause. It was quite obvious how different it was from a formal trial in court. Thus, the members of the 57 Club learned just how political the impeachment process could be. An official could easily be caught up in a complex procedure authorized by the Florida Constitution that was extremely dangerous to his political health. It is worth noting that the whole world—including the full legislature—saw the impeachment process with all its warts and did nothing to change or eliminate it.

## Judge Richard Kelly

In a subsequent session, while a number of the 57 Club members were still in the House, we again saw how political the impeachment process could be. The case involved Circuit Judge Richard Kelly of Pasco County. The charges against him concerned his nasty attitude toward lawyers. The accusations were serious in that, if true, he was abusing his judicial power to the detriment of certain lawyers, their clients, and the judicial system.

The case was heavily lobbied on both sides. The argument against impeachment was to the effect that the process was inappropriate in this case because if the judge were to be found guilty, the only penalty would be his defrocking, which would remove him from office and keep him out forever. That, it was argued, was too severe a penalty in a case in which the charges were all based on the judge's attitude and interaction with lawyers.

Ultimately, the articles came up for debate and a vote in the House. The defense was effective and the vote, while close, culminated in a refusal to impeach. We thought it was over. However, Judge Kelly was overheard by a House member reacting to the decision by saying that, in effect, he would get even with the lawyers who testified against him. His comments were reported to the House members and the reaction was swift. After a motion to reconsider, he was impeached. However, the Senate did not convict him, so he remained in office, but reports from his courthouse indicated that he had changed for the better.

Several years later, Judge Kelly was elected to the U.S. Congress. He was later convicted of bribery.

## Three Supreme Court Justices

As I was experiencing my introduction to the impeachment process, little did I know that in the future—1975 to be exact—I would be retained as general counsel for the Impeachment Committee of the House. This time, the committee was charged with investigating and recommending action concerning three Justices of the Florida Supreme Court. The justices in question—Boyd, Dekle, and McCain—were accused of engaging in inappropriate activities, and the House wanted the committee to advise it as to whether these activities were grounds for impeachment.

Justice Joe Boyd was caught in a situation in which an opinion was drafted by an attorney for one of the parties in a large and important public utility case. Preliminary thinking was that Boyd requested the draft, but after it was seen in his office, he disclaimed knowledge of the circumstances under which it was written and then alleged that he cut it up and flushed it down the toilet.

Justice Dekle, meanwhile, was alleged to have called a circuit judge in north Florida to urge the judge to be protective of a party in a hotly contested lawsuit pending in that trial court. It was suspected that such conversations between judges were widespread.

Justice McCain was suspected of being involved in flagrant and unethical activities relating to opinions of the court.

Justice McCain was impeached by the House and then resigned before the Senate scheduled his case for trial; Justice Dekle resigned before the question of his impeachment was ever put before the House; and Justice Boyd was returned to duty provided that he complied with the committee's recommendations, which involved a variety of tests.

I became so involved with and interested in the subject of impeachment that in 1977, while I was serving as a justice of the Florida Supreme Court, I coauthored with my aide, Marguerite Davis, a *Law Review* article entitled "Impeachment in Florida." The article was published in the winter 1978 issue of the *Florida State University Law Review*. Interestingly, Marguerite Davis, my former aide, subsequently entered the private practice of law but was soon appointed to serve as a judge on the First District Court of Appeal. She has a fine legal mind and is making an outstanding record on that court.

**Interposition Resolution**

Although the Interposition Resolution—which asserted the superiority of states' rights—had come and gone before the freshmen of 1957 first went to Tallahassee, its essence was still around. This resolution declared that Florida interposed its sovereign status between the federal government and the people of Florida. It was a throwback to the Civil War era, when the rights of the states vis-à-vis the federal government were being sorted out.

The title of the Interposition Resolution discloses its purpose:

A RESOLUTION TO DECLARE THE UNITED STATES SUPREME COURT DECISIONS USURPING THE POWERS RESERVED TO THE STATES AND RELATING TO EDUCATION, LABOR, CRIMINAL PROCEDURE, TREASON AND SUBVERSION TO BE NULL, VOID AND OF NO EFFCT; TO DECLARE THAT A CONTEST OF POWERS HAS ARISEN BETWEEN THE STATE OF FLORIDA AND THE SUPREME

COURT OF THE UNITED STATES; TO INVOKE THE DOCTRINE OF INTERPOSITION; AND FOR OTHER PURPOSES.

Representative Farris Bryant of Ocala led the effort to pass the Interposition Resolution. He was, at that time, preparing his campaign for governor, and his close supporters were from the political camp that traditionally opposed the kind of moderate thinking that was making Governor Collins famous. The resolution would help keep the issue of segregation alive. Logically, Bryant would want it alive and on everyone's mind because he would need the votes of all the opponents of integration to win the election.

Favoring the resolution would help to qualify Bryant as the conservative, while Collins, the symbol of reasonableness, would oppose it, making it easy for the Bryant folks to label Collins and his friends as liberals. Although Collins would not be his actual opponent, having a public disagreement with the governor would reinforce Bryant's differences with him and provide a very emotional pretext on which to attack any moderate opponents.

It wasn't that Bryant lacked understanding of the issue. The Harvard-educated lawyer was very bright and well-versed in history. I believe he knew full well that when the Confederacy was dissolved after the Civil War, the notion that superior rights were vested in the states was nullified, and that any attempt to assert otherwise was a waste of time. It appeared that for political reasons, Bryant wanted to distance himself philosophically from Governor Collins, and the resolution served as the tool for doing so.

Bryant knew that Collins would oppose the resolution, but no doubt assumed Collins could do nothing meaningful about it since the governor had no veto power with respect to resolutions. However, because Collins had such strong feelings about the integration issue and detested any attempt to use the resolution as a means of stirring emotions and fostering hatred, he took the unprecedented step of writing his objections in longhand and forwarding them with the original document.

His action demonstrated that there was a serious division of thinking in our state, with a popular governor personally opposing the legislators. The written objection diminished the value of Bryant's effort, but certainly reinforced his desire to be separate and apart from Collins. Separation of powers and the safeguard of checks and balances were real issues in Florida. Governor Collins wrote:

> This concurrent Resolution of 'Interposition' crosses the Governor's desk as a matter of routine. I have no authority to veto it. I take this means, however, to advise the student of government, who may examine this document in the ar-

chives of the state in the years to come, that the Governor of Florida expressed open and vigorous opposition thereto.

I feel that the U.S. Supreme Court has improperly usurped powers reserved to the states under the Constitution. I have joined in protesting such and in seeking legal means of avoidance. But if this Resolution declaring the decisions of the Court to be 'null and void' is to be taken seriously, it is anarchy and rebellion against the nation which must remain indivisible under God if it is to survive.

Not only will I not condone 'interposition' as so many have sought me to do, I decry it as an evil thing, whipped up by the demagogues and carried on the hot and erratic winds of passion, prejudice, and hysteria. If history judges me right this day, I want it known that I did my best to avert this blot. If I am judged wrong, then here in my own handwriting and over my signature is the proof of guilt to support my conviction.

LeRoy Collins, Governor.

May 2, 1957.

Copies of both the resolution and Collins' comments are attached in the Appendix.

## Bryant Wins in 1960

In the 1956 gubernatorial race, Collins beat the entire field of his opponents, including Farris Bryant. At the end of Collins' term four years later in 1960, in a race against Doyle Carlton, Bryant won the governorship and served a four-year term. He was politically wise to have a segregation image that year.

Bryant's Interposition Resolution probably helped. Feelings were sensitive about the issue. For example, I was told by people in whom I had confidence that during the campaign, Bryant—the conservative candidate—was confronted with an allegation that he had attended a luncheon meeting with an organization of black men. He admitted that he had been at the meeting, but forcefully asserted that he did not sit down to eat with them.

## Saltwater Fishermen

On a lighter note, an issue that was barely on the radar screen but proved capable of bringing out the worst in people was known as the saltwater fishing license proposal. In those days, a freshwater fisherman had to buy a license to fish in the lakes and ponds throughout the state. The proceeds from the tax were used to protect freshwater fish and animals in the wild. The agency created to manage that program was the state's Game and Freshwater Fish Commission.

On the other hand, those who opted to fish in salt water—whether in marshes, inland waterways, lagoons, bays, the Gulf of Mexico, the Caribbean, or the Atlantic Ocean—had no such tax burden. There was no revenue source committed to salt water conservation as there was in the fresh water environment.

It seemed to me that this was an imbalance in the political equation and the worst kind of discrimination. I felt confident that saltwater fishermen, being good sports, would willingly pay a modest license fee if the revenue was dedicated to the protection and improvement of salty waterways and the creatures living there. Accordingly, I prepared and filed a bill.

A few of the newspapers wrote about my bill, and then there was a political explosion. One of the many letters I received early on seemed to speak for all those who disagreed with my proposal. It said, "Dear Mr. Karl—Now that you've had your picture in the paper—drop dead."


### Another Fish Story

That reminds me of another fish story—again featuring the fish called mullet. At about the time of the 57 Club, there was an effort to change the public image of the mullet. Representative Baldy Strickland, a 57 Clubber and mullet fisherman by trade, favored the proposal. The main thrust of the effort was to change the name of the common mullet to the more attractive name of "Lisa." But the public relations campaign to cause people to think of the strange fish as "Lisa" and to eat more of it was short lived. It flashed, and then it was gone.

In those days, if one wanted to say something unkind about a newspaper, he would refer to it as a fish wrapper or, in Florida, as a mullet wrapper—with the implication being that it was only worthy of use as a container for smelly fish. Once, in the spirit of cooperation, I awarded AP and UPI reporters with a can of Lisa wrapped in one of the daily papers. It wasn't all that funny, but it made the point that mullet deserved a better image. Ultimately, however, it didn't matter. Smoked mullet with beer reemerged as a great food for some folks, and Baldy kept catching and selling mullet. No one has mentioned Lisa for years.

I presented a tongue-in-cheek award to reporters from the Associated Press and United Press International—a can of "Lisa" wrapped in newspaper.

## Welborn Daniel

A subtle but important incident involved another 57 Club member, Senator Welborn Daniel. In 1968, the people of Florida voted for a new constitution. It took effect January 1, 1969, and has proven to be an excellent piece of work. Interestingly, two other 57 Club members—Jack Mathews and Dempsey Barron—had moved from the House to the Senate and played major roles in drafting and developing public support for Florida's new governing document.

Welborn Daniel was an excellent organizer. He was given the chairmanship of a Senate committee in late 1968 and had the responsibility of leading the reorganization of state government. The 1968 constitution mandated a plan by which some 272 state departments and agencies would be placed under the jurisdiction of not more than twenty-five new departments. Developing, selling, and executing the plan were Daniel's assignments.

One can only imagine the administrative, technical, and personnel problems involved in the task. The elected cabinet officers would preside over many of the new departments, and that raised numerous questions. Which ones would be managed by which officer? Which agencies would form each of those new departments? How would conflicts between those powerful officers be resolved? How could the results of the entire restructuring be made acceptable to a majority of the legislators and the governor?

The enormity of the task seemed to be more than could possibly be handled by a single legislator. Yet Welborn Daniel of Clermont did it. His organizational skills combined with his knowledge of people, his ability to mediate their differences, and his debating abilities all helped. But his best tool—and most powerful weapon— was his cast-iron will. Once he took a position, he was immovable.

Because of the good work of Welborn Daniel, both houses passed the bill recommended by his Conference Committee.

Welborn Daniel was known as an outstanding debater who could use both humor and passion to make his point. (Photo courtesy Florida Archives.)

## An Omission

History buffs will remember that there was one major omission in the 1968 constitution, and that was Article V, the judicial article. Work on that piece was deferred for a few years and left to the legislature to craft. Here again, members of the 57 Club took the lead in constitutionally reforming the court system. Jack Mathews, Dempsey Barron, Welborn Daniel, and I were all in leadership positions in the project, and we had a lot to do with the final outcome.

The system of Florida courts had developed all sorts of problems under the 1885 constitution and was badly in need of repair. The basic structure had been a three-tier arrangement, with the first two tiers being trial courts and all appeals from the circuit court level going directly to the State Supreme Court. Then there were the justices of the peace, or neighborhood courts, that were still around from the days when a trip to the county seat was a major journey.

To make matters worse, over the years the legislature had also permitted a wide variety of specialty courts to be created. Most of the courts were manned by lawyers, but a few of them had no such requirement. Thus, there were cases everywhere in Florida being heard by non-lawyers, and people's rights were being adjudicated by men without any legal training. Also, there was very little uniformity around the state. If there was a need for relief from excessive case loads, whether real or perceived, a new court would simply be created in a given county. There were the County Courts of Record, Criminal Courts of Record, Civil Courts of Record, Small Claims Courts, and Juvenile Courts, to name a few.

## An Example of a Part of the System

One particular Justice of the Peace Court in Daytona Beach illustrates the extent to which the system had degenerated. I can't represent that it was typical of all of those courts in the state, because it was the only such court I had to contend with. However, I heard rumors of misconduct in other such courts that caused me to believe they were all susceptible to the same kind of abuses. In any event, the Daytona Beach example was evidence of the vulnerability of a system that was broken. That neighborhood court was so bad that it was the source of genuine community shame.

Justice of the Peace J. C. Beard presided over his court in an old storefront space on Second Avenue near the railroad tracks that divided the black section of town from the white section, which was all the rest of Daytona Beach. In other words, all the black people were expected to live in one very limited area that was a slum no matter who evaluated it.

Judge Beard was white, and he was seemingly warm and friendly. He flattered everyone he talked with and gave the impression that he genuinely cared about other people. He made it his business to know almost everyone and ingratiate himself into their circles of friends. He did not have much formal education, but he was street smart. He had moved to Daytona Beach from rural south Georgia when he was in his forties and somehow managed to be elected to that neighborhood court in which he made his living and spent most of his time.

The income he received was from fees paid for judicial services rendered. Both the judge and his constable were allowed to charge the people coming before his court a fee predetermined by law for whatever they did. For example, should you be so unfortunate as to get yourself arrested, the judge would earn a fee for signing the warrant, another fee for conducting a preliminary hearing of some kind, and still another for the order binding the defendant over. If the person arrested couldn't pay, the county paid the fees. Imagine the temptation to trump up a charge and arrest some poor, innocent person just to increase the income in a slow month.

Historically, the jurisdiction of Judge Beard's court was limited to misdemeanors and civil cases involving small amounts of money. Naturally, he couldn't sentence a person to prison, but he could order a prisoner held in the county or city jail for short periods of time based on a limited number of reasons. The situation was bad enough on the surface, but if one lifted the lid and took a serious look inside to see how it actually operated, it was positively unconscionable.

When I was just out of law school in 1950, I worked for an older lawyer who had a general practice. One day he called me into his office and told me that one of his good clients was an advertising agency in Chicago that had a contract with a small business located in Daytona Beach. He explained that the local business had refused to pay about $50 for advertising services. My boss had already filed a complaint in Judge Beard's court, and all I had to do was go over there, go through the motions with a representative of our client, and then collect the money. At the very least, I was to bring back a judgment against the local business which would give our client the right to put a lien on the Daytona Beach property, if necessary, in order to collect the money.

I walked into that shoddy courtroom and thought to myself, "Oh man, you have chosen the wrong profession." Toward the back of the area where there had once been a small retail store was a raised platform. At most, it was raised about four or five inches. On that platform were a tattered old desk and a dilapidated chair with a disheveled old man sitting in it. A large mixed-breed dog was stretched out on the platform near the judge and a straight-back chair was nearby for a witness or a visitor if court was not in session. There were about six unmatched chairs out in front of the desk, and they were all occupied by white men who looked as though they had been dropped off by the rotten turnip truck.

Judge Beard recognized me as I entered (I had met him before). He welcomed me and invited me to come up and sit beside him. He explained that the people in the courtroom were his friends who were waiting for a case in which one of the parties asked for a jury trial, or a criminal case in which the defendant was entitled to a jury trial. His friends, he informed me, would serve as jurors. These unsavory-looking individuals were paid a fee for being jurors and, of course, that was why they hung out in the courtroom. Judge Beard explained that he could swear them in without delay and get the trial going in a few minutes. He introduced me to the prospective jurors with a flourish, telling them how he knew and liked my father and mother. He explained about the good work my mother did for poor people as director of vocational education. He finished by telling them that I was a good boy, a veteran and a new lawyer, and that he was going to let me win a lot of cases in his court. They all clapped and warmly welcomed me.

Then he asked me what case I was there for, and when I told him, he explained that he couldn't let me win that one because a northerner was suing a local man and he had to look out for the local person. He was sure I understood how it all worked. And, he added, anytime I sued someone from out of town he would let me win. Then the case was adjourned.

Imagine the trouble I had trying to explain to the client what had happened with his case.

The stories about Judge Beard were as outrageous as they were numerous. The tragedy was that all of them were probably true. A whole series of them involved his dog. It was said that he sometimes called upon that lazy critter to decide the case that was before him. He would tell the defendant—usually a black defendant—that he was having trouble deciding whether he was guilty and that his dog had a great legal mind and he was going to leave the decision up to him. Sure enough, he would ask the dog some question and show him a treat so that the dog would bark. Then Judge Beard would declare that the dog believed the defendant to be guilty, so that was the decision of the court.

There were many variations of the dog stories, but only the non-dog stories seemed to take place when I was present (which wasn't often, thank God). The worst non-dog stories involved questions about the law that was to be followed in that court.

I once heard a lawyer quote an opinion of the Florida Supreme Court in support of his client's case. Judge Beard listened impatiently and then announced that he didn't want to hear "no more of that" because he didn't run his court according to Florida law. He intended to decide the case based upon the Georgia Code because he thought the Georgia Code was better. There were stories about cases in which he actually referred to the Georgia Code in deciding issues or imposing a sentence.

He also had some quaint ways of expressing himself. When speaking from the bench to some hapless person he would explain that he hated to do it, but he was going to have to put him on "the hard road," meaning he was going to jail. The courthouse and the county seat were twenty-five miles away. When a defendant had done some grievous wrong that offended the judge, he would not just say he was going to send him to the county jail, he would say: "You are going to the county jail in the back seat of the constable's car and I order him to drive over there as fast as his car will run so you will be locked up there real soon. And, I'm going to have him blow his 'si-reen' all the way over there so everyone will know you are going to be away for a while."

## The Judge Lost the Election, but the Court Remained

It should be said that all attempts to recall or remove the judge failed, so we beat him the next time he ran for reelection. But the Office of Justice of the Peace survived until the adoption of the new judicial article.

The justice system in Florida was truly in need of reform in the 1950s and 1960s. The fact that legislators had the unusual power to decide whether to form new courts and, if they did so, to determine the jurisdiction, was pretty heady stuff for young legislators, but it wasn't good for our system of justice. And as if that was not bad enough, each delegation could, through a local bill, supplement the salaries of judges paid by the state. That bit of conflict-ridden bad government was also eliminated when Judicial Article V was revised.

Something had to be done to straighten out the confusing court system, but how could the reformers ever overcome the power of those who worked in the system and felt threatened by any suggested change? There were elected judges in neighborhoods of every county, and they could be expected to fight fiercely and enlist secretaries, clerks, bailiffs, and anyone else that was friendly with them or sympathetic to their cause. It was to be a real slugfest.

Apparently, the advocates of reform were heard by the people, because they succeeded. The new structure that emerged from the legislature and was accepted by the people was a four-tiered plan with two echelons of trial courts and two levels of appellate courts. All those homemade courts were gone. A few non-lawyer county judges were grandfathered in, but there were hardly any other significant compromises. The 57 Club members, who were still around, helped to make those important changes.

## The 1968 Constitution

While racial issues were the most pervasive matters and the impeachment of a judge and expulsion of a House member the most dramatic events in the early days of the 57 Club, there were several critical events destined to come to the attention of Club members who served longer terms in public office.

Nothing was more important than the revision of the Florida Constitution. It was accomplished in a two-step process. First were the aforementioned changes in 1968, which did not reform the judicial article. Second was the restructuring of the court system in the early 1970s. The legislators had the responsibility of implementing the new constitution and crafting a new Judicial Article V to take effect as soon as the voters of Florida approved it. Several 57 Club members played major roles in both of those tasks.

## Turnpike Bonds

Governor LeRoy Collins completed a toll road from Miami to Fort Pierce early in his administration. It was a project of the Turnpike Authority which was under his control, and that first segment of the master plan for a toll road to go north through the center of the state was referred to as the Bobtail Turnpike.

Financing was done properly, the bonds that were sold to raise money for the Turnpike Authority were safe and secure, and the interest rate was low. In fact, the road was so successful and the interest rate was so low, that bond buyers couldn't make much money with them. Investors could do just about as well with certificates of deposit, and with far less hassle. It followed that anyone could buy the outstanding bonds on the market at a discount because, as a rule, knowledgeable investors sell any parts of their investment portfolios that don't perform well under the prevailing market conditions. To do that they have to discount their stocks and bonds to a price that will produce an attractive rate of return for the proposed buyer. The investment can then be sold quickly and the seller can invest in more lucrative ventures. For whatever reason, a $1,000 Turnpike bond could be purchased for about $850. The Turnpike Authority was going into the market and gradually buying those discounted bonds, thereby reducing the amount of debt on the Bobtail Project. Had the Authority been able to buy all of the bonds at the discount, the effect would have been to reduce their costs for the project by a significant amount.

Make no mistake about it, the bond market is complicated and reacts to exterior forces and events, so it wasn't quite as simple as it sounds. But there were those who worked in and around bond transactions every day who assured me that under the conditions existing at the time, those savings were available.

In due time, Collins began the task of extending the road from Fort Pierce to Wildwood, where it would join Interstate 75. His announced plan was to finance the extension separately without involving the existing Bobtail bonds or the market price of those bonds, thus leaving open the opportunity to buy the old bonds at the discount. I thought Collins was wise to do it that way for three main reasons. First, the alternative of pledging the revenue from the entire extended road and combining both segments in a single bond issue would make it necessary to call in and buy back the Bobtail bonds. According to the bond covenants signed when the authority received the money to build the first segment, whoever owned the bonds at the time of the call would be entitled to a premium for them, as is customary when the borrower in a bond issue wants to pay off the debt earlier than originally planned. The premium—which of course would make the price more than the face value of the bonds—would put the Turnpike Authority in the position of losing the opportunity to buy the bonds at a discount or below face value. Instead, they would have to buy them at more than their face value. On the surface that didn't sound like a good deal.

The second reason was that, because of market conditions, the interest was so favorable on the Bobtail bonds that it was unlikely to be that low again in the time frame of the refinancing. The Authority would then have to pay a higher

I often visited with Governor LeRoy Collins. He always offered helpful advice.

rate on all the outstanding bonds for the reminder of the life of the bonds. I didn't know with specificity what the respective rates were, so I can't assert with certainty what amount of money was wasted, but it was substantial.

The third reason I liked Collins' plan was that it didn't raise the specter of someone with inside information making a profit at the public's expense. In other words, if the Turnpike Authority planned to finance both parts of the road together, they would have to pay off the Bobtail bondholders by buying their bonds at a "call price," an amount greater than face value. If the person with the inside information went to the market, bought the bonds at a discount, and then promptly sold them to the Authority at the premium call price, there would be a profit of some amount up to around $30 million. That would have a hard time passing the smell test, as they say.

The Bobtail bonds were bearer bonds, which means that they were negotiable just as cash or a signed check payable to "cash" or "Bearer" is negotiable. Only the company or agency issuing the bonds and paying interest on them had a record of who owned them at any given time. Certainly, there was no easy way to determine ownership. Bonds could be held in the name of a bro-

The Grove served as the temporary home of Governor Collins while a new official residence was built. (Photo courtesy Florida Archives.)

ker or a bank, and the only way to know who really owned them was to look at the records of the bank or broker. Those relationships between investors and the institutions they employ are confidential, and the brokers and banks are obliged to keep it that way. The entire bearer bond segment of the investment business is structured so the bonds can be traded easily, and so that those who desire to keep the transactions and ownership confidential can do so comfortably.

Meanwhile, Farris Bryant had won the Democratic nomination for governor and announced his intention to use the alternate plan of financing the turnpike extension with a single bond issue. He even filed a lawsuit to prevent Collins from doing the deal his way in the closing days of his administration. Those among us who were a bit cynical and suspicious wondered if any of the incoming governor's friends—who had access to the governor's plans and the details of the deal to be closed—had purchased any or all of the discounted bonds and were now planning to sell them back to the Turnpike Authority for a profit of as much as $30 million.

I drafted a proposal to create an investigative committee to look into the situation. The committee would have subpoena power so that those who would have had the knowledge and ability to participate could be legally compelled to answer the hard questions about their ownership of bonds and knowledge of others who owned them. I heard that I caused a few hearts to flutter.

Then, seemingly without effort, in a well-orchestrated move, the House leadership amended my proposal in a way that gave the speaker the exclusive right to appoint all of the members of the committee, but limited his power to appoint by including specific prohibitions or conditions. They kept me off the committee through those conditions, one of which excluded everyone who served with certain other groups. One of the groups was a committee on which I served. Then the proposal passed, the committee met, and predictably, nothing came of the investigation.

We will never know who if anyone participated in the $30 million deal. If it all went to the bondholders who bought them in the normal way, so be it. All we can say is that the Turnpike Authority spent all that public money needlessly. But if there was a profit motive and those involved had access to confidential information not available to the general public, then there should have been punishment for the misconduct, and the public should have been given the facts.

# PART 3

*Governors, the Media, and Campaigns*

# 11 *Governors We Knew* ———————————

It is true that the Office of Governor was weak when the 57 Club assembled in Tallahassee in April of 1957, but that did not lessen the interest our members had in the people who occupied the office in and around the time we served. Moreover, two 57 Club members ran for governor in 1964, and one of them ran a second time. There were three men who came to the legislature in our early days and, after serving with us in the House, went to the Senate and were later elected governor. It is fair to say that members of the 57 Club were uniquely privileged to have known and, in some cases, been so close to the distinguished governors of our time.

In as much as many 57 Clubbers were involved in politics in some way before being elected to the House, we will begin with a few tales of Fuller Warren, who was elected in 1948 and, to my knowledge, was supported by some of the 57 Clubbers.

## Fuller Warren (1948–1952)

World War II ended in 1945, and those future members of the 57 Club who were in uniform left the military and tried to reestablish some semblance of normalcy. They had lived through a major war, and, at the very least, had traveled and seen parts of the world they had hardly known existed. Some were in actual combat, where they had been taught to live a cut below human status.

In 1964, six candidates ran to be a "governor we knew" (*left to right*: Dickinson, Burns, Kelly, myself, Mathews, and High), but only one could win and that was Burns.

They were also exposed to cultures and customs new to them. For example, race relations in the service were different from what they had theretofore experienced. For all these reasons, U.S. soldiers were not the same as they were when they first went to war.

The war affected me as well. When the war in Europe ended, I was in Germany preparing to go home and then on to participate in the planned invasion of Japan. My division had been assigned the task of occupying the American sector of Berlin for the month of July 1945, when the Potsdam Conference was being held there, and we had to complete that assignment before going home.

War in the Pacific ended before we left Europe, so we turned in our tanks, wound down our military assignments, and prepared to go back to civilian life. I was certainly one of those changed by military experiences. During the war, I had witnessed the beginning of universal racial integration and was prepared to accept whatever was to happen. I also felt the old calling to politics and began looking to see what offices were going to be available to me.

Like so many of my colleagues to be, I felt that it was necessary to acquire an education and begin a meaningful life of working and giving something back to the country. I was on that track when I met and started to observe Fuller Warren, a candidate for the Office of Governor of Florida. He had a simple form of political organization on the campus of Stetson University, located in DeLand, where I was studying for a degree in law. I heard him speak several times, and he was good. When he spoke, people listened because he put so much into what he was saying. If he told a joke or a funny story, people laughed.

One such humorous anecdote was about two brothers who left their home at about the same time. One went into the military and the other went into the priesthood. They were very smart and talented, so both were successful. After being separated for many years, they decided to meet and selected the lobby of a large hotel in New York City. On the day of the meeting they were both right on time.

The boy who had gone into the military had risen to the rank of general. He had kept himself in good physical condition, so he was handsome, slim, and trim in his uniform. And that was not all. He had medals on his chest as testimony to his courage and bravery.

His brother was a bishop and he wore his cassock with the colorful insigne of his rank in the church. But alas, the bishop had let his body go. He was portly, and his vestments hanging on him barely hid his torso.

When they came together, the bishop was first to speak. He looked his brother over, standing so straight and tall, and said, "Boy, take my bags up to room 2100." The general looked at the bishop with kindness and replied, "Why madam, in your condition you shouldn't even be traveling." As usual when Fuller told this joke, the audience never failed to laugh.

Warren, it was generally agreed, was a handsome, well-dressed southern gentleman. He had a deep, rich voice and a large vocabulary. Because of those attributes, and because he had such an engaging personality, he was quite popular. He was not, however, a great administrator. He was not as careful in selecting people to appoint to the many important posts as he should have been. It seemed that he was a bit too accommodating of people who did not have the best interests of the public as their top priority.

He also had a habit of approaching everyone at a meeting or social event, shaking their hands, and saying, "Hello, I'm Fuller Warren." He would do that even if the person he was greeting was someone he had met before. He did this, he said, because it eliminated the necessity for anyone who wasn't sure of his name to look at his name tag or ask someone to identify him. By doing that it would also lessen the possibility of constituents asking him if he knew who they were.

Fuller explained how much he hated to have a person come up to him and say, "You don't know who I am, do you?" He would tell the story of the veteran congressman who decided to retire and was being interviewed by the press.

"What is the first thing you will do in retirement?" The reporter asked.

The congressman said, "I'm going to go home and walk down the street until someone asks me the detested question about whether I remember his name. Then I will answer the question in a way that I have wanted to reply for years. I will say, 'No, I don't know who you are, and I don't give a damn what your name is.'"

I once asked Fuller how he got started with the practice of identifying himself and being so friendly. He told me in terms I understood without further explanation. He said that he liked people and never wanted to embarrass anyone or cause any type of hiatus in a conversation between two other people. It was just his way.

Two of the issues that confronted Fuller Warren and all other candidates of that time caught my attention. The first was taxation. The state was in need of tax revenue to meet its obligations to provide critical services, especially in the area of public education. A new source of income would have to be generated, and the dispute was about what kind of tax program should be enacted.

Those I talked to about the situation assumed that a sales tax would be put in place. However, it was very unpopular; in fact every proposed new tax was repugnant to those who would have to pay it. No one I knew wanted more taxes.

The second issue—which may seem laughable today—was the proposal to remove cows from the highways. Florida had an open range law at that time, and it allowed ranchers to let cows roam free with impunity. Farmers and ranchers were politically powerful, and they had protected that law against all the attempts to enact changes. It seemed crazy to me that people were being hurt and sometimes killed all over the state because cattle could roam along the state highways, yet they couldn't do a thing about it. In fact, they were quite often made to pay for the cows they hit. Logic and common sense demanded a stop to the mischief on the roads caused by the cows.

This issue and the issue of properly funding public schools called for reform. The more progressive legislators, including then-State Senator LeRoy Collins, were determined to enhance the education system. This would be costly, and they had the pressure on for more tax funds.

Of course, there were many other issues on the agenda, but those two teach us about Fuller Warren. He really did not want to lead the movement for new taxes, but if there was to be a new tax, it could not be a state income tax.

Consequently, he did the politically correct thing and allowed a new sales tax bill to become law. I'm also reasonably certain that he did not want to offend his neighbors in north Florida by making them keep their cows fenced in and off the roads. But there was too much momentum driving the bill and it could not be ignored. As people say today, "It got traction and started moving." Eventually it passed and the slaughter on the roadways subsided.

At the beginning of the 1948 race for governor, Warren made a major speech in Blountstown, his hometown at that time. It was a quaint little town. The Apalachicola River flows from southern Georgia down to Apalachicola Bay. It is the dividing line between the eastern and central time zones. Bristol is on the east bank and Blountstown is on the west bank.

The largest supermarket in the area was a Piggly Wiggly grocery store. Merchants commonly cashed checks for both regular and casual customers. The residents were solid citizens who loved their country and state, and they were masters at dispensing southern hospitality.

It was no wonder that an ambitious politician like Warren picked Blountstown to begin his campaign for governor. The speech he made there in the early days of the campaign was a comprehensive summary of the issues, and included Warren's position on each of the important ones.

Thereafter, when he would be asked for his position on a controversial question, rather than provoke a confrontation or give his adversary a target at which to shoot, he often responded, "I made my position quite clear when I spoke in Blountstown. I have never changed my stance. I stand by my statement."

Warren won the race and served the one term allowed. During his tenure the sales tax was put in place and the open range law was removed from the statutes. Because he did not lead opposition or use his veto power, he was given credit—or blame, as the case may be—for both laws. The voters never forgave him. The people by and large did not like the way those things were done, but accepted the new laws. We still have the sales tax, and those who own cows must keep them off the roads.

Fuller Warren moved to south Florida when his term expired. Later he tried to win another four-year term in the Governor's Office but made a poor showing.

## Daniel McCarty (1952–1953)

Dan McCarty was elected to succeed Fuller Warren. He was elected during the time when Florida was a one-party state. By no means did that mean that all voters were of the same political philosophy. Neither did it mean that there was harmony among the voters of the state.

Within the Democratic Party there were factions and classifications. Some were for convenience or because of a particular issue; others existed in recognition of a political or financial philosophy. Still others were based on such issues as racial integration and reapportionment. There was even a "good guy vs. bad guy" classification by some folks.

Dan McCarty was from the east coast city of Fort Pierce in St. Lucie County. His family was affluent and respected. Politically he was in the camp of the most moderate thinkers. He did not qualify as a radical conservative or a radical liberal. For those who thought in terms of "good vs. bad," he was on the good side. He was conservative in fiscal matters, but advocated liberal spending for education and certain social services.

In terms of his supporters in the legislature, McCarty counted as his friends Senators LeRoy Collins of Tallahassee, Ed Price of Bradenton, Doyle Carlton Jr. of Tampa and Wachula, and Verle Pope of St. Augustine.

Also among his supporters was the powerful and successful Tallahassee law firm of Ausley and Ausley. Charles and John Ausley, senior partners in the firm, were well known around the state for their fundraising ability and political expertise. Senator Collins was a partner in the firm, and that added to its stature.

The campaign in 1952 separated the voters into those groups that were satisfied with the bombastic Fuller Warren and his small county outlook and programs and those that thought the citizens of Dade, Broward, and Palm Beach counties on the lower east coast, as well as the residents of other heavily populated areas, were entitled to have their voices heard in the legislature. It was not exactly a liberal vs. conservative split, although there were those who saw it that way and attempted to hand out labels accordingly. Most of the daily newspapers endorsed McCarty, as did leaders in education at all levels.

When the votes were counted and McCarty declared the winner, his followers celebrated the victory as though progress and enlightenment were coming to Florida soon and would stay forever. Generally speaking, the "ins" of Warren's administration were about to become the "outs" of the McCarty era.

Meanwhile, the men who dominated the Senate and represented the counties with small populations elected Senator Charley Johns as their president. Johns' district included Bradford County, where Raiford, the state prison with the electric chair known as "Old Sparky," was located. It would be an understatement to say Johns was not a supporter of McCarty. Because of their differences, Johns' election as Senate president would have been trouble for McCarty in any event, and that would have tempered the McCarty enthusiasm and hope for a new way of doing state business. Sadly, the total effect of their differences was much more significant and complicated.

Shortly after his inauguration in 1953, Dan McCarty suffered a heart attack and died. Charley Johns became acting governor, and for all practical purposes the decision of the voters to have a governor who was not beholden to the small county leaders was reversed. Instead of a governor elected statewide who would represent the thinking of all parts of Florida, they would be governed by a man elected by a relatively small number of people in the northern part of the state.

Although McCarty did not live long enough to put his ideas and programs into effect, he is remembered as one who would have been an outstanding governor. He is credited with gathering good people and integrating them into a fine campaign organization.

Strangely, the organization did not dissolve when McCarty died. Rather, it was preserved, strengthened, and enlarged during the two years the state was controlled by Charley Johns and his friends, then was called out and used by LeRoy Collins to defeat Johns.

When the 57 Clubbers were getting their feet on the ground and learning where the restrooms in the Capitol were located and other important facts, John McCarty, the personable brother of Dan, came to Tallahassee. He seriously explored, with his brother's friends, the possibility that he could be the one to pick up the McCarty flag and attempt to carry out the programs and plans of the deceased governor. However, in spite of the relationship, his wonderful reputation, and all his other qualities, John was not able to move into a position of leadership in the organization, nor could he stir any real enthusiasm for his potential race for governor. It was sad thing to watch, but such is the way of politics.

## Charley Johns (1953–1954)

Before Charley Johns chaired the infamous committee that was informally named for him, he was the man who happened to be President of the Senate when Governor Dan McCarty died in office, and he automatically became acting governor. The title implies that Charley Johns was somehow something less than the elected, regular governor. Not true! He was only in the office until the next general election, but that was the only distinction.

Johns was invested with the full panoply of powers and authority just as any other governor. He was fully aware of what he had inherited, and he moved quickly to take control of the office and all of its accoutrements, as well as the apparatus that supported it. All of the key McCarty appointees such as the governor's staff, Road Board members, and the like were replaced by Johns' people who, by and large, were not cut from the same bolt of cloth as McCarty's.

It must be understood that generalizing in this situation is as unfair as any other generalization. Therefore, it would be wrong to characterize the transition from the McCarty camp to the Johns people as a movement from good to bad or from liberal to conservative or from progressive to regressive. It was truly a change of personnel, and there is no denying that the collective thinking about governance of the Johns followers was different from that of McCarty's disciples. Obviously there were both good and bad, and some of most any quality that comes to mind in each group.

My fellow 57 Club members and I were not in office when Johns was acting governor, so we did not observe him in action from a good vantage point like the incumbent legislators. However, we were all interested in politics and were attracted by the unusual and dramatic turn of events that put Charley Johns in charge of our state.

I was a junior partner in a small law firm in Daytona Beach, and I had two senior partners who were legal scholars. One of them was very private about his politics. He never said which candidate he favored or what issues he felt were most important. In the twenty years we practiced together, I never knew for sure whom he voted for in any given race. I'm not even certain he voted for me when I was a candidate.

On the other hand, the partner who was the oldest and had more seniority than anyone in the firm was acutely interested and involved in politics. He loved it. He could never get enough conversation about what was going on. I found myself with one senior partner who took a special and exclusive interest in the operations of the firm and another who—while a bright and capable lawyer and an effective business magnet—so loved politics that he gave it a priority position in his thinking. That made our firm a profitable and politically potent organization. You might say that I had the best of all worlds, so far as my personal political environment was concerned.

For reasons I never knew and could never understand, the politically active senior partner was a supporter of Charley Johns. He had known Johns before he became the acting governor and kept in touch with him from time to time. My partner was a decent man, so there was no question about the sincerity of his sadness and regret over the passing of Dan McCarty, but he was elated that Johns came to power.

It was hard for me to participate in the early preparations for unseating Johns when my friend and law partner—twenty years my senior—was on the other side. As if that was not bad enough, my barber, an outspoken segregationist, was also a committed supporter of Johns and let me know it whenever I needed a haircut. Frankly, I dreaded the next election season.

I did not know who would challenge Johns, but I assumed it would be one of my acquaintances from the McCarty group. I was not politically significant enough to meet those people on their level, but I had sort of fallen in with them and felt at home there. I could not oppose my political friends, and I hated the thought of publicly supporting a candidate for governor who was the political enemy of my own law partner.

There was yet another problem for me in that situation. In DeLand, the county seat of Volusia County, there was a political strongman, Francis Whitehair, who, like my senior partner, made me very uncomfortable with my decision to oppose Charley Johns. He was an alumnus of Stetson University and an active supporter of the school. He was also a member and active supporter of my social fraternity.

He had always been supportive of our law firm and had actually sent good cases our way. He was politically oriented, although controversial. Knowing I would someday run for office, I was reluctant to alienate such a person. He was close to Johns, who asked him to accept an appointment to the Road Board—a very important and prestigious position at that time.

The Road Board was doubly important to a county like Volusia that was so dependent on tourism. Good roads to and from the county were essential. Also, the cost of road construction was so high that the work going on in any given county affected the entire economic environment at a time when every county needed all the help it could muster. There was no minimizing the positive impact of having a native son on the Road Board. That exacerbated the troubles flowing from my opposition to Charley Johns.

I knew myself, and I knew that I could not support Johns. Predictably, I would oppose him in 1954, so I went ahead and participated in the preparations to unseat him. I did not enjoy the feelings of betrayal I endured or the knowledge I had about the embarrassment I caused my partner. I survived the whole process without serious damage, although I always knew that neither of those men ever fully understood my decision nor forgave me for my action.

Johns' time in the Governor's Office was unremarkable. There was harmony between the governor and those in control of the Senate. He worked closely with the anti-McCarty groups, both within and without state government. The contrast between McCarty and Johns was to some of us stark and bad news for the state. The lamp of progress the McCarty people thought their man would bring to the office and with it lead the state to new heights was snuffed out.

Then came 1954 and the long-awaited showdown between two factions in the same political party. When the smoke cleared, a battle emerged between the incumbent, Acting Governor Charley Johns, and State Senator LeRoy Collins.

The two Democrats had served together in the Senate, but they had little else in common. Johns, as has been mentioned, was a fire-eating speaker who could sound and act like an evangelical preacher. Collins was a soft-spoken, articulate orator with something of a southern drawl. Collins directed his campaign at all the people, calling for patience, progress, and moderation. Johns stirred fear and suspicion, and at the same time promised roads and other improvements everywhere he went.

Television was in its infancy as a political tool in 1956 and 1957. That is to say, in 1956 it was used very little in local campaigns and not much more in statewide races. However, the Collins/Johns race in 1954 was something of an exception because of an important incident.

Collins and television fell in love at first sight. He was at ease in front of the cameras and looked good on the screen. Most who were following the Collins/Johns campaign agreed that television was an important factor in Collins's victory, and that the turning point of the campaign was a TV program that originated in Miami.

Johns had been reluctant to debate Collins and seemed to be enjoying the frontrunner position because he was the incumbent. Then, late in the campaign, a joint television appearance in Miami was agreed to by the candidates' political teams. The Miami station agreed to feed the program to several stations around the state.

That evening as Collins arrived at the station, he picked up an early edition of the next morning's newspaper, and to his surprise found that the Johns campaign folks had bought an advertisement wherein they claimed a grand victory in the debate that hadn't yet been held. Collins did not disclose the fact that he had the boastful ad until they were on the air and pretty far into the program. Then with a dramatic announcement, Collins unfolded the newspaper and let the cameras zoom in on the advertisement as he pointed out how deceptive Johns was to attempt to convince voters he had won the debate when it had not even started.

That incident was the critical point in the campaign and helped establish television as the dominant medium for presenting candidates' messages to the voters in state political campaigns.

Finally, the votes in the election were counted and Collins was the winner. Those who had supported McCarty and were disappointed when Johns dismantled McCarty's governance team were celebrating once again. The Johns appointees worked hard right up to the last minute before the curtain came down, trying to make the administration a memorable one. On the other hand, the Collins group seemed to take a holier-than-thou attitude and approached the first Collins year as something different and better than the Johns era—and even a cut above what McCarty had promised.

## LeRoy Collins (1954–1960)

LeRoy Collins won a two-year term as governor in the 1954 election, filling the office for the remainder of the unexpired term Dan McCarty won in 1952. From the moment of his election he seemed to know exactly what had to be done. He wanted to accomplish his goals for good government, lead the state safely through the turmoil caused by reactions to the U.S. Supreme Court's decision on desegregation of public schools, and improve the image of the state in the eyes of those considering moving business to Florida.

Furthermore, he had to prepare for reelection in 1956, conditioned on the Florida Supreme Court's holding that he could run for his own four-year term under the constitutional provision that specified term limitations.

Collins had to move quickly and carefully. It would have to be his administration, not Dan's. They had shared many friends and supporters, so the differences between his team and McCarty's were small when compared to the McCarty/Johns governance organizations. To avoid disappointing his own campaign leadership, he also had to be certain his longtime supporters were appointed to the key positions and that there were more Collins supporters than their McCarty counterparts.

Having to make the appointments so soon after the conclusion of the hard-fought campaign against Johns was a good thing. The need for qualified, competent people to fill administration positions was urgent, and with the next general election on the near horizon he had to have a team of effective fundraisers, campaign organizers, and campaign officials ready to go. Being obliged to select them in such close proximity to the campaign emphasized the importance of what he had to do, and it kept him focused on doing it with sensitivity and without delay.

Reapportionment of legislative power was an important issue in Collins' mind. He knew from his experiences in the Senate that the senators from counties with small populations were in control and that it would be difficult if not impossible to induce them to give up that control. He and his small band of crusaders in the Senate had been unable to move them in years of trying, but now with his statewide victory behind him and the power of the highest executive office in state government at his disposal, he had hope.

After about a year Collins came to grips with reality and decided that the only way he could win the reapportionment battle was to keep the legislature in session until it got the job done. After trying every tactic he knew, and in near desperation, Collins called a special session and asked the leadership to enact a plan to fairly and constitutionally apportion legislative power. He kept them in Tallahassee under his mandate almost a year, but still the legislators would not compromise.

Meanwhile, the U.S. Supreme Court handed down its famous decision in *Brown v. Board of Education* during Collins' first term, and it set the woods on fire. Many Floridians were anxious to see their political leaders stand up to the federal government and stop the movement of African Americans into the American mainstream. Southern governors generally took stands against the trend of integration, but not LeRoy Collins. Although a southerner with a record of opposing sudden change that would disturb the peace, he took a very moderate view of what was about to happen and encouraged Floridians to do the same.

The position he adopted took a good bit of courage on his part because it wasn't the popular approach to integration, and it had the potential of defeating him if he ran for election for a full four-year term. None of that deterred him. Collins approached the issues of race with the same excitement and determination as all his other legislative initiatives. He set a tone that was good for the state, but it put him at odds with some important legislative leaders.

As expected, Collins asked the Florida Supreme Court for an advisory opinion on the question of the legality of his running for his own full four-year term. The court held that the one-term limitation for the governor did not prevent Collins from running for a full term even though he was elected to serve two years to finish Dan McCarty's term.

Collins ran for the full term in 1956, and that campaign is where we really began to get acquainted and become friends. During the campaign and in the years that followed we spent time together when it was mutually convenient. We often talked of public service. It was his favorite topic. Leadership in public service naturally surfaced.

Collins believed that a good leader was always ahead of his people, leading them toward the objective. I could agree with him on that proposition because it squared with my early leadership training in the military. I was in medium tanks during the war, and the platoon leader, which was my position, always led the way. Never did we say, "Go get them." We said, "Follow me."

More than once, Collins spoke of not getting too far out ahead of those who are being led. He would say that if you get too far out there, you go over the horizon and lose your people. He was pretty far ahead of his people on integration, and I thought that at the time he was reminding himself of the danger of going over the horizon.

Another peripheral issue that created a diversion of attention was the condition of the building in Tallahassee known as the Governor's Mansion, or perhaps it should be called the governor's residence. When Collins took over from Johns, everyone who worked in the Capitol seemed to agree that the official residence for the governor was in deplorable condition. I was never inside the old place, but I believed the story because a decision was made to build a new mansion on the same site as the old one. I was new in politics, so I didn't think anyone in government would construct a building using taxpayers' money unless it was badly needed. In many respects I was naive.

It happened that there was a beautiful home on a corner very near the Capitol building that was suitable for the governor on a temporary basis. It was named the "Grove," and it was owned by none other than the Collins family. Mrs. LeRoy Collins was related to an early governor of Florida, and the Grove had been his home. It had been acquired, restored, and preserved by the Collins family, and they graciously agreed to live in it until the new mansion was constructed and ready to receive the first family. The Grove was a source of pride for Floridians. It was large, historically important, and in all respects appropriate as a governor's residence.

Collins entertained at the Grove and invited us to visit him there quite often for lunch or strategy sessions. It was a genuine pleasure going there. The meetings or social events were pleasant and productive; the ambience was unique; and just the notion that a young state representative was attending functions at the invitation of the governor was exciting to me.

One day early in my legislative career I was working in my Daytona Beach law office when Governor Collins called to tell me that there was a vacancy on the circuit court in my area, and that he was willing to appoint me if I would accept the appointment. That was before the Judicial Nominating Committees came into existence, so there was no formal procedure as there is at the present time; therefore, the governor could pick possible candidates himself and put his choice on the bench without input from the Florida Bar or anyone else if he cared to do it that way.

As it turned out, I couldn't accept the appointment, as badly as I wanted to do so, because the salary of a circuit judge was $12,000 a year. I was making about twice that amount in my law practice, and I had four little children. I just could not afford to take a 50 percent reduction in income at that time. He and I were both disappointed. Parenthetically, he later offered me an appointment to the agency that regulates utilities, known today as the Public Service Commission. I declined that opportunity for the same reason.

Collins served with distinction. (His good work is mentioned in other chapters, and is reviewed in some detail in a well-written book by Martin Dyckman entitled *Floridian of His Century*.) When Collins left the office in early 1961, he was well known throughout the country. He had been on the cover of Time magazine, was asked to address the Democratic National Convention when John F. Kennedy was nominated, and in a good many political venues was talked about as a person with the qualifications to hold a major national office. But sadly, as is often the case in politics, he had left a trail of political activists who were wounded by his strong leadership in racial matters and others who were jealous of his national prominence, and they were not supportive of his continuing desire to serve.

One of the positions Collins took was as the executive head of the National Association of Broadcasters. He didn't stay there very long because he poisoned the well for himself by condemning smoking and suggesting that the members of the association he chaired should stop the advertising of tobacco products. The fact that he was right on the issue did not soften the reaction of his associates who were broadcasters and dearly loved the revenue derived from the tobacco industry.

Collins once told me that he knew full well what to expect when he proposed the termination of a very important stream of revenue for radio and television stations, but he said that he had no choice. He believed it was wrong to use advertising to induce people—including youngsters—to smoke when it was so harmful, and that made unthinkable his silence on the issue. He tendered his resignation and it was accepted.

Then, following the assassination of President Kennedy, President Lyndon Johnson appointed Collins as Undersecretary of Commerce. Collins never expressed to me any negative thoughts he had with respect to that position, even during personal visits to his home in Georgetown. However, knowing him as I did, I felt that he was terribly uncomfortable working as a member of the Johnson team. Having to be a good soldier and preach the party line was hard for an individual with such strong feelings about the current issues and who was accustomed to speaking out on them in his own way. I'm afraid he did not heed his own advice about getting so far out ahead of supporters that you go over the horizon and lose them.

President Johnson asked Collins to go to Selma, Alabama, for the Rev. Martin Luther King Jr.'s march. He went willingly and represented the president courageously. I feel certain that he knew the picture taken of him at Selma would surface like a raging underground river rising and breaking free of its barriers if he ever ran for public office again, but he had confidence in the rightfulness of his position and in the people of Florida, so he didn't shirk his responsibility or try to avoid the photograph. It was a major factor in his defeat when he ran for a seat in the U.S. Senate.

As will be discussed elsewhere, Collins helped me in various ways when I ran for governor in 1964, and then he received a blow that was as hurtful as anything that ever happened to him.

I had salved the wounds incurred in my campaign to be governor and went on to serve four years in the Senate when, while sitting in my Tallahassee law office, I had a personal visit from Collins. He knew I had an interest in the Supreme Court of Florida, and he said he was there to talk about his possible appointment to fill a vacancy that had recently developed. First he asked if I intended to apply for the appointment and assured me that if I was interested he would not apply. I told him that I would like to be a justice on that court, but I was not ready just then. So Collins decided to apply, and I agreed to do what I could to help.

His first step was to apply for the appointment. Once in the system, every applicant goes through a process that involves one or more interviews, a background check, and, finally, the selection process. The Nominating Commission serves up a minimum of three names to the governor. The theory is that the screening process winnows out all who are unqualified, so any person nominated by the commission has at least the minimum qualifications and the governor can be comfortable appointing any one of them. The final selection is exclusively in the hands of the governor.

The system is not perfect in that it does not guarantee that the best candidate is ultimately appointed. There is enough subjectivity to leave room for mischief of various types. It is said—although never proven—that the nominating process is permeated with partisan politics. But for all its faults, it works, and it is much better than when there was no nominating system and raw politics could dominate the entire exercise.

In those days, one had to judge the quality of judicial appointments by the quality of the governor. A so-called good governor would strive to appoint high-quality people to judicial positions. An obviously bad appointment could bring criticism to the governor from the Bar groups or from knowledgeable newspaper editorial writers or columnists.

One newspaper executive who served with distinction on a nominating commission was James Clendenin, editor of the *Tampa Tribune*. He thought the appointing authority given to the governor in the Florida Constitution was of great importance, and of course it was. He felt that for the system to work, every facet of it must work as intended. He saw to it that any commission he sat on preformed in keeping with the Florida Constitution, and not just the letter, but the spirit of the basic document.

Collins was so conscientious as governor when it came to judicial appointments that I believe he assumed everyone must feel the same. He was blindsided in some way. The committee did not even send his name to the governor. He was wounded and hurt to the quick. He certainly had the education and law experience to qualify him for service on the court. His integrity and judicial conduct were not issues. He had the credentials, but he was passed over.

How could that be? Like Collins, I was passed over for an appointment to the federal bench and again for the Florida Supreme Court, although I was a finalist in both of those selection proceedings and my name was sent to the respective appointing authorities. But Collins didn't have the satisfaction of being declared competent and qualified to serve before being rejected. Again, my rejections were justified because the U.S. Attorney was appointed to the federal court from my group, and it was no surprise that a person who had many years of service in the system would have the edge. When I missed out on the Supreme Court appointment I was trying to recover from a very serious illness, and the governor had an opportunity to appoint the first black justice to that court, and he was healthy.

Collins could not understand why he was not even given a chance to compete as a finalist. The only thing I ever heard about the situation was that Collins' age was a factor. The governor at that time, so the story went, wanted the youngest justices he could appoint so his influence would remain as long as possible. That unofficial reason was most likely without merit. In the end it didn't make any difference what the reason was, because nothing could take the sting out of it and there was no recourse.

Collins survived the slight and went to his grave knowing that he would be held in high esteem by all who knew his story. He counted for something important.

## Farris Bryant (1960–1964)

The governor's race in 1960 attracted attention. Feelings were strong for and against the things Collins was doing with respect to racial problems. The Collins faction within the Democratic Party was supporting Doyle Carlton Jr., the son of Doyle Carlton Sr., who had served honorably as governor from 1929 to 1933.

It was said of the senior Carlton that he was so honest that being the Governor of Florida left him without enough money to move his family back to Tampa. He was so broke that he had to borrow money from his friends to be able to vacate the governor's residence. I don't know anything about his financial situation, but he did have a reputation for honesty and he was a very decent person. I met him a time or two when he visited Stetson University while I was a student there, and later when he visited the legislature while I was a House member. He had a marvelous sense of humor.

Doyle Jr. was the beneficiary of a wholesome legacy of integrity, instincts for good government, humor, and other attributes of his father. He was also fairly well known. He subscribed to the moderate approach that Collins took. He was bright and, by that time, affluent. He was a formidable candidate. I was one of many legislators supporting Doyle Jr.

On the other side was Farris Bryant. His home was in Ocala, Marion County. He was very intelligent and well educated, having received his legal education at Harvard University. He had been an effective leader in the House and left it before the 57 Clubbers arrived. In 1956 he ran for governor, but Collins won that race. Collins was the well-known incumbent and therefore the favorite. However, Bryant ran a second time in the 1960 election and was favored to win because he had run before, as well as because he had spent his time during the last four years of Collins' term preparing for the contest, criticizing and otherwise separating himself from Collins.

As Bryant and Carlton faced off, there were many important issues about which the candidates disagreed. Taxes, funding for education, and alleged redundancy of employees in state government were among those issues, and they were well debated. Bryant staked out a conservative position and then attempted to force Carlton to wear the liberal sign.

In addition to those issues, the one that was most crucial to victory was racial integration. Bryant had developed an anti-integration image. He had the enthusiastic support of those who felt threatened by and angry about integration of public schools. Moreover, he said and did various things that conveyed the message of his fiscal conservatism to everyone interested, and, because of his Harvard background and other sophistication, he was attractive to moderates.

As noted earlier, there was a story that came out of Bryant's campaign that I believed to be true, and it illustrates just how illogical and cautious politicians of that era were prone to be. Farris was accused of speaking to an organization of African Americans in Jacksonville. The implication was that he was fraternizing with them. To set the record straight and preserve his conservative image in racial matters, Bryant is reported to have admitted to attending the meeting and making a campaign speech, but denied sitting down at the table or eating with them.

History tells us that Bryant became governor, moved his family into the official residence, and took the reins of state government in early 1961. We who were members of the 57 Club were as divided about our relationships with Bryant as we had been with Collins. The difference was that under Bryant the Collins "ins" were now the "outs." Life in the legislature went on and most activities were about the same, notwithstanding the change of faces in the governor's suite in the Capitol.

During Collins' administration he appointed me to the Southern Regional Education Board's Legislative Advisory Board. I liked working with my counterparts from the other fifteen southern states and the very competent and imaginative staff assembled to operate the SREB. I must have had a measure of success because the members elected me chairman. The schedule called for me to assume the office in 1961, provided the governor of Florida appointed me to a second term as a member of the advisory group.

That appointment says a lot about both Governor Bryant and me. I wanted the appointment so much that I was willing to ask him for it even though I had done everything in my power to keep him from being governor. He was big enough to put away his natural inclination to give this token of "spoils" to a friend rather than to an adversary, and appointed me. We were both influenced by the facts that it would be good for the image and status of the state for me to be in that position and that I had already gotten a commitment from the SREB group to have a meeting of all members in Tampa. He was magnanimous and I was grateful.

We operated at arm's length through the '61 and '63 sessions and things went fairly well, except as noted elsewhere. Over time we got along just fine.

Many of my legislative friends such as George Anderson of Monticello, Lawton Chiles, and John Crews were close to Bryant, and that caused our paths to cross frequently. Then I offered my support to him when he ran for a seat in the U.S. Senate, and his daughter took an important role in my campaign for the Supreme Court.

## Hayden Burns (1964–1966)

During this period Democratic officeholders at the state level were also the leaders of the state Democratic Party. To protect their elected status, they came to believe that state and local offices should not be filled in the same years that the country elected the president of the United States, and soon a process was in place to shift the elections for Florida governor and the Florida cabinet to the off years. It was argued that all too often local candidates would not support the national ticket, and the fear was that the Republican Party would make inroads in state and local offices if a change was not made.

History tells us that none of this mattered because Republican candidates eventually took control of local offices in many counties across the state. In any event, the change was made so that in 1964 the gubernatorial candidate would be elected to a two-year term, and then in 1966 the term of office would shift back to four years.

I can testify that this is what they did because I was one of the candidates for governor that year. There were six of us who qualified to run in the Democratic primary. The winner was slated to run in the general election against the Republican nominee, who turned out to be Charlie Holly, a lawyer from the west coast.

I was the first to announce my intention to run, but it was always understood that Jacksonville Mayor Hayden Burns would also be a candidate. I felt certain that Fred O. (Bud) Dickinson, an attorney from Palm Beach County, would be in the race because he had been a candidate in the 1960 race that Farris Bryant won. Bud had made a good showing his first time out, and he was able to raise a sizable war chest to finance his campaign.

Scott Kelly, a developer from Lakeland, Polk County, entered the field fairly early and complicated things for the early entrants. I was quite confident that Jack Mathews of Jacksonville would not run, but he would not promise that he would stay out, so we considered him a possibility until the weekend of the University of Florida's Homecoming when he decided to announce his candidacy.

And finally there was Miami Mayor Robert (Bob) King High, who conducted himself as a non-candidate until the week President Kennedy was assassinated in Dallas, then went to the funeral in Washington, D.C., and cried (on camera). Soon he announced that he was the one who had to take up the Kennedy banner and march with it. He joined the campaign late but with a flourish and really fouled things up for the rest of us.

When the qualifying book was closed, there were six Democrats in the primary. The winner would surely be the governor for two years following Farris Bryant, because the Democratic nomination was tantamount to election. Moreover, if the first two years of the new administration went well, reelection for a four-year term was a good possibility.

Those running represented the entire spectrum of thinking about racial matters. Hayden Burns started using a slogan that sent out the segregation message loud and clear. He often reminded anyone who would listen that "A man's home is his castle." The message was that he was opposed to such things as forced integration of residential areas, but it was much broader by implication and suggested that he was as tight with the white supremacists and segregationists as one could be. He appropriated the far right position, and was welcomed into it by those who believed that preserving segregation was the right way to govern the state.

Scott Kelly challenged Burns for that position but was not successful. He was a dynamic speaker and used all the catch words and phrases, but couldn't get his campaign off the ground. He made most of his progress talking about fraud and other mischief in state government, which he promised to clean out while punishing the guilty.

Bud Dickinson held himself out as a moderate, but in fact he tried to be all things to all voters. He had the advantages of name recognition and statewide campaigning experience. His campaign was well financed and he had no visible opposition. However, his campaign lacked purpose and passion.

Jack Mathews, on the other hand, had dedicated and devoted supporters, and his whole campaign was well run and chock full of substance. His trouble was that there weren't enough people who subscribed to his philosophy to do him any good after Bud Dickinson took a piece, leaving the balance to be divided up among Jack, me, and, to some extent, Bob High.

When I announced my candidacy I was the favorite among the public school teachers, which gave me supporters in every nook and cranny of the state. And, on the philosophical scale, I was the only candidate who qualified as a moderate but could also attract support of all who were left of the moderate line. When Jack Mathews came in, he challenged my friendly status with the daily newspapers and the teachers. I found myself pushed a little left of center, and I began to sense disaster because my core support was being wooed by Mathews, Dickinson and, to a lesser extent, by Kelly.

The death blow to my campaign came from High. He took a stance that was more liberal than mine, and he was virtually unchallenged out there on the far left. The trouble intensified when he made a bid for the support of teachers and moderates, particularly in Dade County where he had the "Favorite Son" status.

The campaign was most interesting, and some of the choice anecdotes from it are included later in this book. As it progressed, Burns showed us what a well-oiled machine could do in a campaign. It warded off all attacks on him, and the nickname "Slick," given to him during the campaign in an effort to reduce his stature and imply that he was something less than forthright, failed to stick. He had lots of money, his organization was the best I had ever seen, and he had committed city officials in every municipality.

His political position on racial issues was as popular as it was cruel. It was even a bit deceptive because he knew full well that to buck integration was to fight a losing battle, and yet he campaigned as though he could deter the activists. He was clearly in first place through the first primary, even though he was dragging a lot of baggage he had picked up while serving as Jacksonville's mayor.

Second place remained in doubt until toward the end of the primary. Dickinson and Kelly had money and hard-working staffs. High ran surprisingly strong. He gathered the liberal and black votes and developed heavy miscellaneous support from all groups with his misleading slogan, "Reduce Taxes, Vote For Bob High." Dickinson ran a good race, but couldn't cope with Burns on the right or High on the left. He concentrated on the center, but so did all the rest of us.

Campaigns like that one can get a bit boring when fatigue overtakes the candidates and they have to listen to the same political speeches over and over until they could switch places and give an opponent's speech without missing a beat. It is during times like those when the Devil takes control and mischief is done.

To provide some context, we must be reminded that Bob High was a very short person. Someone had started referring to him as "Chest High High," which he took in fairly good spirit. Then there was the prank. High was not the most popular candidate on the circuit; the way he had entered the race and conducted himself disqualified him from the Mr. Congeniality contest.

We had all noticed his habit of gathering telephone books to sit on whenever we were making joint appearances on TV. That trick made him appear to be as tall as the rest of us. One evening in Miami, a few of our staff people conspired to remove his prop and leave him in a reality situation showing the disparity in size. Just prior to turning on the cameras, High noticed that the telephone books were gone and he was furious. He ranted and raved, but to no avail. He had to sit on a bare chair and let the world know what we knew about his size.

When the votes were counted at the close of the first primary, the winner was Burns, with High second, which under the rules at the time put him in a runoff with Burns. Jack Mathews and I—the two members of the 57 Club— ran fifth and sixth. Our supporters assured us that we were the best in the field of candidates, but nothing they said helped. Burns beat High in the runoff three weeks later. He also beat Charlie Holly, the Republican nominee in the general election, and became the governor of Florida.

For two years Burns paved a lot of roads, had the state borrow a ton of money, and otherwise worked toward his reelection.

Meanwhile, those who were attempting to break down racial segregation in Florida did not let up. Both sides of that issue kept the pressure on. At the same time, considerable work on a new constitution was going on behind the scenes.

There were many other adjustments taking place in Florida and throughout the country as we tried to get used to the idea that the president was Lyndon Johnson instead of John F. Kennedy, who had been assassinated during the early days of the gubernatorial campaign. Also, reapportionment captured the attention of the governor and the legislature as the federal courts intervened and the state officials sought in vain to find a way to comply with courts' opinions without completely shifting the legislative control of the state to the more populous counties.

Burns made two appointments that had us wondering what was going on. The first was when he named Fred O. (Bud) Dickinson the state comptroller. Dickinson had been a staunch opponent of Burns in the 1964 campaign, and yet he was appointed to a very important cabinet post. We concluded that it had something to do with Dickinson's support of Burns in the runoff. The other one was my friend and loyal supporter, Representative Woodie Liles of Plant City, Hillsborough County. He was appointed to be a judge and fill a vacancy on the Second District Court of Appeal. I wasn't aware that Woodie had supported Burns in the runoff, if in fact he did. Woodie was too good a friend for me to ask him about it, and he never saw fit to explain it to me.

In retrospect I have come to believe that there were two reasons for the appointments. The first was that Burns was looking ahead to his campaign for reelection, and the supporters of Dickinson would be pleased and presumably willing to help Burns out of gratitude. The same general logic can be applied in Liles' judicial appointment. Although Liles was not a candidate himself, he was known to be my friend and very influential in my campaign. So the appointees and their supporters were valuable in terms of the future, and it was reason enough to appoint people who had not been with him in the campaign.

The second reason had to do with the personal popularity and presumed competence of the appointees. It spoke well of Burns and his interest in having a high-quality governance team that he would look outside of his political staff for popular appointees.

Meanwhile, High made ready to attack Burns at the end of Burns' two-year term. When High took on Burns, it was a mean campaign. High was the attacker, and he made Burns look awfully bad. He brought him down in the 1966 Democratic primary. When his work was done, High assumed that he would be the governor for the ensuing four years. He celebrated and developed in his mind and heart the expectation of an inauguration.

Unfortunately for him, High would never be the governor of Florida. He was defeated by Republican Claude Kirk in the general election of 1966. He later suffered a heart attack and died shortly after he lost the race. Some said he died of a broken heart. I don't know about that, but I can state without fear of contradiction that he was bitterly disappointed when he was rejected by the voters. He thought he had it made.

## Claude Kirk (1966–1970)

Claude Kirk was the Republican nominee for governor in 1966. He was not a typical Republican, nor was he a typical candidate for governor in Florida. As a matter of fact, he was not a typical anything. He was a unique person. He was as bright as any gubernatorial candidate I had known and was as flamboyant as Fuller Warren. His sense of humor was always on ready; he was outspoken; and he loved confrontations. I'm afraid he wasn't taken seriously by the Democrats who assumed that he didn't have a chance.

By the time Democratic candidates Burns and High were finished with their campaigns for the party nomination, there was so much animosity that reconciliation was impossible. Burns, the loser, was so bitter that he didn't feel bound by party loyalty, and to say that he was unwilling to support High was an understatement. He was hurt and disappointed by the loss, of course, but what really embittered him was the way High and his people had attacked him. Burns came out of the campaign looking like a crook. They colored him with indelible ink. It was a vicious attack.

Kirk naturally took advantage of the situation and gathered the bitter friends of Burns to help him win the general election. He became the first Republican governor of Florida since Reconstruction.

When Kirk was approximately at the midpoint in his four-year term, I was a candidate for the Florida Senate. The district was comprised of five counties: Volusia, Lake, Sumter, Citrus, and Hernando. It stretched from the Atlantic Ocean to the Gulf of Mexico. Two incumbent senators represented the district (single-member districts were not yet mandated), and when I decided to run, Welborn Daniel of Clermont, Lake County, had already announced his intention of running against one of them. Thus, my opponent had to be the other one who was a Republican, a lawyer, and a Good Old Boy. The last quality of my opponent was my reason for worrying whether I could win.

One day I went to Tallahassee to call on Governor Kirk. The conversation was brief but poignant. I told him that I hoped he would not campaign too hard against me because I expected to win and would like to be in a position to help him with some of his legislation, provided it squared with my own philosophy. Kirk replied that he would not be supporting my opponent because he did not like him. It was as simple as that. I could run against a Republican and not have the power of the Governor's Office against me. He was as good as his word.

Kirk's method of governing was as unique as his personality, and he set out to demonstrate his homegrown approach to the whole process. One of his first acts after being sworn in was to issue a call to the legislature to meet in special session—then he left for a vacation at a time that would cause him to miss the special session he had called.

Meetings of the cabinet were worth the price of admission. Kirk presided over a body of six Democrats who were accustomed to sharing the executive responsibilities. As mentioned, he loved confrontations. Those meetings provided unlimited opportunities for him to practice his skills. They met every two weeks and Kirk never missed an opportunity to shoot at them over some issue. Sitting through one of those meetings was very difficult for those who liked peacefulness and harmony.

Once, Kirk was accused of trying to improperly influence a county judge. Conveniently, the legislature attempted to raise its own pay at the same time, so he used the legislative pay raise and his criticism of it to preempt all the news for a few days. He used his people skills to attack the legislators. Kirk was so effective and so resourceful that he soon had the people of the state thinking legislators were all money grubbers and unworthy of public office. He escaped harsh treatment and negative reactions regarding his tampering with the judge, which surprised everyone, probably including the governor.

Much of my experience with Kirk related to his crusade to suspend local public officials for inappropriate action. The 1968 constitution continued the traditional authority of the governor to suspend public officers, but the provision was updated and slightly modified. Article IV, Section 15 of the constitution of 1885 was replaced by Article IV, Section 7, of the constitution of 1968. It provided the governor with the power to suspend a local or state officer upon his finding that the official was guilty of malfeasance, misfeasance, neglect of duty in office, commission of any felony, drunkenness, or incompetence. Those grounds for suspension were defined by the Senate in special session, February 1969, when the report of the select committee was adopted.

In the 1969 regular session of the legislature the procedure to be used in suspension cases was written into Chapter 112, Florida Statutes, on the recommendation of my committee—the Senate Select Committee on Suspensions—with help from the attorney general. The statute recognized the suspended officials' right to due process and equal protection. To that end the statute provided for a summary suspension without a hearing, but mandated a hearing to make the suspension permanent.

The constitutionality of the prescribed procedure was tested by Jim Fair, the Hillsborough County Supervisor of Elections who was suspended by Kirk. Fair sued and argued that the summary suspension denied him his guaranteed right to due process. He lost every round, but persisted and went all the way to the U.S. Supreme Court. The court upheld the statute, and its decision made clear that the post suspension hearing satisfied the due process requirement.

For the remainder of my term in the Senate, and in my capacity as chairman of the select committee, I participated in every case that came before the Senate. Every case held my attention, but a few of them were particularly interesting. One of the most interesting involved the Sheriff of St. Johns County. The sheriff had been in office for many years and was very popular. At one point he was indicted for bribery, but was acquitted in just seven minutes. However, as a result of the indictment and speedy acquittal, Governor Kirk's people found evidence of other misbehavior and the governor suspended him from office.

I presided at the hearing where we received the testimony of a room full of important citizens from the sheriff's home county, and the select committee found a genuine paradox. On one hand the sheriff was an asset to the county and the state in that he successfully conducted many youth programs and other meaningful and wholesome projects. Generally he was a good law enforcer. Many leaders of the county thought of him as an excellent role model. But on the other hand, he was a corrupt public official who protected certain people involved in gambling and prostitution.

The committee recommended permanent removal from the office. We all wondered how Verle Pope, the veteran senator from Johns County, would vote. It was obvious that his constituency was divided on the issue. When the case came up for consideration by the full Senate, I made the report and recommendation, and Pope spoke with his usual preacher-like style. He explained how hard the decision was for him because he had friends on both sides, but that he had confidence in his Senate colleagues who served on the committee. Since they had found corruption he had no choice but to support the recommendation. The Senate also voted to approve our work and the sheriff was removed from office.

Before my responsibilities as committee chairman ended, I had presided over some fifty-two suspension cases. At that time, most of the public officials on the local level were Democrats. Although many did misbehave and deserved to be suspended, Kirk was accused of trying to create vacancies in offices held by Democrats so that he could appoint Republicans to fill them. I saw no evidence of his doing that. Every suspension case was supported by some evidence of misconduct.

Kirk married while he was governor. He always seemed to be able to keep folks—including the press—focused on activities that he selected and laid out for them. It was hard to induce people to be interested in some important but mundane issue when the air was full of flying debris from one of Kirk's real or contrived crises. His whole approach to problems seemed to be that life in the capital was some gigantic game to be played by those in government against the people.

### Reubin Askew (1971–1979)

Reubin Askew came to the House of Representatives about a year after the 57 Club members, so the members and the future governor became pretty well known to each other. Although he was not there in time to be a member of the Club, he was so personable and competent that he fit right in with the members—and after a while it was impossible to distinguish him from us.

After serving in the House, Askew moved to the Senate. He was an active member of both houses and established an unblemished record. His leadership qualities were as apparent as the light in a lighthouse on a dark night. He excelled in his work on reapportionment, congressional redistricting, and appropriations.

As far as I could tell, he was respected by every legislator in office at that time. People are always inclined to start thinking a person like that has no enemies. It is all right for friends and supporters to have those thoughts, but the candidate dare not have them. The candidate needs only to look at the vote count in his last run for office to see that all those who voted against him are not truly his friends. Any public servant who has reached any significant goal or accomplished anything meaningful has made enemies along the way. Reubin was not naïve; he knew he was very popular and generally well liked, but he also knew that there were a few out there who did not wish him well. Happily, he was realistic about how the public viewed him, and he conducted himself in a way that was appropriate. He had just the right balance of self confidence and humility.

Those of us who observed him from a position of close proximity knew that he understood those fundamentals of politics, and we were not surprised when he let it be known that he was going to challenge Claude Kirk for the governorship. Neither were we surprised when Kirk, in a moment of complete candor, evaluated those who were rumored to be his opponents when he would run for reelection and announced that Askew was the one who worried him the most.

Reubin defeated Claude Kirk in the 1970 general election for the Office of Governor and was inaugurated in early 1971. He served eight years and did a fine job. He left a trail of successes and left his mark on such issues as civil rights, capital punishment, fiscal responsibility, and reapportionment. He did so well that he was seriously discussed as a possible candidate for president of the United States. He went out during the primary season and sampled the situation, but it did not seem right to him so he aborted the effort and returned to Florida, where he continues to contribute to good government.

## Bob Graham (1979–1987)

All of the members of the 57 Club who were still in office when Bob Graham was elected to the House came to know him quite well. He was from south Florida, obviously affluent, friendly to all he encountered, and smart. He made no excuses for his political ambition, which was visible at all times but never responsible for any bad votes. That is to say, he was never guilty, in my view, of voting against his conscience or the public interest because his political ambition dictated it.

We were all curious when we heard that he was related to Catherine Graham, the publisher of the influential *Washington Post* in Washington, D.C. We wondered how he might use it and what advantage, if any, it would give him. He never made reference to that relationship, nor did he try to use it in any way. His immediate family was an exact representation of the typical American family. In so many ways he seemed to have it all.

I heard him in debate shortly after he arrived and was impressed with his knowledge, sincerity, vocabulary, and stage presence. It was rather obvious that he would succeed in politics.

His primary interest in the legislature was education, and he became an expert on it. He was also interested in environmental problems, and when he took an interest in a subject he found the time to do his homework and develop a sound and reasonable approach to it.

While in the Senate he was relatively quiet. He probably devoted most of his time to preparing for his race for governor. His contributions to education, social programs, and the environment established a solid foundation for his effort to be the governor.

Once, while we were both in the Senate, I was planning to drive from Tallahassee to the Orlando area immediately upon adjournment for the weekend. Bob asked to ride along, and my wife and I were happy to have the opportunity to get to know him better. We were in the front seat and Bob took the back seat, only he didn't use much of it. He settled on the front edge of the seat with his arms on the back of our seats in a way that put his head between ours. Both of us could hear whatever he said and he could hear us.

The ride that night was in excess of five hours, and he never moved out of his original position. We talked seemingly forever and then we talked some more. We covered every politically oriented subject one could imagine. We discussed people, places, and issues. On arrival at our destination I felt that I knew him very well. I had the feeling that this was not the first time he had endured the physical discomfort of leaning on the back of a seat in front of him and spending several hours with the same couple in such a prolonged conversation. It was just another evening for him. For us it was an event of some magnitude, and one we discussed many times while he was governor and then our U.S. senator.

When first he was governor, Graham's office coordination was virtually nonexistent. Everyone I knew who had business with the office complained about some aspect of the operation. There were no allegations of corruption, discrimination, or anything unsavory. The problem seemed to be office management. Soon he corrected that problem, and for eight years he governed the state with class and competence. It was not a surprise when he went to Washington to join that exclusive club known as the U.S. Senate.

As the end of his tenure as governor approached, Graham decided that he would leave the office a few days before the end of his term so he could take the oath of office with others joining the U.S. Senate in early 1987. As I understood it, seniority was very important in the Senate. Had he served his full term as governor and allowed the other freshmen senators to be sworn in ahead of him, he would forever have been ranked below them for such purposes as committee assignments, committee chairmanships, and other important matters, probably including parking spaces and the like. And so it was that Lieutenant Governor Wayne Mixson moved up to the Governor's Office on January 3, 1987, and served as governor until January 6, 1987, when Graham's successor, Robert Martinez, was inaugurated.

### Robert Martinez (1987–1991)

Quite a few members of the 57 Club knew Bob Martinez while they were in their formative political years. We knew him in the '60s as a Democrat and as the executive director of the Hillsborough County Teachers Association, and then later as the Mayor of Tampa.

He became a Republican and was elected governor to succeed Bob Graham. Martinez was the second Republican Florida governor since Reconstruction.

By 1987, when Martinez assumed the office, most of the members of the 57 Club had moved on. However, it is fair to say that his administration was a good one. He hit a few bumps along the way in the area of taxation. The biggest of the bumps was related to the sales tax. The legislature—with Martinez' support—passed a bill that took away several exemptions from the sales tax. Exemptions such as professional services and newspaper advertising would produce a large number of dollars in revenue, but they were very controversial. When the lawyers, newspapers, and others who were touched by the bill released their pent up energy, there was a lobbying display the likes of which we had never seen. The law was repealed and the governor lost a bit of face.

### A Party at the Governor's Mansion

Before the lights went out for the Martinez administration and while Martinez was serving as the state's CEO, I was living and practicing law in Tampa. My wife and I met and became friendly with Ms. Jennie Tarr, a niece of Governor Martinez who was employed by Hillsborough County as an assistant county attorney. When she planned her marriage, her uncle—the governor—offered to have a reception in her honor at the governor's residence in Tallahassee. My wife and I attended, and it was a gala affair. Jennie was beautiful and a very pleasant and poised guest of honor. Mrs. Martinez and the governor were wonderful hosts. The party was well attended and everyone had a delightful evening.

As Martinez' term in office progressed, something happened between him and the *Tampa Tribune*, the daily newspaper in his hometown, which caused most of his political trouble. Perhaps it was related to the attempt to tax newspaper advertising, or maybe it was because of differences of opinion on other issues. In any event, it was serious. Even a casual observer could sense his weaknesses when the paper—which was thought of as a moderate Republican media outlet at that time—started jabbing him in hurtful ways.

As the end of Martinez' first term approached, both Lawton Chiles and Buddy MacKay were considering a run to unseat him. Martinez' vulnerability was apparent, but it seemed that a hard fight was in store for two strong and popular Democrats who would surely weaken each other and perhaps have the effect of saving Martinez.

But that was not to be. Chiles and MacKay got together and agreed that Lawton would be the candidate for governor and Buddy would run as a part of Lawton's ticket as lieutenant governor. They were described as the "Dream Team" by the media, and they successfully unhitched Bob Martinez.

### Lawton M. Chiles Jr. (1991–1998)

One day I was having lunch at the Governor's Club in downtown Tallahassee and Lawton Chiles was there, too. It was always good to see him. He was so courteous and considerate and always seemed to enjoy our meetings as much as I did. Our conversations were comfortable and tension-free. We had a relationship that was arm's length when I was representing a client and petitioning him for some help for the client, but in casual meetings such as this one we could talk straight and freely share information.

Chiles was a U.S. senator at that time, and he was a leader in that body. He had enormous responsibilities with respect to the budget. His influence was widespread and his image was wholesome. He had a reputation of competency and honor. However one looked at him, the conclusion was the same: he was a decent human being and a very important person in America.

I believe that every member of the 57 Club who knew Chiles while we were young state legislators held him in a similar position of high regard. I asked him if he was considering a run for governor when he completed his current term in the U.S. Senate. I indicated that I thought he should do it, and I volunteered to support him in every way I could.

His answer was thoughtful and unemotional; it was also quite clear. He said that he considered his position as a U.S. senator to be the best job in the country, what with fair compensation, opportunities to know many interesting people, duties that were critical to the country and very satisfying, and all that ego stuff that is so important to most politicians. He said he wouldn't give it up for a chance to be Florida's governor.

I accepted his answer and the decision he had apparently made. That is to say, I accepted the fact that he was telling me the truth as he knew the truth on that day. I was politician enough myself to understand that nothing he told me would preclude a change of his mind at some future date. I was certain I had understood his answer when he said as we were parting company that day: "If I change my mind I'll let you know and take you up on your offer to help."

Of course, he changed his mind, and his friends were happy he did. We rallied to his support and he was elected. He served almost the full eight years he was allowed by the Florida Constitution, but died in office a few days before the end of his term. He was alone in the gym at the Governor's Mansion when he collapsed and died alone.

His administration was a good one. He and his fine works are mentioned throughout this book, so there is no need to belabor the point. He kept his steady hand on the controls, which made for a smooth journey for the state. He took care of the people's business effectively and in the sunshine.

Florida has had outstanding governors since the formation of the 57 Club, and Lawton Chiles was one of the best of the lot.

I don't play the game of "What If?" But if I did, I would wonder what would have occurred if we had not been blessed with the good governors we have described. I'm afraid our state would be in a different place, and we would no doubt be bemoaning the damage that was the result.


## Kenneth (Buddy) MacKay

Buddy MacKay was elected with Lawton Chiles as lieutenant governor and became governor when Chiles died in office. It is appropriate that he be included with the other governors we knew because he was our contemporary and our friend. He went on to the Florida Senate before becoming governor.

MacKay became a House member well after many of us who were 57 Clubbers moved on; he later went on to the Florida Senate and to the U.S. Congress. He was planning to be a candidate for governor, but as noted earlier, decided to join Lawton Chiles as a lieutenant governor candidate.

When Buddy was in the House and I was a senator, we worked together on Florida's famous no-fault automobile insurance laws. It was quite an experience. The Florida Bar—the lawyers' professional organization—was against us as was the Academy of Florida Trial Lawyers, a very effective lobbying group that spoke for the trial lawyers. They fought hard to preserve the old tort system that was so full of inequity and unfairness that I always wondered how anyone could defend it.

A Volusia County native named Bill Gillespie was chairman of the House committee that worked on the no-fault law, and I feel certain that he was somewhat involved in crafting the bill, negotiating support for it, and debating its merits in the House.

It was Buddy MacKay who actually delivered the House proposal to the Senate for consideration. Buddy was active and effective. He did yeoman's work on a bill that has survived for more than thirty-five years and has saved Florida's drivers an enormous sum of money—and, at the same time, brought fairness and compassion to the system. He should be commended for leading the fight in the House for that major piece of legislation.

Buddy was always working hard on meaningful projects, and his work was effective. It would have been better if he had been a member of the 57 Club, and he would have been a fine governor in his own right.

# 12 *The Role of the Media* ────────────────

When the 57 Club was born and while it was in its infancy, everything was changing. Integration of the races was imminent; the state was maturing and experiencing rapid growth; a new Capitol was on the drawing board; the residual effects of World War II were fading away; and the whole apparatus for gathering news and disseminating it to the citizens was beginning its metamorphosis.

In our 1956 political campaigns, the term "news media" was interchangeable with the press. Newspapers were the dominant source of daily news. Television was in the process of proving its relevance and was showing signs of being able to reduce radio to a new and subordinate role. Newspapers were also moving into the sights of the young upstart, television. Leaders in the media saw the changes coming and began preparations for them. Mergers and purchases were transforming Mom-and-Pop newspapers into subsidiaries of media giants.

## The First Amendment

The First Amendment of the U.S. Constitution has always been the protector of the media, and the judicial interpretations of the First Amendment have set the parameters for the interface of government and the news media. The media was partially protected from retaliation by those rulings, as well as the ones construing the libel laws. One of the results of that protection was that the media was extremely active on the national level. Aggressive reporters for a major newspaper in Washington, D.C., were working on the current administration, and scandals at every level of government were being uncovered for the world to see. Florida was also experiencing the same sort of traumatic discovery of official mischief.

Occasionally, representatives of the press made news instead of reporting about the actions of others. A good example was the time reporters broke the Florida Senate of its historic habit of going into executive session and transacting the public's business behind closed doors.

Rules at that time permitted senators to vote to clear the chambers, including the area set aside for reporters, and meet in executive session (secretly). This procedure was regularly used to discuss and decide the fate of public officials suspended from office by the governor. Senators swore that they would not disclose what transpired in those closed sessions, and they were careful not to violate their oaths. Outsiders knew almost nothing about what went on in those sessions. There was speculation that when considering a suspension case involving a local official, the senator who represented the district in which the local official lived had the last word, and that he had but to give a thumbs up or thumbs down and the full Senate would vote accordingly.

A group of reporters set out to challenge the Senate's right to close the doors when they were engaged in the public's business, and when the sergeant at arms attempted to clear the chambers, the reporters sat at their desks and refused to leave. They made big news on a statewide basis. Many senators were outraged, and I feel certain they considered their options for retaliation and discovered that there was not really anything they could do. They couldn't have the reporters arrested, and complaints to the bosses of the reporters would certainly fall on deaf ears. LeRoy Collins was governor at the time, and he believed in openness. So, in the end, the Senate gave in and terminated the practice of secret sessions for all practical purposes.

## The DeLand Newspaper

In the wake of the Great Depression, my family functioned on the edge of insolvency. The once-profitable business my father and grandfather owned and operated in Michigan was sold and the proceeds invested and lost in bad real estate deals in Florida. My father took almost any job he could find and tried to recoup some of the lost money. One of those jobs was as circulation manager of a small daily newspaper in DeLand, Volusia County. That was my first encounter with newspapers. I would often join my father for his twenty-five-mile commute from Daytona Beach to DeLand and spend the better part of the day selling the papers on the streets of the county seat.

The courthouse was across the street from the newspaper, and a few of the most successful law firms in the county had offices in close proximity. I would start in the courthouse and then go through each of the law firms before hitting the streets. The newspaper offered movie passes and beach parties for those who delivered to homes and also for salespeople like me. I was younger than most of the paper boys, but they talked to me just the same because my father was their boss. I became fascinated with the newspaper business and, unlike most of the kids I knew who wanted to be police officers or sailors in the Navy, I vacillated between hoping to be a priest or the governor, and also dreaming of owning my own newspaper someday.

Later I furthered my interest by delivering the *Daytona Beach News Journal*. I had the best route in town, with 200 customers who received the morning, evening, and Sunday papers at their doors for a mere twenty-five cents a week. My part of the quarter—assuming I was able to collect it—was nine cents for twelve separate newspapers delivered to their doors every week.

When I ran for office the first time in 1956, both newspapers were politically active. The DeLand paper endorsed me, but the Daytona paper supported the man I defeated in the runoff. Thereafter, however, both newspapers supported me with enthusiasm in every race I ran. Moreover, they supported my positions on almost every major issue. Perhaps it was a residual benefit of having been a good carrier. It certainly was a bit of serendipity.

The grandson of the publisher of the *News Journal* was in my class in high school, and my parents knew his parents quite well. For those and other reasons they took an interest in me as I developed, and they spent time teaching me about the business and allowing me to participate in the editorial endorsement procedure. They also allowed me to help broadcast the election results on their radio station. All of that activity helped me to become known in the community and enhanced my fledging status.

## Media Melodrama

Generally speaking, I developed great relationships with all the newspapers in the state. They were almost always fair to me. However, when they were against me on a particular issue, they could be fierce and sometimes unfair. I was seldom treated unfairly, but when it happened it made me angry. I could take plain old criticism, but unfairness by a major news outlet was different. I abhorred unfairness.

Because I believed so fervently in the fairness of the press, I did not fault the papers in my 1964 race for governor when they passed me over for someone they thought had a better chance to win. Intellectually, I could understand their desire to back a winner, and I accepted the fact that some of them preferred one of my opponents after an evaluation of my candidacy in comparison with theirs. And it goes without saying that I was extremely happy in 1976 when, as a candidate for the Florida Supreme Court, I received the editorial endorsements of all but one of the major daily papers in the state.

But when I felt that media criticism was unjustified, unpleasant, or worse, I was disappointed in their expressed opinions. Obviously I was aware that the press would not always be totally objective and that we would occasionally disagree, but when it actually occurred it was still a shock. The story of a situation that illustrates the point is worth telling.

As explained earlier, one of my assignments during my time in the Senate was to chair a select committee on suspensions. My committee heard the evidence in all of the cases of officials suspended from office by the governor. We then recommended to the full Senate either the reinstatement of the suspended person (if we found him innocent) or his permanent removal from office (if we found evidence of guilt).

One of those cases comes to mind. It illustrates one particular example of strong criticism by the media and how the media reacts when they are criticized. The case involved Lloyd Early, superintendent of schools in Palm Beach County. The case was very problematic, but I still firmly believe that we reached the right conclusion, even though the afternoon paper in West Palm Beach disagreed and in my opinion punished me for what I wrote in the report to the Senate.

Lloyd Early was elected by the people in Palm Beach County, but during his term of office Governor Claude Kirk issued an order of suspension. From the allegations in the order, one could conclude that the Palm Beach County School District was in turmoil and Lloyd Early was among those responsible for the trouble. It also appeared that there was serious friction between Early and the members of the school board, but the conclusion of the order was that Early was basically inept and that the voters obviously made a mistake when they elected him to that very important post. Although the governor's attorney tried to stretch the evidence to prove that there were constitutional grounds for the suspension, it just wouldn't stretch that far.

The afternoon paper in Palm Beach County had been on a crusade to induce the governor to suspend Early. They were critical of almost everything he did. They pointed out his "warts" by featuring them in published editorials, political cartoons, columnists' opinions, letters to the editor, and even articles that purported to be straight reporting. Early's attorney collected all of these articles and arranged a display in an anteroom near the room where the committee conducted the hearing. There was enough to cover all the walls, tables, and any other surface that could be found. There was an awful lot written about Early's shortcomings, as well as his amateurish reactions to the first several attack articles. Early's attorney characterized the representation as excessive and unfair.

We understood that Governor Kirk was reluctant to use his constitutional power to suspend in this case, but the pressure from the newspaper was so great that he gave in and had a suspension order prepared and filed. Because of the importance of the office and the nature of the charges, we scheduled the case for a hearing at the earliest practicable date.

The case was tried in a professional manner. Charlie Miner represented the governor. Miner—son of a former member of the House—was at the time general counsel for the Department of Education, and, not too long after the hearing, was seated on the circuit court and, subsequently, on the First District Court of Appeal. Joseph Farrish, a Palm Beach attorney with extraordinary trial skills and a reputation for successfully handling large and high visibility cases, represented Lloyd Early. The result was that the select committee members received a heavy load of competently presented evidence.

After deliberation, the committee asked me to draft the report and recommendations, and, without delay, all of the members (except one who had missed a part of the hearing because of a death in the family), approved what I prepared even though they knew it would be controversial.

### The Senate Report on Lloyd Early

The select committee's report summarized the evidence, including the room full of acrimonious media coverage. It quoted one witness as characterizing the situation as "One of the most dreadful times in the history of the county."

The report further described a committee created by the school board and referred to as "a general investigating committee roaming through the school system striking the same kind of terror in the hearts of the staff and instructional personnel as the citizens experienced with vigilantes of another era."

The summary in the report concluded: "Perhaps a more experienced superintendent could have performed more efficiently under the circumstances. Perhaps a stronger, more decisive man could have stopped the encroachments of the board and its committee at its inception. But such a man was not elected as Superintendent of Schools in Palm Beach County."

We also found that the newspaper's crusade was excessive and most likely responsible for the issuance of the executive order of suspension. Then we explained our interpretation of the constitutional provision and the applicable statutes that granted the governor the power to suspend. We said that the constitution should be construed as requiring a finding that the suspended official was guilty of one or more of the constitutional grounds for suspension, which precluded suspension and removal for any other reasons.

We made it clear that the suspension process could not be used as a method of recall to correct mistakes made in the election. We concluded that there was no proof of guilt on any of the constitutional grounds for suspension, and that Lloyd Early had been required to defend himself in a case that was brought for the wrong reasons, and, therefore, that he should be reinstated and paid a reasonable amount as attorney's fees.

The full Senate met and the members asked several questions when I concluded the report, and then voted to approve it. The case and the outcome were news. The report was widely distributed. We didn't mind the attention, but I'm certain that the folks on the newspaper staff didn't appreciate the report crossing the desks of their counterparts in papers across the state.

As if to rub salt in the wounds, Early sued the newspaper and won a judgment of $1 million, although it was subsequently taken away by the appellate court. I heard that the people at the paper were not happy about the way I handled the case and blamed the Senate's actions for the $1 million hit they thought they would have to pay.

I guess what I heard was substantially correct, because when I ran for a seat on the Florida Supreme Court and visited the editorial board to request the endorsement of both the morning and afternoon papers, I overheard a conversation in the hall among employees in which they had some unkind things to say about me and indicated that I would not receive the endorsement. Sure enough, the afternoon paper endorsed one of my opponents. It was disappointing and hurt my feelings that they took my conduct as something personal against them, and that they could be so vindictive. However, the loss of their endorsement didn't affect the outcome of my election, nor damage me in any other way as best I could tell.

I expect that every person who has run for public office has been criticized by the press. Sometimes they deserve it, and other times they may not have misbehaved at all. Whether unfairness is real or imagined doesn't really matter because strong and/or continuing criticism can be hurtful—even politically fatal—depending on the track record of the politician. When that happens, the person targeted must cope with it and devise some way to calm down the close supporters and prevent their defection. It is not an easy task.

Legislators could ask for permission to speak to all members on a point of personal privilege. Permission was normally granted and the offended member was accorded the privilege of speaking from the lectern. When someone requested that privilege, the other members took seriously the entire matter and started paying attention. Those who had been reading the morning papers put them down. The youngsters who were selling boiled peanuts suspended their operations for the duration of the speech, and as far as I know there has never been a protest or discourteous act in the chambers when a member was speaking about his frustration or his anger aroused by the press. The speaker has a moment in the sunshine when he can vent his angry thoughts. He can actually treat it like a bully pulpit because he has the lectern all to himself and it appears to be an official function in which he is speaking for the leaders. But such an outlet for rebuttals is not always available or appropriate.

In those cases the responses are just words or phrases that can do no more than console the victim over the crisis instigated by the press. One popular defense is to say: "There is nothing older than yesterday's newspaper." Or an offended politician might explain to his friends his non-action when he has been punched in the gut by printed words by saying: "I can't fight with them because they have an unlimited supply of ink." A less cautious politician might explain why he can't fight back by saying: "Everyone knows you can't win a pissing contest with a skunk." Those and other negative clichés are like using a toothpick to hit a fastball thrown by a big league pitcher. But they must do some good, because they are used on a regular basis.

## The Capitol Press Corps

Members of the 57 Club had frequent contact with news people in Tallahassee. Reporters who covered the legislature fell into one of several groups. There was the Capitol Press Corps, made up of the Associated Press (AP) representative and the person who ran the operation for the United Press International (UPI). Also, a few other chain papers and an occasional newspaper company kept someone in Tallahassee most of the time. That group did not limit itself to covering the legislature. They reported on everything that happened in the Capitol.

And then there were many other reporters who were often present. Each was there to do a specific job, and their employment arrangements ran the gamut from college newspapers with volunteer student reporters to experienced, highly-paid, and talented writers sent in for specific stories. These reporters were not a part of the recognized Capitol Press Corps, but they shared office space with them and all seemed to work together very well in spite of the ongoing competition.

Finally, there were reporters who worked for local papers throughout the state and were sent to Tallahassee during regular sessions of the legislature to write stories about what was going on there, with a special emphasis on legislators from the newspaper's hometown.

The *Daytona Beach News Journal*, the largest newspaper in my home county of Volusia, regularly sent one of its most experienced reporters or editorial writers to cover each session of the legislature. The presence of such a person was a real convenience and was very helpful to the legislative delegation. It made possible in-depth coverage of all the things we were doing and provided opportunities to explain the motivations or reasons for our important activities.

In addition to the newspapers, which were referred to as the print media, there were radio reporters, independent or freelance television reporters who sold stories to various stations, and television stringers who were not employees of any station but had contracts with a station or two to furnish a specified number of stories relating to legislative activities.

Again, those who were employees of newspapers, as well as the radio and TV people, were not integral parts of the Capitol Press Corps. But they hung out at the press corps building and were invited to sit in on press conferences held there, where they could pick up copies of announcements and other communications set out for the press corps.

When the legislature was in session, the press corps' offices were beehives of activities. Legislators who had been in office long enough to know reporters pretty well would drop in to check the latest wire stories and pay their respects to the reporters. Representative Bob Mann from Tampa was good at that sort of thing. He would just show up as though he was one of them, but not everyone could comfortably do that. It is certainly true that a shy legislator is an oddity, and yet there was a feeling that those impromptu visits could be perceived as transparent attempts to solicit personal publicity. That situation bothered some of us, and we were reluctant to expose ourselves to possible ridicule or unflattering mention in some paper.

In addition to the activities caused by or designed for the drop-ins, there were press conferences scheduled by legislative committee chairs and others who were anxious to have people know about an important meeting or some other happening. And it was a common occurrence for a candidate to stage a kick-off press conference to attempt to generate favorable publicity for her/his candidacy. It was a busy place.

My experiences with the press corps and others who had offices there were positive. That is to say, they usually treated me fairly. However, it would be wrong to represent that legislators or other public officials were good friends with press corps members because reporters normally did not let that happen.

I observed that the most successful reporters kept a respectable distance between them and public officeholders. There was not necessarily antagonism or animosity, but rather a shield of skepticism. The good reporters could be warm and friendly without letting down their guard or allowing a public official to co-opt them. Early in my public career I decided that a good Capitol Press Corps was a necessity for the people of Florida. It could keep them informed about their state government and do it in a professional manner. The passage of time proved me right.

It is too bad that there isn't an alumni association for members of the Capital Press Corps who have gone on to bigger and better jobs in journalism. I knew Frank Trippett, capital bureau chief of the *St. Petersburg Times*, who wrote a book entitled *The States, United They Fell*. It was a fine piece of work that pointed out how the states—because of lack of interest and failure to act—had allowed cities to connect directly with the federal government, leaving the states virtually impotent and certainly irrelevant. He was later retained in a fairly high position by *Newsweek*. Another outstanding reporter I knew quite well left Florida for a post with the *New York Times*. I kept in touch with both of them for a while, but soon realized that, for the reasons mentioned, there was not a strong friendship bond, and we lost contact.

A more recent example of the quality of the Capitol Press Corps is Martin Dyckman. He was a full-time reporter for the *St. Petersburg Times* but stayed in Tallahassee most of the time and was considered to be a member of the corps. I watched him carefully as he moved around the Capitol. While working on a story about some aspect of current legislation, Dyckman would sometimes stop me in the hall and ask me a hard question about whatever he had on his mind. Generally he either already knew the answer to his question and was seeking to verify what he had been told or was checking to see who would lie to him. He was too smart to be fooled and too well informed to permit anyone to feed him the wrong information. Skepticism seemed to be his watchword. I never tried to mislead him or ask him for any favors. He served his paper and the public very well.

He did such a good job in Tallahassee that he was promoted and began spending most of his time in St. Petersburg, where he wrote about subjects that were important and complex. When he retired he moved back to Tallahassee, where he authored two books that have taken their place in the history section of public libraries. The first one is entitled *Floridian of His Century*, and is an excellent account of the personal and political life of Governor LeRoy Collins.

Collins was arguably the best governor Florida ever had, and Dyckman made the case for him. His book is well written, informative, and accurate. It is well worth reading.

His second effort is a book about the Florida Supreme Court at a time when the court was in crisis. The title, *A Most Disorderly Court*, is quite appropriate. Dyckman, as an investigative reporter, exposed the unacceptable conduct of three of the justices who were on the bench at that time. Simultaneously, the House of Representatives appointed a committee to investigate the possibility of impeachment. Dyckman's description of the court leading up to the crisis, his account of the work of the House Impeachment Committee, the resignation of two of the three justices, and his treatment of the court and its members as the court went through a reformation, is an excellent read. I was appointed general counsel to that House committee and served until a serious health problem took me out of action for a while, so I can testify that the book is accurate in all respects.

### A Well-Known Member of the Media

I also found representatives of the news media around the state to be as competent and conscientious as their colleagues in the Capitol Press Corps. There are many good examples, but I believe the best one for this purpose is Larry King, who is now well known for his work on CNN, where he presides over the program they call *Larry King Live*.

During the 1963 and 1964 governor's campaign, King was writing a political column for the *Miami News* and doing a radio talk show that originated in Miami Beach. He invited the candidates, including me, to be on his program from time to time. I was his guest several times, and it was always a thrill to be on with him because he had the reputation of knowing more about the candidates and the issues than we suspected. It was said that he knew where all the secrets of the community were hidden.

The callers could ask anything that was on their minds, and predictably, they did just that. King had it in his power to make a person look bad, no matter how smart or experienced the guest may have been. Similarly, he knew how to make one look good, even though he/she might not deserve it. But to my knowledge, that rough and tumble young man from Brooklyn never intentionally built up or diminished a candidate. Instead, he was always matching wits with his guests. He asked questions and follow-ups that were searching and challenging. He never let a guest bluff him or his listening audience, but he was never rude or unfair. His broadcasts were good programs and had thousands of regular listeners. He was a fine journalist. No wonder he has been such a success.

When the campaign for governor was over and I was licking my wounds, we exchanged a few words of praise and gratitude. Then he published a column in one of the papers he wrote for, and that pleased me very much. He made positive comments about me and predicted that I would be heard from again. I was flattered and grateful, but it didn't take the sting out of my loss in the campaign.

As with all other aspects of politics, those who wrote about it were not all work and no play. Most of the press people I knew best were not affluent when I knew them. Some, I am certain, accumulated wealth after all of us moved on. I came to believe they were taught in college that high earnings were not what counted and that they would be better media representatives if they were hungry. Nevertheless, they knew how to have a good time.

I was with them in all sorts of situations over a long period of time, and I am comfortable making that statement. One of my favorite memories is of a party at the home of a non-affluent member of the Capitol Press Corps. Popcorn was both hors d'oeuvres and entrée. The home was poorly furnished and modest in size, but it was one of the best evenings I spent in Tallahassee. The beer straight from the keg was delicious and refreshing, and the conversations were stimulating and enlightening. When I think about that evening and others like it, I am always reminded of my late brother, who was regularly short of money and had an effective way of describing his near-poverty status. He used to say: "If a trip around the world cost a dime, I couldn't get out of sight."

## Press Corps Antics

And who could forget the media skits? Each year there was a coming together of the press corps and public officials for the purpose of presenting skits that were witty comments on current events. I was never bored. Each one was thoughtfully prepared and skillfully presented. There were no holds barred on skit night. Everyone and every issue was fair game. There was speaking, singing, and dancing. Every skit was the product of many hours of preparation and endless hours of rehearsals. It was always worth the price of admission.

## Weekly Print Media

There were also weekly newspapers that coexisted with the daily papers and the growing television industry. They came in all forms and with an infinite variety of content. Some were entertaining, some were angry, and others made us think. For years I regularly read one of those newspapers that made me think. It was published in North Carolina under the name of the *Carolina Israelite*. I looked forward to each issue and read every article with interest.

Then there was *La Gaceta*. It was—and still is—published in Ybor City, known as the Latin Quarter of Tampa. Today it is owned and operated by Patrick Manteiga, who is carrying on in the tradition of his father, Roland, and grandfather, Victoriano, both of whom published the paper and were known statewide for their fearless politics. When the 57 Club was formed, I began reading it regularly and found that quite a few Club members did the same. It is a trilingual paper. The principal English feature was a front-page column entitled *As We Heard It*. It was nothing more or less than a political feature, but it was well received by politicians because it was skillfully written. Surprisingly, that little newspaper was read and catered to by some of the most powerful people in the state, and because of that fact it was unique.

Another contributing factor to its uniqueness was the arrangement it had at La Tropicana, the popular Hispanic restaurant in Ybor City. The owners kept a table reserved for Roland whenever they were open. The sign on the table made clear that it was off limits to anyone else. There was even a private telephone at the table for his exclusive use.

## The Future of the News Media

As I record my observations and memories concerning the news media, I am personally troubled by what I understand to be happening to the newspapers today. I knew them when they were the strongest opinion makers in the state. I credit them with being at least partially responsible for most of the progressive changes that occurred as the state was maturing.

They taught us. They entertained us. They helped protect our freedom and watched those of us who were in politics to be certain we behaved. What will we ever do if newspapers are diminished so dramatically that they lose their influence and are forced to play smaller and smaller roles? What will politics be like if the present trend of newspaper management continues and good reporters, columnists, and others in this field keep leaving to find employment in a more stable industry, and the papers are forced to hire people who can do no better than write and print mediocrity?

# 13 *Anatomy of a Campaign* ————————————

Political campaigns play a significant part in the overall system of government. It is through them that we select our leaders, and the pressure of a coming election or reelection tends to shape the voting or performance of those who are politically ambitious. Virtually everyone residing in this country is—or has the opportunity to become—a registered voter and an integral part of the process in which public officials are selected. For those reasons and others, the more voters know about the way campaigns are managed and what really happens in campaigns, the more likely they are to make a sound and informed decision.

It has been said that there is nothing like a campaign; that seeking elected public office is a unique experience that calls up the best and the worst in those who opt to run. Winning a campaign causes a euphoric reaction unlike anything else; losing is political Hell.

I ran as a candidate in seven races. My score was six wins and one loss. I can testify that it is a lot more fun to win than to lose. I also participated to some extent in the campaigns of friends who I wanted to see in office. Based on my experience, I agree with all the above truisms about campaigns.

It is my observation that most people don't stop to think that when a person qualifies to be a candidate for an elective office, his/her life changes in some very important ways. First, the candidate puts everything he or she has on the line and at risk, and that makes for tension. The candidate's family is injected into the fray regardless of whether they want to be there.

The candidate automatically becomes a "public person" under the libel laws, which means, in effect, that the media and the citizens can say or write most anything they choose about the candidate with impunity. The only time a libel suit is available is when the person making the statement knows or should know that the damaging statement is untrue. It is a tough test, and libel suits by candidates—which are the only recourse against damaging statements—are seldom won. This public vulnerability invites slanderous allegations that can threaten the candidate's reputation.

Furthermore, it is self evident that a campaign is a financially dangerous undertaking. The campaign organization is typically assembled in a hurry without adequate time or proper resources to check everyone thoroughly, and the opportunities for mischief are plentiful. Viewed in that light, the wonder is that anyone volunteers to run for public office.

In spite of the risks, however, people do seek public offices. A few succeed, and regrettably they are not always the best in the field. The campaign should expose all the political warts and winnow out the unqualified and untrustworthy candidates, but the system is imperfect and a few bad apples slip into the barrel once in a while. When that happens, we need to be ready to find ways to rid the system of the likes of them. We should never give up or let the bad ones have it all their own way.

The fact that our country is more than 200 years old and has survived thousands of elections at all levels tells us that we have a workable system, and that if we regularly correct the glitches as we discover them and remain on the alert for ways of refining and improving our system, we will be well served in the future.

With that in mind we will focus here on a campaign for the Office of Governor that occurred in Florida in the early '60s. It should be entertaining and perhaps a bit educational to review anecdotes (as I remember them) from what was my first statewide campaign. The really important happenings of that race, like who won and who lost, have been reported and hashed over many times, so we will concentrate on important but lesser known parts of one of the most interesting political events of that time.

I selected for discussion this particular race for several reasons, not the least of which is that two members of the 57 Club were candidates. Moreover, racial integration and legislative reapportionment were major issues, and both of those subjects were prominent in the days of the 57 Club. Also, the governor's race of 1964 provided an insight into what candidates and future political leaders were saying in respect to the political environment, and that was relevant to the rest of the history of that tenuous organization.

## A Little Background

I was a member of the 57 Club and the Florida House of Representatives for eight years, from November 1956 to November 1964. I was politically active from the beginning of my career in the House, and I experienced a rather rapid rise to a midlevel political rank.

One of my greatest concerns in the political arena was education. My mother had been active in education, and I grew up on her teacher's salary. Interestingly, during WWII my pay as an eighteen-year-old lieutenant was $125 a month—the same salary that my mother earned as an experienced full-time teacher.

Many family friends were educators, so I had a natural affinity for education as a legislative subject. It was not surprising that as a legislator I was appointed to leadership positions where I could develop my ongoing interests and help to improve the system. Neither was it a surprise when the educators began to recognize me as a legislative friend. That was the first hint that I was nearly ready to run for a higher office.

People interested in politics began talking about the possibility of my running for governor. A few Capitol correspondents picked up on the rumors and wrote about it. One in particular was Allen Morris, who at that time wrote a syndicated column about political events and politicians. He was an important figure in press circles and was generally respected. Just for the record it should be noted that he later became the clerk of the House of Representatives.

One Sunday morning Morris featured me in his column and said some very nice things about me. He said that I was of the Collins, McCarty, and Carlton ilk—a group of respected and very serious political movers and shakers who represented the moderate thinkers—and he conveyed the thought that I would be a strong candidate for governor. I did not object to what he said, and that tended to give the rumors credibility. Subsequently, the possibility that I might be a candidate for the Office of Governor took on a life of its own, or as is said today: "The rumor got legs."

## Decision to Run

The first and most important question one must ask at the outset of a campaign is: "Can I win?" There is no sure way to know the answer, so one does the best he can to make an educated guess. In my case it was too early in the political season for polling, so in the 1964 race I evaluated my situation based on several pieces of information. The first goal would be to win a place in the runoff. Florida was a one-party state at the time, and winning the Democratic nomination was about the same as winning the general election. The party had its primary election, sometimes called the first primary, in May. If no one received a majority of the votes cast, the two top vote getters ran head to head in a runoff election three weeks later, which was sometimes referred to as the second primary.

Anyone running for a major office learned the applicable rules and planned the campaign accordingly. In my case I started with the assumption that I would carry my own county in a big way, and that because of my tight relationship with the Florida Education Association (FEA) I would have teachers/supporters in every county. After all, I handled all their legislation in the House and was their strongest advocate for improved school funding, including increased teachers' pay.

I never took seriously the advice I received from some of the more seasoned legislators to the effect that I should not count on educators to campaign for me just because I had been a faithful supporter of their legislative package. In retrospect, I should have heeded that advice, because most educators do not vote in a block or for a particular candidate out of gratitude for legislative help.

In addition to my own county and the teachers, I surmised that I would have good support from a few of my House colleagues, plus several senators. The House members were not expected to do much, particularly if they had opposition themselves, but their endorsement was valuable in my view. Those who made up the House delegation of Hillsborough County—Bob Mann, Woodie Liles, Louis de la Parte, Rene Zacchini, and others were the most enthusiastic of all.

I also had reason to believe that I would receive a fair amount of the minority vote, although everything was changing and no one knew with any degree of certainly whether African Americans would vote in a bloc or whether they would be unduly influenced by the old-fashioned political precinct workers who gave them a ride to a voting place and once in a while slipped them a little token of gratitude for voting the "right" way. I didn't even know if they would be disillusioned or if they were interested enough in the whole process to bother with voting.

Finally, I rightfully assumed that I would be strong in Dade County. No one from that area of the state had given any indication that they would compete for the Governor's Office. Furthermore, I had numerous commitments from prominent residents of Dade County and a few public officials, including the mayor of Coral Gables, a politically oriented community. Not only that, but the afternoon paper, the *Miami Daily News*, which seemed to love Governor LeRoy Collins, told him that they planned to endorse me because of my record in the House. I confirmed that fact with the man who would write the editorial. For all these reasons, I believed that I was well connected in Dade County and that those connections could be quantified in terms of votes.

When I estimated the anticipated total number of votes and how many candidates would be in the race, and then calculated how many votes I would have to receive to be in the runoff, I was surprised at how few would be needed. Then I calculated how many votes I would likely receive from each of the groups or areas where I was strong, and I ultimately concluded that I had an excellent chance of being in the runoff, provided, of course, that my estimates were accurate.

Because I believed in my political calculations and seemed willing to take action based on them, one might question my judgment. I was not totally lacking in common sense, although I really wanted to be the governor, and such ambition often blinds an amateur such as I was at that juncture. However, as a safety measure, and before committing to be a candidate, I took two other giant steps. First, I reviewed with politically sophisticated friends and others—including prominent media people with whom I had good relationships—what was known about my potential opponents. I also invited a representative group of folks who regularly involved themselves in governors' races to meet with me in Daytona Beach to probe the possible availability of quality support and campaign funding.

The issue of prospective candidates was critical. I understood that there were people in politics who were not completely honest when answering specific questions about their future political plans, but I needed the best information available when making the important decision then confronting me. There seemed to be good news about the potential candidates. It was theorized that Mayor Hayden Burns of Jacksonville would run, as would former State Senator Fred O. (Bud) Dickinson, but there were mixed views about Senator Scott Kelly. Some thought he would run, but others did not. I knew him quite well and assumed he was going to be a candidate.

With just the four of us in the race, I would have an advantage in that I was the only one with direct connections to the people considered to be the moderate thinkers—in other words, the former supporters of Dan McCarty, LeRoy Collins, and Doyle Carlton Jr. Those people could never support

Burns, Dickinson, or Kelly, I thought. Also, it appeared that I would have little competition for the votes of the educators and minorities. From reading the editorials and talking with editors and others who were informed about the inner workings of the statewide daily newspapers, I concluded that most of them would never support Burns, Dickinson, or Kelly over me, and that I would have a good chance of receiving their endorsement.

There was also good news about support beyond the media as well as possible financial support. My Daytona Beach meeting was well attended, and the makeup of the group indicated that we were correct in the assumptions about who would run and the base of support of each opponent. Those assembled urged me to run. They were fearful that if I didn't declare my intentions soon, others would probably throw their hats in the ring and split the support that seemed to be mine. However, a few argued that it was still very early, and that perhaps it would be smart to wait since it was only the early fall of 1963—more than eight months before the first primary.

A large room full of influential friends telling a candidate to go ahead and run is a pretty heady thing. I knew it would be almost impossible to turn them down when I thought running was a grand idea as well. Then the question of money was put on the table and I picked up the first negative vibes. No one actually refused to commit to financial support, and more than $50,000 was pledged for startup expenses (equal to just about $500,000 in today's dollars), but no one left any significant amount of money with my treasurer. I was somewhat concerned, but rationalized that it was still early and perhaps my campaign staff and I had not done a good job of demonstrating the urgent need for immediate funding.

In any event, that day I passed the point of no return. I agreed to be a candidate for the Office of Governor. There would be no turning back.

The potential candidate I was most concerned about was Jack Mathews who, like me, was a member of the 57 Club. The investigation of our campaign committee had concluded that he would not run in 1964. That made sense to me because he and Jacksonville Mayor Burns were from the same county, so I theorized that Mathews could never be the "favorite son." The best he would be able to do would be to share that status with Burns.

The fact that we would be running for a two-year term instead of the usual four years was seen as a deterrent to someone like Jack because of his current legislative status and his family's political reputation, as well as his obvious political ambition. There was also the matter of timing. I believed that Jack had waited too long to declare and had allowed me to commit too many of our mutual friends. Still, I was concerned. We had similar voting records, numerous mutual friends and supporters, and if both of us were running at the same time, we would likely divide the available support and that would not be good for either of us.

From the time of my original Daytona Beach meeting with supporters until mid fall, I heard nothing from Mathews nor anything specific about his plans to run. Therefore, I went on my merry way raising funds, planning the dissertations (known as white papers) I would write, publish, and distribute to explain my positions on the issues, and otherwise devoting my full time and best efforts to projecting my name out to the potential voters.

## Campaigning by Air

There was a lot of travel involved in those early efforts. When the travel was to a place only a short distance away, we went by car. However, it was not unusual to have to attend meetings in several cities or otherwise cover a large number of miles in a single day, which necessitated using an airplane.

At first I used the aircraft of a small charter company, but the bill was growing rapidly. Fortunately, my advisers found a way to ease that pain. They solicited and were able to secure an in-kind donation of a small two-engine plane manufactured by the Piper Company. We would have to hire our own pilot and pay all the operational and maintenance expenses, but those expenses were more manageable. Having the full-time use of an airplane even back in 1963 and 1964 was an important resource in running a statewide campaign, and it gave me the ability to cover a lot of ground in a short period of time.

Much of the drama of a political campaign is related to the airplane. For example, I considered myself very lucky to find an Air Force pilot who was leaving the service and looking for a job just like the one I had to offer. We struck a deal and integrated the plane and the pilot into our planning process. However, on the first flight I began to wonder whether I had made a mistake about the pilot.

The problem was that while he was in the service he flew only B-52s: the largest airplanes in the Air Force. Everything he knew about flying (other than what he was taught in basic flight training) he learned at the controls of that giant aircraft, and practically all of his flying experience was in it. He had a problem adjusting to our small plane. The takeoffs were not bad, but when he came in for a landing, the big ship technique was all he used. That maneuver involved cutting the power before the landing gear touched down so the plane would drop to the runway. I have never been a pilot, nor have I had any pilot training, so I was at his mercy.

I review a campaign speech during one of my many airplane trips across the state. (Photo courtesy Florida Archives.)

I was told that the reason for the frightening landings was that the large, heavy military aircraft couldn't land with the same precise control as the small ones, so when pilots land one of those big planes, they drop it in before they run out of runway while trying to bring it close to the ground. I wasn't certain I was given straight information because I had flown on large commercial flights that were famous for their soft landings. However, I was so preoccupied with the affairs of the campaign that I did not investigate and foolishly assumed that the pilot would soon adjust to the small plane and all would be well.

He did not adjust.

For as long as he worked for me, I held my breath during every landing. He would bring the plane in quite fast and when we finally touched down it was with a jolt that punished both the plane and the passengers. I wondered how the landing gear on that little plane could withstand the beating he gave it. Moreover, my campaign chairman was so frightened that he refused to ride in the plane after a really scary landing on a grass runway near Miami.

As it turned out, that pilot did not stay very long. He took advantage of one of my rules, and I caught him at it. The rule was that the pilot—and no one else—made the decision to fly or not if the weather was marginal or if there was any question about the airworthiness of the plane. One evening while we were in Tallahassee, and anxious to return to Daytona, he told me that the weather was too bad for us to fly. I accepted his decision and everyone traveling with me, except the pilot, spent the night in a hotel.

His absence struck us as unusual and we wondered where he was. One thing led to another and someone suggested we call for an updated weather report ourselves. The call was made and the report was that there was no weather problem and that there had not been one all day. First thing the next morning, I confronted the pilot and he admitted that the proposed flight had interfered with his private plans, so he used my rule about who decides when to fly to require us to spend the night in Tallahassee.

I relieved him of his duties in the lobby of the hotel and took the keys to the plane. There would be no more rough landings. I was able to replace him promptly. His replacement stayed with me to the end of the campaign and had no flying habits that put us in danger.

## Campaign Opposition Revealed

During the 1963 campaign, the University of Florida had its annual homecoming in the fall. It was a popular event in the lives of the students and those active in the alumni association. Thousands of people assembled in Gainesville for the fellowship and to watch the Gators play football.

Homecoming was also one of the biggest and most significant political affairs. All of the political powerbrokers were there, as were all the candidates for statewide offices. The press was also there because that was where the action was on that weekend. No serious candidate for governor would dare be absent. I was there in 1963 with an ample contingent of my support team around me, and we planned to make a showing of strength. The other announced candidates were also there and in full view. I heard that Jack Mathews was attending, and I assigned someone to find out if my information was correct and, if so, to arrange a meeting between us. I expected that he would support me, and I intended to tie that down.

The meeting was arranged, and Jack surprised me with the news that he had decided to run. The conclusion my team and I had reached about Mathews' intentions was dead wrong. By the time our meeting was over, I knew he would be an opponent, that there was nothing I could do to change the situation, and that his involvement was not good for my campaign. In my wildest dreams I did not guess how much trouble his entry would cause me.

My political staff and I decided that Mathews becoming a candidate was not fatal and that we could adjust to it. There was no interruption in our campaign activities; however, another airplane incident during that time almost gave me a heart attack.

It was a very hot year and even in the fall the temperature was unusually high. One day I was flying out in the airplane and because it was so warm I took my coat off and hung it on a hook just to the rear of the door on the passenger side. Then I held the door open as we taxied to the runway so the cabin would cool off a bit. The meeting I was going to in Miami was a fundraising session, and it was extremely important to my campaign. Leaders in business and politics would be there. I wanted to look my best, so I was trying to avoid wrinkles in my clothes as we flew the 250 miles down the coast. When we reached our scheduled altitude, I reached for my coat to take something from the pocket and realized that the right sleeve had been caught in the door as I closed it for takeoff. The sleeve of my new suit was on the outside of the plane flopping around in the wind.

The remainder of the flight was terrible. There wasn't time to go back and change. I had no luggage with me, and there wasn't time to buy a new suit. I pictured the sleeve all torn up from being pounded against the plane and, at best, wrinkled. I knew it couldn't be worn like that and I dreaded going to the meeting in shirtsleeves because back then a gentleman wore a coat no matter what the temperature. I also knew that canceling the meeting was not an option, so I resolved to go without my coat and just make the best of it.

I must have been living right that day because when we landed and I had a look at the coat, I found that it was in great shape. One button was missing, but otherwise it was OK. Somehow it had not taken the beating I predicted. The folks at the meeting were amused by my story about the coat, and the fundraiser was a success.

It was not long before I received another shock from the Mathews camp. I learned that a small group of his key supporters were visiting all the editorial boards of the daily newspapers and saying that I planned to withdraw from the race and support Jack. I had never said I would do such a thing, and I believed they knew it was a made-up scenario.

No matter how the rumor started, it was devastating. I had worked my heart out on the daily newspaper circuit because I knew their endorsements would be important to the campaign. Now the newspapers weren't sure whether I would even be in the race at endorsement time. I assumed that Jack's campaign staff was saying the same thing to others around the state, and I soon confirmed that indeed they were. I knew their malicious story had to be answered.

Without hesitation I scheduled a meeting with each of the editorial boards and started rebuilding my status as a viable candidate. To their everlasting credit, no newspaper printed a story or reported on the subject, so I felt that there was a chance I could recover. Nevertheless, my campaign was shaken to the roots. I developed the hope that some or all the papers would write a story or an editorial exposing the dirty trick and give substance to my denial, but they did not do it because there was no proof one way or the other and it was Jack's word against mine. They would not be the adjudicators and decide who was right and who was wrong, and certainly they would not say who said what at our meeting in Gainesville. They went as far as they could, so they said.

## A Major Endorsement

It was around that time when I learned that a new magazine, *Florida Trend*, was building a statewide readership and had decided to endorse a candidate in our race. They had selected me. The magazine had never before endorsed a candidate and, in doing so that year, the editors interviewed each gubernatorial candidate. It was a coup. Their decision to support me was a lifesaver and helped me through that very dark period. The editorial endorsement was a thing of beauty. It helped me convince others that I would not be dropping out.

Word of the untrue rumor initiated by the Mathews people spread even though it was never published. My key supporters in Miami heard about it and asked for a special meeting to discuss the issue. I stood firm and assured them that there was nothing to the story and that I would not get out of the race no matter what else happened. However, trying to stop the spread of the story was like trying to extinguish an electrical fire with a garden hose. I had much work to do and I had to do it thoroughly and with a vengeance.

I was in the process of getting the campaign back on track and feeling good about it when I had an experience in Blountstown, a north Florida community, which tested my resolve in another way.

Blountstown had a very small airport. In fact it was tiny and had a grass runway. On the day in question, we flew in for an afternoon meeting and planned to take off before dark and head back to Daytona. By this time, I had replaced my first pilot and my new one was wonderful. He was confident of his ability and proud of his flying skills. He was fearless, but smart enough to avoid taking any unreasonable chances. Flying with him was, for the most part, a pleasure, but not without incident.

As should have been expected, we were late getting back to the airport. It was not only after dark when we arrived, but it was a really dark night. There was no light in the sky. The pilot took me aside and said he was concerned about taking off after dark because the little airport had no lighting and there was a power line at the far end of the runway that we had to clear just after takeoff.

He asked me if I would induce my friends from Blountstown to park their cars under that power line and turn on the cars' lights so he could guide on them and know where the electric line was located. He never said a word about possibly canceling the flight. I raised the question by asking him if it was safe to take off under any conditions that night. He assured me that everything was fine and that he would have no trouble getting airborne if I could arrange for the lighting he requested.

He very carefully explained how he would manage the takeoff. According to him, he would start as far away as possible from the end of the runway where the power line was hanging. He would then set the brakes and rev up the engines as high as he could. Thereafter, when we were ready, he would let the brake off and sort of jump start the plane. He said that while he had been waiting for us in the afternoon he had walked the grass landing strip and was satisfied that he could get up enough speed to lift off and clear the wires at the end of the runway.

We did not discuss the consequences of any miscalculation or any failure of the plane to perform as expected.

Because of that hair-raising experience, I am living proof that it is possible to take off at night and miss the power line at the airport in Blountstown. I guess I am also living proof that a non-pilot who does not particularly like heights can survive a tension-filled experience if he has enough confidence in the pilot. Incidentally, as we were striving to be airborne that evening, the pilot turned to me and with an impish grin on his face said: "Did you feel a bump right after we left the ground?" I answered: "No, I didn't feel a thing."

"That's good," he said. "I guess we missed the power line."

## William France Sr.

Early in the campaign, Bill France Sr., the man who formed the National Association for Stock Car Auto Racing (NASCAR) and built the Daytona International Speedway, took an interest in my candidacy and supported me with enthusiasm. He even let us use the grandstand of the speedway to hold a picnic and rally, to which we brought people from around the state. We wanted to impress everyone and demonstrate that the campaign had substance.

Bill France helped my campaign by sponsoring a rally for me at his Daytona Speedway. (Photo courtesy Florida Archives.)

The outdoor rally was a success and a high spot in the campaign. The people who came contributed money and we made a showing of strength. Later France gave me a speaking role in a ceremony that was held just before a big race, honoring a famous driver who had pulled another driver out of a burning car. The ceremony was well received by the crowd of nearly 100,000 race fans, and it was great exposure for me because it was such a meaningful gesture honoring a courageous man. My part was quite long with the hero of the day standing with me for most of my time at the mike.

Perhaps my biggest thrill was the time Bill France personally flew me from Daytona to Tallahassee in his private airplane. Bill was a race driver, as I described earlier, and he was also an excellent pilot. And that was not all. He was a great conversationalist, and it was a genuine pleasure visiting with him for the one-hour flight. Then, as one might expect given my track record in flying, the weather took a turn for the worse. I had visions of another situation wherein a delay was imminent and I would be sitting there in the plane hoping we would make it to the airport of our destination.

France never missed a beat. He told me that he was a pilot qualified to fly on instruments, and that the plane was equipped to fly in any weather and had been switched to instrument control. He explained the technique of relying on the instruments instead of the pilot's eyesight in which he finds his path and direction by locating landmarks and goes from one landmark to another.

With complete confidence, France approached Tallahassee from the south. When we were approximately twenty-five miles to the south we were over the coast by the Gulf of Mexico. The instruments controlled the direction, altitude, angle of decline, and speed. As if by magic the plane's instruments flew us right to the southern edge of the runway. We were high enough to miss the tree tops and at a speed that kept the plane in the air, but slow enough to permit the descent and allow the landing gear to touch down gracefully.

I was impressed with his flying skill, but not at all surprised because France was a big man, as strong as an ox, courageous as a knight, and smart as a wizard—and he seemed to win in every game he played. I was one of those who were happy that he did so well and made such a huge fortune, and I am happy that his family is still enjoying the fruits of his labor.

Campaigning went on at a ferocious rate. Each candidate tried to outdo the others in every important way. We all had fundraisers; we all pretty much concentrated on our strengths; we delivered policy speeches; we shook hands at every place where large numbers of people were employed; and we continued building our organizations. We did everything we could think of, and

During my campaign for governor, I shook hands with everyone, even if they were too young to vote.

most everything our staffs could think of, to get free publicity in the newspapers and free time on the TV news programs.

As the fall of the year began to mature and we started in to November, the pace was picking up and the candidates were being categorized and classified by the media. Hayden Burns was the conservative and the one to beat. I was pushed to the left further than I intended to go, and to save the minority votes I allowed people to think of me as the most liberal candidate in the race. My friends and I thought that since Burns was on the right and I was moderate-to-left, he and I would be in a Burns-Karl runoff.

Down deep I knew a runoff was unlikely. Jack Mathews was encroaching on the support on which I had counted. He had a fine record on financing education, and the senators who were helping him were also connected to educators. I had no doubt that the core group of teachers on which I had depended was going to split between us. Moreover, Mathews' people had de-livered that near-fatal blow to me when they insinuated that I would withdraw if he became a candidate. Consequently, no matter how many times we said we were not getting out, we still had trouble un-ringing that bell. The senators supporting Mathews were political pros and they knew what they were doing when they created doubt about my staying power, and they did it well. But I still had hope, so we kept on fighting the good fight and we made some real progress.

On a more encouraging note, my organization was growing fast and effectively in Miami. One key supporter, Ed Sirkin, was a former resident of Volusia County. He had lived in Daytona Beach as a youngster. It happened that when I was in high school, I delivered newspapers to his family, and Ed, who was now grown up and practicing law, volunteered to help me because he said he had fond memories of how decently I had treated him during those days as I delivered papers from house to house. More important, he also thought I had the right political philosophy.

## A Leader of Men

Ed Sirkin was not the only former native of Daytona Beach who was now living in south Florida and supporting my candidacy. Three others, all of whom were in my senior high school class, were there as well. Lester Force, a close friend since we were in kindergarten, was living in Fort Lauderdale and his sales territory included Dade County. He pitched in and proved once again what a good friend he really was. Dick Talton, a fine friend, was a banker in south Florida and was great help. The other was Dan Paul. Dan was the one who, as editor of our high school yearbook, wrote the caption for the picture of Lester's former girlfriend, Florence Currier (she later changed her name and became the well-known singer, Jane Morgan) and me, explaining why we were selected as the most versatile in our class. As to me, he wrote several flattering things and then said I was "A leader of men and a follower of women."

I was always glad that none of the voters had access to our yearbook, but not withstanding that rather embarrassing caption, Dan Paul was extremely helpful to me in the campaign.

Paul was a graduate of Harvard Law School and enjoyed a very successful law practice. He accomplished many significant political tasks, including drafting and overseeing the constitutional amendment that allowed Dade County to have a charter and Home Rule power. One of his clients owned *Look* magazine and other media companies. Dan arranged, through them, for me to go to New York to meet his clients and take a crash course in how to act and what to wear when on camera in TV stations.

They tested me, trained me, and gave me a prescription for TV success. The prescription included such advice as I should always wear a dark suit, white or light blue shirt, a tie that did not attract too much attention, and that I should never wear a handkerchief in my lapel pocket because it would be a distraction from what I had to say. A colored backdrop should always be behind me. Another piece of the advice was to never allow a TV cameraman to set his camera below my line of sight. The camera should be looking down on me because of the configuration of my neck. My loss in the 1963 gubernatorial race wasn't the fault of my TV trainers. They did the best they could with what they had to work with.

## Perry Nichols

Another person who was active in my Miami organization was Perry Nichols, a well-known trial lawyer. He was a graduate of Stetson University, as I was, but he was older. He was a very fine attorney who had organized a large and successful law firm that concentrated on plaintiffs' personal injury cases. He was something of a pioneer in that field and had perfected techniques that gave him a national reputation. He is the first person I ever heard use the old saying: "Among the graduates of any good law school, the A students teach law, while the B students work for the C students." He was a C student. He certainly was helpful and loyal. He never wavered, not even in the dark days after Mathews' people did the job on me.

It is interesting to note that my campaign attracted young people who were on the way up. Bill Sadowski was later elected to the Florida House of Representatives and served with distinction. His most important achievement came after he left the legislature and agreed to head the Department of Community Affairs. He led the department for several years and distinguished himself by developing and installing a plan that required, among other things, that each county and city prepare and adopt a comprehensive plan to govern and guide them into the future. He died in an airplane crash at St. Augustine.

Another person on the campaign was Sandy D'Alemberte, who was elected to the Florida House of Representatives and did a fine job. Thereafter he became dean of the FSU Law School and after that, president of FSU.

Jack Peoples was a friend and confidant of Governor Collins, and at Collins' request he served as director of the Department of Beverages. Then he organized and led an outstanding law firm that represented major clients such as a nationwide brewery company and a large and well-known developer.

Ron Silver subsequently served in the House and the Senate. There were many others and I very proud of every one.

It was not just in Miami that I had noteworthy support. There were supporters in most of the major communities who were destined to do outstanding work in the future. Members of the Tampa group were particularly endowed with the qualities that make for success, as were the folks in West Palm Beach, Fort Lauderdale, Orlando, Jacksonville, and, of course, Daytona Beach.

A key factor in the campaign was the enormously popular Governor Le-Roy Collins. Naturally, he did not attend meetings or make speeches for me, but he was quietly active. He was always available for consultations, and he influenced many of his supporters to help me. However, no matter how popular or influential he was, we could not overcome the damage done by Jack Mathews' friends.

Then we received the worst news of all: President John F. Kennedy had been assassinated. It cast a long shadow across the political spectrum. Almost all of my people were emotionally upset. A sort of paralysis set in. Nothing was happening, and I was forced to spend most of my time trying to refocus everyone without being disrespectful of President Kennedy. We were as stunned as was everyone else. We didn't know who was responsible or whether we were about to be attacked by our Cold War adversaries. The country was in turmoil, and so were many of my key campaigners.

### Bob High Announces His Candidacy

Before the Kennedy funeral was over, Miami Mayor Bob High had entered the race. I thought there had been an understanding that he would not be running and would support either Jack Mathews or me. Obviously, my understanding was not well founded. I confronted one of his ranking supporters and was told that, as a result of the assassination, the entire situation had changed and all bets were off. Bob had gone to Washington, D.C., for the funeral and, when he came back, it was with the message that he had an obligation to run for governor and that he was the only one who could carry the Kennedy banner—or words to that effect. Now there were six contenders.

### A Key Person

A person who was involved in the campaign from beginning to end and played a key role the entire time was an interesting man named Radford Bishop. I met Radford in Tallahassee in 1959. His family home was in Daytona Beach, but I did not know him or anything about him before our first meeting. I knew a little about his affluent and respected family that had been in Volusia County for two or three generations. They had the reputation of being good citizens and decent human beings, and I quickly learned more about them as we became better acquainted.

Radford and his family were staunch members of the Baptist Church, and they took their religious obligations seriously. They were interested in politics for all the right reasons. They wanted their government operated by honest and competent public servants, and they supported candidates who had those credentials. They asked nothing else of their elected politicians.

Radford was a student at Florida State University studying business, no doubt preparing himself to take over the management of the family's substantial land holdings. He walked into my legislative office in the Capitol one day and told me that he would like to volunteer to help me with my work. I explained that the state did not provide us with any paid assistance or assistants. He already knew that and assured me he was not looking for compensation and would work for nothing. That was a refreshing surprise. As he explained about his family's attitude about public service, I became convinced that he was sincere and to paraphrase an old saying, he was ready to put his energy and talents where his mouth was. Thus began a strong and lasting friendship as well as a trusting and supportive political relationship.

He was a quick study and learned well my idiosyncrasies as they related to my official responsibilities. I often told people that he was my Bobby Kennedy, referring to the then-popular belief that Jack Kennedy, as president, appointed his brother, Robert, to be the U.S. Attorney General and head of the Justice Department because he needed a person he could trust unconditionally to be near him in the administration and invested with significant power in his own name so he could help the president with important, sensitive matters. Radford did all that for me and was an effective troubleshooter.

He was a confidant concerning my decision to run for governor. He helped with the scheduling and transportation problems. He often traveled with me and when he did he saw to it that our baggage was where it needed to be at the time it was required. He very carefully and discretely enforced a campaign policy that I was never to be left alone.

We found that there were always unexpected questions or unfriendly assertions about my activities that required note taking or help with little known facts and, from time to time, there would be a person—usually a female—who was overly friendly and sometimes seemed determined to maneuver me into a position that might be misunderstood. He successfully protected me from real or perceived enemies.

Those and other responsibilities kept Radford very busy, but he still found time to bring campaign workers into the organization, including members of campus organizations from most of the universities in the state. A good example of his campus-related work is what happened at the University of South Florida. There, in addition to inducing students to register to vote and encouraging them to actually vote on election day, he had them arrange for

Two men who proved invaluable to me in the legislature were Radford Bishop and Harry Landrum. I referred to Bishop (upper right) as my Bobby Kennedy because I could trust him unconditionally. Landrum was one of the good guys and the real hero in helping me pass needed revisions to the state insurance code.

me to become acquainted with faculty members as well as university staffers so I could ask them for financial support and advice about the issues. I was always right at home on that campus.

Radford did the same things at Florida State University. Although I never enrolled at FSU, he arranged for me to receive honorary membership in the Garnet and Gold organization, the leadership group on that campus.

Back at USF, Radford developed leadership volunteers. He recruited John Grant, a young Democrat, as chairman of the Fred Karl for Governor Campaign at USF. John, in due time, graduated from college and practiced law in Tampa. When the Republican Party began to grow and the two-party system was becoming a reality, John became a Republican, or I should say he registered as a Republican, because he may have been one all along but played the one-party game when necessary. Anyway, he later served in the legislature representing Hillsborough County. When my wife and I moved to Tampa in 1988, John was in the Senate and quite successful.

Radford survived the gubernatorial campaign and its aftermath. Later, we worked together through my legislative time in the Senate. Then we went our separate ways. He died of cancer while still relatively young.

## Foreshadowing of a Two-Party System

On the campaign trail I picked up evidence that the one-party system was not likely to last. One incident in particular brought this fact to my attention. Governor LeRoy Collins had introduced me to a friend of his who managed a hotel in Mount Dora, a delightful little city in Lake County, located in central Florida. His friend had served in an appointed position in the Collins administration and he had agreed to help me.

I found the governor's friend to be a very persuasive person and one who I believed might be able to help a lot. He started by taking me on a walk in downtown Mount Dora to meet some of the townspeople and some of his hotel guests who were also walking around. The first person we met was a well-dressed, elderly lady. She had that wonderful "Aunt Bea" appearance and personality. My new friend introduced me to the lady and gave her a short description of my accomplishments and told her that he was helping me become the next Governor of Florida. When he finished, he offered her one of my cards.

She didn't take it, and instead said to me, "And to which party do you belong?" I told her I was a Democrat. Then she said, in a manner that left no room for doubt as to her sincerity, "I can't vote for you, because I only vote for Republicans." She left without further conversation and without my card. You may be sure I did not carry Lake County.

## Advice from George Wallace

During my campaign, I met and received advice from the infamous Governor of Alabama, George Wallace. The meeting occurred while I was attending a function at a hotel in Miami Beach. As it happened, Governor Wallace was attending the same affair and we had a brief, unscheduled, and informal meeting in the lobby of the hotel. I asked him a question just to make conversation and he reacted as most politicians do with a long answer. He was already prominent on the national scene, so he probably thought he was helping a person in need of advice.

He advised me that if I wanted to win I should pick an issue—an emotional issue like segregation, the one he had selected—and concentrate my campaign efforts on that issue rather than using a broad, multi-issue platform. His point was that if the issue selected is sufficiently emotional, it is all that is needed and those voters who are involved in the issue in some way won't really care what position is taken on the other, customary issues.

I got the impression that it was not necessary, in his view, for the candidate to sincerely believe in the selected emotional issue so long as enough was known about it to defend the position taken. I watched him campaign, especially in 1968, when I was running for the Senate, and it seemed to me that he was following his own advice.

## A Christmas Party

I spent part of the 1963 Christmas season in North Carolina at the invitation of a good friend who owned a lodge. Some of the other guests were supporters of Bud Dickinson, one of my opponents. It was a nice holiday and there was no trouble, but it was hard to have a good time because the campaign troubles preempted everything else. The most fun I had was having my picture taken with the Dickinson supporters to send to Bud.

The remainder of the campaign was exciting and many interesting things happened, but we were politically wounded and we were having trouble healing, which was no secret.

## A True Supporter

Still, there were a few lighthearted times. One of my Tampa supporters, the wife of a high school friend, had an attack of appendicitis during the campaign and was taken to Tampa General Hospital for surgery. When they undraped her for the surgery, the operating room staff and the surgeon discovered that she had a bumper sticker advertising "Fred Karl for Governor" plastered across her abdomen. I was told that the news of it traveled through the hospital and was better advertising than a TV spot.

A copy of the campaign bumper sticker one of my supporters wore when going into surgery.

## An Update of the Story

Bob High received the endorsements of the Miami newspapers. After all, he was the hometown boy. High and Mathews split most of the other endorsements with me. I got the small end of the stick because by that time the die was cast and editors, like everyone else, wanted to be with a winner. In fact, we had one report that we believed was authentic, in which an editorial endorsing me was written and approved, but the board decided the day before it was to run that Jack Mathews had a better chance of winning, so they just changed the name of the endorsee and used what had been written about my activities to endorse Jack.

Hayden Burns was the strongest candidate and ran ahead of the rest of us. The wonder was that he didn't receive enough votes to win without a runoff. Bob High finished second and Kelly, Dickinson, Mathews, and I split what was left.

Meanwhile, I endured two other airplane incidents. The first was in north Florida, when the flight instruments indicated that the nose wheel of the landing gear would not go down to support the plane upon landing. The runway was in a pasture and was surfaced with clay. We could see it had ruts in it. There was no tower on that field and we had no communications with anyone on the ground, so there was no way we could verify the trouble or have any other help.

The pilot recommended that I authorize him to try to land. He explained how he would keep the nose up as long as possible and then set it down gently. That way, if the nose wheel collapsed when he put weight on it, we would probably survive because of the reduced speed. I told him to do it, and he did. There were many times I was especially happy to walk away from the plane after an unusual landing, but that one took the prize. I wasn't just happy to be down, I was also very grateful to the pilot.

The other incident was over Fort Lauderdale at about 4,000 feet when the right engine (the one next to where I was sitting) developed trouble and was smoking as though it might be on fire. We had few options about what to do. There were no parachutes, which was no big deal as far as I was concerned—I would have had a hard time jumping. Anyway, there was no way out on my side of the plane because the smoke was everywhere. I had been told that the plane would fly with one engine, and it would be an understatement to say I was hoping that the guy who told me about it knew what he was talking about. Once again the pilot demonstrated his expertise by calmly feathering—or shutting down—the right engine. Luckily, it did not catch on fire. The airplane flew pretty well on one engine and the pilot brought it into the Fort Lauderdale airport where the emergency crews were out waiting for us.

There was never an accident in the plane, but I'm sorry to say that there were several accidental happenings involving people working inside the campaign. In every case something I said or did was taken as a personal offense, and the person or persons offended ended our friendship. Repairing the damage was time-consuming and usually unsuccessful. The best example of those very painful experiences involved a couple I had counted as friends since we were in grammar school together.

This couple was unusually successful in business while we were all quite young. They used me as their lawyer in all transactions, and I patronized their business and did all I could to help them through the legal and governmental sand traps along the way. We had something of a social relationship; we went to the same church; we helped each other through personal tragedies; and we even fished together. In 1956 when I was just starting my campaign for the House of Representatives, they were among the first to agree to help me, and they worked hard in the campaign. When the race for governor came along they were once again there for me.

It happened that during the governor's race they had a serious problem with the city and they sought me out to help solve it. At the time, I was out of town and fully engaged in the campaign. Obviously, my time and attention were dedicated to the effort to be elected. However, because of our relationship they assumed that I would do whatever was necessary to accomplish what they wanted. Conversely, I felt that because of our relationship and their demonstrated interest in the campaign, they would understand my preoccupation with the campaign and my inability to cancel all plans to come in and take care of their problem.

I asked the senior partner in my law firm to help them and he agreed to do it. But the couple had information to the effect that my partner might have some kind of a conflict of interest. Admittedly, there was a failure on my part to properly communicate with them, and they were unhappy with the referral to my partner. Meanwhile, I was out there campaigning my heart out without knowing that the situation was infected with misunderstandings and was festering.

The matter with the city wasn't solved soon enough or in a way that satisfied my friends, and they held me responsible. When I heard that they were bitterly dissatisfied, I called on them personally. I explained my understandings and my actions. I apologized profusely. We parted as something other than friends.

For more than forty years after that incident, they were against me in everything I did. Frankly, I could cope with their opposition when I ran for a seat in the Florida Senate or a seat on the Supreme Court, but the loss of the close, personal relationship bothered me a lot. It was a casualty of a political campaign and I knew those things happened, but it didn't help. Although time healed the wounds to some extent, things were never as they once had been, and they can never return to the original status.

## The Day I Would Like to Forget

Finally, the day came when the voters spoke and the votes were counted. I've tried to forget that day ever since. It was the beginning of a very dark time in my life, not just because I lost so miserably, but because I soon discovered that my organization had spent more than it had taken in. Everyone shook hands, wished me well, and left me to cope with a deficit of $75,000. Considering that my earned income from my law practice in the early 1960s was in the $25,000 range, and considering inflation, it appears that in today's dollars I owed around three quarters of a million dollars. And, as if that was not a hard enough punch in the gut, I learned that during the campaign I had spent everything I had saved, including my equity in the law firm.

The largest piece of the debt was a result of spending the same money twice. Toward the end of the campaign, I approved a plan in which my finance group would approach individuals and ask them to sign a note for $1,000 payable in six months with minimum interest. A friendly banker would take the notes and give my campaign the full $1,000. If the campaign raised enough money to pay the notes off within six months it would do so. If not the person signing the note would pay the bank. I was told they raised $52,000 under that plan, and I assumed the money would be deposited to the statewide account. I authorized the team in the headquarters to buy last-minute TV spots and other things, and then learned the money had been distributed to county organizations to buy the same sort of things out there. I was out campaigning so I didn't see it coming, and still don't know exactly how it happened.

The unpaid bills left for me to deal with included a $5,000 telephone bill, utility bills, a $6,000 American Express bill which included charges for campaign workers' hotel and restaurant bills, and a wide variety of small bills for such things as bumper stickers, hand-out materials, and office supplies.

Election laws prohibited the extension of credit to a candidate or his campaign organization. I felt secure in the knowledge that I could not be required to pay all those people, but I was concerned that they, in good faith, had extended credit in my name and if I didn't pay them, they would not be paid. Moreover, I believed that I had a moral obligation to protect them.

I concluded that they must be paid, and I wrote to everyone to verify the amount due. In the letter, I told them about the law that made the accounts uncollectible, but promised to pay them in full if they would be patient and give me a reasonable time to work it all out. Only one person took an unreasonable position and required immediate payment. I was angry enough to refuse to pay him and to turn him in as a violator of election laws, but I felt sorry for him. He was desperate, and so I paid him before I paid the others. I hated the appearance of favoritism and it bothered me for a long time that I seemed to be rewarding his impatience. But the fact is that what I did was right, all things considered, and one cannot do any better than that. So my decision stands.

I was true to my word in that I paid every bill. I borrowed enough to pay the utility companies and the credit card company, because they were legally unable to wait for me to do it my way. Then I developed a monthly payment plan and executed it. After several years every account was satisfied. Paying those accounts with after-tax dollars was hard. It was like paying an old whiskey bill.

## Getting Back on the Horse

Losing a political campaign is like being thrown from a horse. The only sure way to live in peace and bear the humiliation is to ride that horse again. I knew I would have to run for office again, and I did. Four years later I ran for the State Senate. I won that race and served a four-year term. Then, in 1976, I ran a successful statewide nonpartisan race for a seat on the Florida Supreme Court. No other member of the 57 Club was ever seated on that court.

# 14 *A Justice Is the Sum of His Past* •————————

In January, 1977, about thirteen years after I unsuccessfully ran for governor and five years after I finished my term in the Senate, I was sworn in and seated on the Florida Supreme Court. I was fifty-two years old, and for most of my adult life I had been working to achieve this major goal. It was the highest court in the state system and there were only seven members. I thought I had arrived. I was euphoric. As I will explain, I had the distinction of being the last elected justice in Florida.

## The Story of a Journey

My journey to the Florida Supreme Court started when I was a young man who had just returned from WWII and was studying law at Stetson University in DeLand. Stetson was the first and therefore the oldest law school in Florida, and enjoyed an excellent reputation. The entire time I studied law there it was located in buildings at the DeLand Airport that had been built for the Navy. During the war the Armed Forces trained their pilots at many of the airports in Florida, including the one in DeLand. Years after I graduated, the law school was moved to St. Petersburg in Pinellas County, where it has prospered. At the time I was in law school, four of the seven Florida Supreme Court Justices were graduates of Stetson.

One of the programs organized by the university for the law students was

I took my place on the Florida Supreme Court in January 1977. I was the last elected justice.

a luncheon with three of the four members of the court who had received their legal education at Stetson. Each of them spoke briefly about his life on the court, sort of a personal insight into what went on in those hallowed halls. I was impressed and went away with thoughts of what an interesting and rewarding life they lived. It combined the best aspects of politics—or public service if you will—and work on a professional level. Their responsibilities were important and meaningful, with time to think and write.

There was also time for social events such as attendance at receptions in the Governor's Mansion, functions sponsored by the Florida Bar, the governor's State of the State report, and other important activities in the legislature. It couldn't get any better than that, I thought. I wondered whether I would ever have the opportunity to be a justice on that court. I can't say I maintained that goal as my sole plan for the future, but it certainly was my "Plan A." Those thoughts were ever present in my mind from that day on.

It was only about six years following my graduation from Stetson Law School before I was a member of the 57 Club and a practicing attorney. Both of those achievements, in some ways, were further preparation for the Supreme Court. Then, as noted earlier, Governor Collins offered me an appointment to a circuit court—a court that had trial jurisdiction. However, presiding at trials was a totally different occupation, in my view. I enjoyed trials, but what I longed for was the life of an appellate judge who reviews the record made by a trial judge and also decides legal issues.

Legislative experience, most of my colleagues agreed, would help prepare me for a judicial career. Many of the legislative duties and experiences, including public speaking, would be helpful on the court. And, most important, the Supreme Court was the administrative head of, and set the tone for, all courts. Moreover, justices petitioned the legislature for help in the form of new judges, needed equipment, office space, and other resources to make it possible for the courts to function and cope with an ever-increasing work load.

To lobby the House successfully, members of the court had to understand the culture of the legislature and how it functioned. What better way to prepare for judicial service than to be a legislator for a while? I felt that I was doing the right thing, and so did members of the 57 Club in whom I confided my ambitions.

Shortly after leaving the Senate, there was a vacancy on the federal bench. I applied for an appointment as a federal district judge to fill that vacancy. The process was similar to the state appointment system. I went through the entire procedure knowing that the odds were against me because the current U.S. Attorney was also a candidate. He was a part of the justice system in that circuit, and the nominating committee would know all about his qualifications and just how good he was.

My application received high marks from the nominating committee and I was selected as one of the finalists. Thereafter, my application was passed on to the U.S. Senators from Florida for their consideration and selection of a nominee who would subsequently be recommended to the president for his appointment. As I expected, the U.S. Attorney was appointed. However, my selection as a finalist by such a distinguished committee encouraged my judicial dreams, and I considered the entire process I had just endured to be an exercise that further prepared me for my ultimate goal.

## A Committee to Consider Impeachment

Early in 1975, I had another good lesson in preparation for service on the Supreme Court. Three justices were investigated by an impeachment committee of the House of Representatives, and I was asked to serve as general counsel to that group of legislators. I learned a great deal about the court, and my work with the committee refreshed my knowledge of the impeachment process.

Martin Dyckman, a veteran investigative reporter, was responsible for the House action. He dug out the facts and reported them, leaving the House no choice but to investigate. His book, *A Most Disorderly Court*, contains all the details of that episode and is a must read for any serious student of Florida's judiciary.

After all of that preparation, I was ready to find a way to serve on the court. However, my doctor discovered that I had a growth on my esophagus which needed to be surgically removed. I reluctantly submitted to thoracic surgery after being assured that I would only be in the hospital seven to ten days. To my horror, things did not go well. My esophagus was ruptured (the mortality rate was about 75 percent) and I virtually did not wake up for about a month. Hospital confinement lasted more than six weeks, and then I was burdened with a recovery period of several months. I was on my knees physically, emotionally, and financially. Thus, while I was professionally well-prepared for judicial service, I was in no physical condition to take a seat on the court.

Nevertheless, I longed to start my judicial career, and I was anxious to be appointed or elected every time there was an opportunity. I didn't want to miss a single chance for fear that it would be my last. So I just waited for the next opportunity.

As I was recovering from my medical ordeal, a vacancy opened on the Florida Supreme Court and, because of the juncture in the incumbent's term when the vacancy occurred, it was required to be filled by appointment. I applied, and although still struggling to recover my health, I was deemed to be qualified and was certified to the governor as one of the finalists. As explained earlier, Governor Reubin Askew selected Joe Hatchett, a relatively new face on the scene, but certainly a qualified candidate. It was a great disappointment for me, but I chalked it up as one more step in the preparation for my goal.

## A Prospective Vacancy

Then, late in 1975 and much to my surprise, I received a call from Justice B. K. Roberts, who told me that he had decided to step down from the court. He said he believed in the election of judges and would time his departure so that the vacancy he would create could be filled by the voters and not by the governor. He informed me that he had called most of those who had been finalists in the appointment process and shared with them his intention to retire.

Roberts accomplished his objective of letting the people elect his replacement by stating publicly that he would not be a candidate for reelection to another term. He created a situation very much like a prospective resignation in which the holder of an elected position picks a date in the future which is after the next general election and resigns as of that date. He continues in office until the date specified, but the law creates a fictitious vacancy that can be filled by the general election.

Stated another way, an officeholder does not create a vacancy as of the date of the announcement that he will not run for a new term, so his successor cannot be appointed. However, by announcing that he will not be a candidate for reelection he triggers an opportunity for those who want to succeed him to run in the general election that occurs before his last day in office. The winner of the election then takes office on the date specified or after the last day of the term of the incumbent. For the governor to have the power to fill a vacancy by appointment, the vacancy must actually exist.

For the next few days there was nothing else on my mind. I wondered to myself if this was what I had been waiting for. On one hand, it looked that way. If there was to be a vacant seat, that meant there would be no incumbent to unseat as I had to do in my bid for the Senate. Also, I was one of the first to know about Justice Robert's plans, so if I moved soon I might limit the opposition.

However, on the other hand there were many negative factors to consider. My health was not particularly good. Could I physically tolerate a campaign? Money was another serious consideration. I was earning around $150,000 a year in the law practice. Could I reduce my needs and obligations to my children for their education so as to be able to live on the annual judicial salary of $40,000, the amount paid to each member of the Supreme Court in 1976? If not, would my modest assets be sufficient to supplement the judicial salary for enough years to keep me going until the legislature raised the salary or until I had put in enough time to make my pension adequate for the future?

I carefully considered all the personal factors and concluded that it was doable. It would mean sacrifices for the entire family, but everyone was in accord that I should go for it. There were some risks to be sure, but we were used to taking risks. My entire life was a story of risks I had taken and survived.

The weakest point in my campaign was my health. I faced that issue head on. My decision, with the blessing of my family, was to take a chance. If I had no opposition, I felt I could make it for sure. If there was opposition, I could push myself to run a respectable campaign. Most important, I convinced myself that I was feeling good. My health decision was an educated guess at best. I really wanted to join the court, and I probably fudged a bit on that issue. At any rate, I decided to make my bid for a seat on the court.

I announced my intention to run and began preparations not only for the campaign, but also for the closing of my law practice if I succeeded. Those preparations were not easy. They entailed such things as a complex agreement that my practice would be assumed by my partners on January 2, 1977, provided I won the election; but if I lost, it would remain all mine. In that event, I would not interrupt my ownership or control, and in the end I would remain the sole owner. The terms and conditions of the transfer were difficult to negotiate because of all the business and ethical considerations. It was doubly hard at a time when I was totally focused on the campaign, the result of which I knew would make the full-time practice of law difficult throughout the coming year. Either one of those tasks could take all my energy, but adding my health situation and having to conduct a statewide campaign while maintaining my responsibilities to my clients, made it, to say the least, a daunting undertaking. However, with strong support from my family, I did what was necessary and the campaign began.

This campaign for the position of justice of the Florida Supreme Court would be the seventh time I had campaigned for an elective public office, and my second statewide campaign.

As I stood at the threshold of the campaign, I mentally reviewed the other campaigns in which I had been a candidate and the many other races in which I was an active supporter of another candidate. As I scrolled through my experiences, I remembered that I had been in both partisan and nonpartisan elections.

Strangely, the nonpartisan contests were often the most difficult. That was particularly true when judges were being elected. Although I was preparing to ask the people of Florida to elect me to a judicial office, I thought then—and I still think today—that it is a mistake to elect judges. As a matter of fact, in the year I was running for a judgeship, there was a constitutional amendment on the ballot that would change the method of selecting appellate judges (Supreme Court Justices and Judges of the District Courts of Appeal) from elective to appointive. I was a supporter of the amendment, and fortunately for the integrity of the judicial system and the people of Florida, it passed.

I supported the amendment because I believed that it was best for the judicial system, best for the state, and best for the candidates. It is not a panacea for the system, but it is far better than electing judges.

I've already explained what a hardship it is to have to campaign for a judgeship. The lawyer/candidate virtually gives up his law practice if the campaign is long or contentious. He cannot practice with any degree of efficiency and campaign at the same time. Something will suffer, and it's not fair to clients that they be subordinated to the lawyer's ambition. Even if he wins, his valuable law practice is likely to be in shambles when the campaign is over. If he loses, he probably will have neither the judgeship nor the law practice. I'm sure good lawyers are turned off by the risks they must take and the loss of income while campaigning. It follows that we should expect to have a better set of judges if they are appointed instead of elected.

I suspect that the campaign itself keeps good lawyers from trying to be in the judicial system. Most folks don't like to lay their private business open to the public. I know very few people who enjoy putting themselves up as fair game for opponents to shoot at whether the shots are deserved or not.

## Campaign Temptations

The process of electing judges is tough on the candidates and may reduce the quality of the judiciary, but what about the temptations to which the candidates are subjected? For instance, a lawyer familiar with my financial situation at the time offered to underwrite my entire campaign. The campaign was having money troubles because of the lack of interest in judges as candidates and because of the limitation of a $100 maximum donation I had imposed.

I rejected the offer immediately, so I don't know exactly what he had in mind or what the quid pro quo would have been, but I was glad I wasn't so desperate to win that I was tempted to go against my better judgment. I am satisfied that other candidates would react the same way. However, I could see how a candidate under somewhat different circumstances might at least be inclined to consider the offer.

In the same campaign, a potential supporter who was also a lawyer refused to contribute anything unless I would accept a $5,000 contribution from him. And there were others who were much more subtle but just as insidious. In my view it would be better to have a permanent vacancy on the bench than to have a judge who was in any way beholden to someone who had invested large sums in his campaign.

The other reason I prefer to see judges appointed rather than elected is that, in my opinion, the campaign diminishes judicial candidates. Who wants judges who make decisions ranging from who lives and who dies to how the Florida Constitution will be interpreted to have to go hat in hand looking for money to finance their campaign? Judges should not have to "kiss the ring" of professional politicians to induce them to help. And what kind of judges can we expect from a system that potentially exposes them to the dirty tricks and mudslinging which candidates are prone to employ when they become desperate to be elected?

## A Frugal Campaign

Things were moving fast for me in the Supreme Court campaign. My first goal was to try to minimize or avoid competition. It was one thing to give up a law practice in order to take an appointed seat on the bench, but it was quite another to spend almost a year campaigning for a position that I might or might not win, and then, if I was successful, to close out my law practice or what would be left of it after the campaign.

Certainly, the hardship and risk created by the need to campaign warranted serious consideration by lawmakers and judicial scholars on the question of whether to continue using the election process as a means of selecting judges. The decision to run not only creates a severe risk for a candidate, but it makes it very difficult to chart out any meaningful plan and prepare for service on the court.

At the outset of my campaign there was no opponent, so I concentrated on organization and fundraising in the hope that a show of strength would discourage other candidates. Hindsight proves that it didn't.

At first there was just one opponent. He was Charles Holly, a former legislator who had been the Republican candidate in my ill-fated 1964 governor's race. He was a plaintiff's trial lawyer living in Naples. I knew him well and felt confident that I could beat him, but his presence in the campaign eliminated any question as to how I would spend my time between then and the November election.

At that juncture, all planning had been for a one-on-one statewide campaign that promised to be a tough, year-long fight. Later on, Judge Richard Swann from Miami, who had served on the Third District Court of Appeal, qualified and turned everything upside down. It was now a whole new contest, with the very real possibility of a runoff. Judge Swann had actual judicial experience and promised to be an aggressive campaigner.

In the early days of the race, I took a few very important steps. First, I limited campaign contributions to $100 per person. There were good reasons for that limitation. I didn't want anyone—particularly lawyers—to feel that they could buy influence with campaign contributions. I felt that large contributions were inappropriate in a judicial race. I also thought the voters would be more comfortable with me as a justice if they knew I had not taken significant campaign contributions from anyone.

Neither of my opponents set any voluntary limits or did anything like that; in fact Judge Swann started his campaign by disclosing a large, but legal, contribution. Thus, I knew from the outset that my campaign would be a frugal one and that I would be outspent. My strategy was to make campaign contributions one of the issues in the race. In keeping with my decision, I talked about my limit on contributions whenever I could.

In recognition of the ethical considerations which prevented us from saying how we would rule in major cases (such as those involving capital punishment, abortion, reapportionment, and the like), I resolved that I would not talk about such matters nor would I focus on the Democratic Party or identify myself as a Democrat since it was a nonpartisan race. However, I adopted a slogan that enabled me to convey to the voters some idea as to my positions.

## My Slogan

The slogan I selected for my judicial race, "A Justice Is the Sum of His Past," developed into the actual theme of my campaign, and I used it in as many places as I could. I spoke at luncheon clubs, rallies, debates, and anywhere else that I was able to wrangle an invitation.

First, I would remind my audience that a person running for a seat on the court would still be the same person after he was elected and had donned the judicial robe and taken his seat on the bench. The robe, I speculated, might make a judge look important and dignified, and it might well serve to keep him warm, but it couldn't make him one little bit smarter or improve his judgment. A new justice would still be the person he was before his election.

Then, to further explain the parameters within which judicial candidates must campaign, I would tell my listeners that they could not ask me or my opponents about attitudes or opinions on possible issues that would come before the court. Therefore, it was going to be difficult for voters to evaluate the candidates. However, as far as I was concerned, my record was available to them. Should they want to know what I would likely do in the future, they should look at what I had done in the past. A justice was truly the sum of his past, and what he had done prior to becoming a justice was, in all likelihood, what he would do in the future.

I further explained that if they were interested in my ability to write, they could look at what I had written for the Senate in suspension cases, as well as the *Law Review* article at the University of Florida. They could also read things I had written for trade associations and media outlets. I shared with the voters that while in the legislature, I voted on just about every issue one could imagine, and that my voting record was a public record that was available for examination.

With that approach I made them understand that I was not trying to hide behind the rule that limits what judicial candidates can do in their campaigns, and that I was actually inviting them to look at my past activities and use them as points of reference when they attempted to identify the candidate they would favor with their votes.

It was a good slogan, and my presentations about how to use the idea suggested by the slogan were well received. The editorial boards of the statewide newspapers seemed to like it too. I felt I had done a good job on that part of my campaign, so I gave myself an appropriate compliment. To quote John Crews, that outstanding orator who I thought was such an effective debater when we served together in the House, I told myself that "Even a blind hog roots up an acorn once in a while."

## A Family Affair

Another early decision that worked well in my campaign was to make it a family affair. I couldn't afford to personally pay for solicitation mail-outs, a driver, other staffers, or anything with a high price tag. It was apparent from the inception that mainly lawyers and a few knowledgeable people were really interested in the race.

Political campaigns in general had become so focused on money, and the level of pragmatism had risen so high, that contributors tended to ask, "What is it that you can do for me that warrants my substantial contribution?" Since I couldn't offer them anything, and because I had deliberately limited individual contributions, I concluded that I was not going to receive enough money to do many of those desirable campaign things like hire people to stuff

My wife, Merci, and I greet Supreme Court Justice Joe Hatchett.

envelopes, arrange meetings, and work out speaking engagements. For those reasons, I knew I'd have to look to volunteers to staff my campaign, and what better volunteers are there than one's own family?

My wife's name is Mercedes, but we call her Merci. She took an active, partnership-like role in the race. Throughout the campaign we often talked about our joint effort to secure my judgeship and, after the race was over and I took my place on the court, I presented her with a golden charm engraved, "Justice with Merci."

My daughters Debbie and Tami and sons Rick and Jim were all very active in the campaign. They gave up their own interests to help me. They not only gave their time, but also successfully recruited their friends to help. Merci did most of the recruiting herself, but the volunteers the children brought in were hard workers and very helpful. Those volunteers, under Merci's leadership, answered the phones and talked with visitors who came to the headquarters; they folded and stuffed mass mailings; they ran all the errands; they went for pizza for all the volunteers so no one would go hungry—because Merci's deadlines didn't allow time to go out to eat. They did so many of the tasks that are so tedious but also so important. If we had paid for everything they did, it would have cost us thousands of dollars.

In addition to Merci's work with the volunteers, she filed all the reports on the money that came from contributions and managed all the financial details of the campaign. Her job was a hard one as it is in any campaign because it involves some fundraising and a whole lot of checking to be sure we didn't accept any amounts over the limits I had established, and that we didn't take it from the wrong people.

The law governing campaigns is complex and voluminous, but Merci became an expert. Just so she wouldn't run out of tasks, she had her own travel schedule. She never missed an event where wives were expected to be present. She and our youngest son, Jim, would regularly travel to important receptions to set up a giant collage display that featured my campaign slogan and a picture story of my previous activities. At other times, Merci accompanied me as I attended fundraisers and spoke with well-wishers, prospective supporters, and current supporters like Bill and Grace Nelson from Brevard County.

Bill Nelson of Melbourne played an important role in my life long before he was elected to the U.S. Senate and ultimately played an even more important role on the national scene. He was—and has remained—a popular, well-respected Floridian, and his popularity in Brevard County worked in my favor during the 1976 Supreme Court race.

Happily, Nelson combined his popularity and his desire to see me seated on the court into action and announced his unconditional endorsement of my candidacy. He and his wife also hosted a delightful Sunday afternoon ice cream social in my honor and invited many of their friends and business acquaintances to attend.

The event was held on a warm summer afternoon, and it was well-attended. The physical surroundings were attractive and the hall was beautifully decorated. It certainly promised to be a pleasant occasion. Then came what my wife, Merci, considered to be a near disaster.

There she was chatting away with a group of attendees as I was escorted by another group of the Nelsons' friends to see the special cake that had been created for the event. I was impressed with the baker's design and motioned to Merci for her to come and see it. As she walked from the carpeted area where she had been standing and onto the highly polished wooden floor where the cake was displayed, she turned an ankle, fell to the floor, and came sliding toward me as she struggled to maintain a ladylike demeanor—not an easy task, but I think she was as successful as anyone could be under those circumstances. In any event, she was not seriously hurt and was a real good sport about what was one of her most embarrassing moments.

In the fashion of a real trooper, she allowed us to help her to her feet and then oohed and aahed about the cake that almost ruined her afternoon.

To this day, when we talk about the Supreme Court race, the ice cream social stands out in our memories—not only because of the near disaster, but because it is a reminder of the many special friends, like the Nelsons, who helped me realize my long-held dream of serving on the court.

Rick, my eldest son, traveled with me quite a bit. He drove the car, toted the luggage, manned the portable telephone, and looked out for me. He saw to it that I was where I needed to be at the time I was due to be there. His was not an easy assignment. Rick heard the same speeches over and over and put up with all the tension that campaigns generate. He also managed to get a good start on an article he was writing about the campaign—an article that was subsequently published under his name with the title, *The Last Elected Justice*.

There was no way I could have run my Supreme Court race without my children and without my wife, Merci and her troop of volunteers.

## The Relevance of the Press

The news media played an inordinately critical role in judicial campaigns. Without the press, voters simply did not have a satisfactory way to find out about the candidates on their own. For the most part, the electorate was not all that interested in who would be on the Supreme Court. The typical voter wasn't likely to have a case that would go to the Supreme Court and, I dare say, there weren't many who were willing to take the time to understand the jurisdiction of the four echelons of courts as they were established in the early 1970s.

Lawyers, of course, have a keen interest; particularly those who have an appellate practice and are in frequent interaction with members of the court. But all lawyers are involved when the Florida Bar conducts a survey of lawyers, asking them to rate or rank judges. When this occurs, all lawyers are invited to participate, but again, only a relative few have practices that require their appearance before the Supreme Court.

In fact, it is fair to say that most lawyers do not appear in any court representing clients in litigation. The lawyers who do not have litigation practices spend their time on real estate transactions, intellectual products, bond issues, corporate transactions, probate matters, and other non-litigious legal services, so many of them know little more than non-lawyers. And yet, the results of the polls are published for the information of the public.

Therefore, when I was a candidate I was of the opinion that the newspapers and media in general played the biggest role in the election of judges. I spent a great portion of my time preparing for and participating in interviews by newspaper editorial boards.

## An Opponent Attacks

Incidentally, one of my opponents obviously understood the importance of those newspapers, because when he set out to attack and attempt to discredit me, he took his allegations to them. Judge Swann asserted that a man named Pat Tornillo, who was executive director of the Dade County Teachers Association at that time, had filed suit against one or more newspapers, and the outcome of the litigation could possibly damage the protective structure of the First Amendment of the U.S. Constitution.

Swann implied that Pat was not in favor of the First Amendment, which would make him an undesirable and a bad influence on those with whom he associated. Then he tied me to Pat Tornillo by pointing out that Pat had supported my gubernatorial campaign and was supporting me in the Supreme Court race. Every paper gave me an opportunity to rebut his far-out notion of my unworthiness by reason of Tornillo's support of my candidacy.

I worked very hard to dispel any idea that I was in any way antagonistic toward the First Amendment. Using my slogan that a justice was the sum of his past, I cited cases I had handled, papers I had written, and my legislative record. I did everything but violate the ethics rule which forbids campaign representations or promises about something to be considered by the court.

None of the papers fell for Swann's scheme. I believed they knew me well enough to be comfortable in their belief that I wasn't an opportunist or one who wanted to score points on them. They each had my responses which cited public documents and other materials explaining my opinions and positions vis-à-vis the First Amendment.

From my experience in 1976, I can testify that those press interviews and the related inquiries they routinely conducted were as thorough and as searching as the evaluation I was subjected to by the judicial nomination committees when I applied for appointments to the bench. I have since concluded that editorial endorsements are the best protection voters have when judges are elected.

There were daily newspapers in almost every one of the sixty-seven counties during my campaign. Those without a daily edition of their own had access to one or more from nearby cities, and some had a weekly paper or two which often printed information about candidates gathered by their affiliated daily newspaper.

As a candidate, I visited every editorial board at least once and sent them material that I thought would help them make the decision as to which of us to endorse. Because of my belief in the importance of the press in the election process, informing the print media of my qualifications was a major component of my campaign effort.

In my previous campaigns, I had observed the seriousness with which the editorial board members approached this part of their work, but I was somewhat surprised at the extra effort they expended on the Supreme Court race. They quizzed me about the ethical considerations that kept judicial candidates from campaigning in the usual way. From their probing questions, I gathered that they wanted to be sure I understood that rule and would respect the prohibition against any discussion of issues that might come before the court in the future. It was as though they were the enforcement arm of the Florida Bar.

They also tested my knowledge of the constitutional provisions in Article V, the judicial article that established the four levels of courts and assigns jurisdictional limitations. They wanted to know if I understood the change in jurisdiction and the other effects of a proposal that Justice Roberts had initiated which involved the court in hundreds of cases that would otherwise be resolved at the Court of Appeal level.

The questions they asked me ranged from why I wanted to be on the court to whether I would be a conservative justice and limit my rulings to interpretations of the constitution, or be an activist justice and legislate matters expanding the power of the government.

I was asked to discuss my favorite member of the Florida Supreme Court. They asked specific questions about justices who were off the court. I believe those particular questions were for the purpose of determining how interested I was in the history of the Florida judiciary. In any event, the questions were numerous, of varying subject matter, and seemingly went on forever.

After exhausting queries regarding the state courts, they would shift to the federal court system and probe my knowledge of justices and former justices of the U.S. Supreme Court, the structure of the federal system, and the historically important cases such as *Brown v. Board of Education*, as well as the court's intervention in reapportionment and landmark cases interpreting the First Amendment.

I perceived that they were interested in the whole person who wanted to be a justice: not just the lawyer, not just the political figure, and not just the personal side of the candidate. They wanted a look at us from every angle so they could know such things as what kind of education we had acquired, whether we were empathetic, whether we were biased in our thoughts or actions, and just what kind of a human being was inside each of us.

Within the ranks of the editorial boards were some smart, thoughtful, and caring individuals who obviously wanted to change the Florida Constitution so that judges would not be selected in the election process. I believed—based upon what was said and done while I was with them in the conference rooms—that for as long as judges were elected they would screen the candidates for judicial office and report their findings to the people so a better-educated electorate could cast informed votes. That was a meaningful public service they provided.

## Professional Dilemma

The campaign lasted for almost a year, and there was generally a full schedule every day. Nevertheless, I could get into the law office once in a while to answer phone calls from clients wanting to know the status of their cases. I would remind them that I had their consent to bring another lawyer of the firm into the case and that I had done so. I would promise to make sure that the substitute lawyer called with the desired report as soon as possible. I would put that note on the list of legal matters I would talk about with my partners.

I would look over the list of calls that had been received at the office, return those I could, and delegate the others to my law partners. Although there was some time in which I could have engaged in some aspect of the practice of law, I had to face up to the realization that it was not practical for me to do much of the day-to-day work required by my clients. In the first place, I was so preoccupied with the campaign that I found it difficult—impossible, actually—to do much legal work, especially anything that required concentration and absolute focus.

The urgency of the issues and magnitude of the risks related to the campaign demanded top priority. That's the nature of political campaigns. But no client was hurt by that process. They were not always happy about having their lawyer out on the campaign trail while their matters were in the hands of a lawyer they did not retain. However, their interests were always protected by a competent attorney.

It goes without saying that I earned little revenue during that time. The arrangement among my law partners is best described in the vernacular of the business of the law firm: each lawyer "eats what he kills." That is to say, each member of the firm contributed to the overhead and could keep the net revenue he earned from legal fees. Because I was spending almost all of my productive time campaigning, I had no kills and, therefore, nothing to eat.

There was some equity in my law practice to be sure, but it was in my accounts receivable, work in progress, and escrowed fees. It was a substantial amount, and it was an asset I counted on when I decided I could run. However, I did not accurately evaluate the intensity of the campaign I would have to conduct, so I didn't take into consideration the fact that I would be living on the equity in the law practice for about a year.

Upon examination of my situation, it appeared that valuable asset would disappear before the campaign came to an end. That was a serious matter because there was no way I could meet my obligations and live on the $40,000 annual salary that was the standard pay for justices at the time. Without a doubt, if I succeeded in winning the judicial seat, there would have to be a supplement to my future income.

The other ongoing worry that was critical to my future career and the future of my family—and the one that detracted from the campaigning—was my health and the residual effects of a recent surgery that had resulted in a ruptured esophagus. I had been warned that the repaired rupture might have caused permanent damage and that the extent of that damage could not be accurately measured. The specter of that possibility, while disturbing, did not deter my eagerness to sit on the court.

I had experienced practically no health problems in the thirty years prior to 1975, so the warnings didn't mean much to me. That is, they didn't mean much until I began having problems on the campaign trail. I knew something was wrong because I had little strength, no endurance, considerable pain, and I felt rotten most of the time. As luck would have it, I was experiencing a series of internal problems that ultimately resulted in surgery in early December 1976, a month after the election. Through it all I kept going right to the end of the campaign.

Other than that brief timeout for surgery, everything else went well. The campaign developed nicely. Organizational efforts we had engaged in were well spent. There was some form of campaign organization dedicated to achieving victory in virtually every county. I was able to renew friendly relationships with many of my supporters from the governor's race. We had no money to speak of, but hard work and wonderful volunteer support put me out front, and I was looking like a winner. It looked and felt so good that my staff and family began dreaming of success without a runoff.

And then came the day for counting the votes. I was leading, but there weren't quite enough votes to win in the primary, so we were catapulted into three more weeks of campaigning. The next day we got ourselves together and hit the road again. It was a long, hard road to victory, but it was all the sweeter because it was so long and so hard.

## The Investiture

When the general election votes were counted and the campaign was officially over, I was declared the winner and I was feeling great. I was very grateful to the people who voted for me and to those who worked so hard to help me execute my "Plan A" for service on the court. I experienced exhilaration as never before.

Being the pragmatist I am, and knowing myself better than anyone else knew me, I was also full of humility. While the campaign was a wonderful experience and allowed me to finally put the loss of the governor's race in its proper place, it also taught me again about my shortcomings and weaknesses. I reviewed them regularly and it helped to keep me humble.

The next step was the investiture. I was given the privilege and responsibility of helping to plan the event. The chief justice was actually the one in charge.

Merci helps me with my robe during the investiture ceremony.

He was thoughtful and generous in granting me a measure of autonomy and control. The program we arranged was outstanding. The speakers were top leaders in the Florida Bar and in state government. Merci put the robe on me for the first time.

I was correct in what I said during the campaign: I wasn't one bit smarter with the robe than I was the day before. I was the sum of my past, nothing more. But after sitting through the ceremony in the main courtroom of the Supreme Court building for a couple of hours and hearing all the flattering things these fine leaders said about me, my feelings of pride and excitement were at a new high. That was very heady stuff.

Those feelings were short-lived. Following the election— but before I was actually a member of the court—I had been given my first assignment. I was to review the complete record of a case in which the criminal defendant had been sentenced to death. My responsibility was to be sure there were no fatal errors in any part of the trial or sentencing proceedings.

The appeal to the Supreme Court was a legal right, so we had to do more than review the briefs of the attorneys. We were obliged to read every word of the entire record and reach a conclusion as to whether the defendant received a fair trial and whether all of his rights were accorded. The record, when neatly arranged in one stack, was at least three feet high. I read most of it prior to the investiture, but I received my first indication of the urgency of those death cases when I learned that I was expected to be finished with the case and have an opinion drafted and ready for circulation to the other justices by the time I took my seat on the court. I was full of remorse and afraid I was starting off on the wrong foot.

The second jolt to my ego came with a bucket and mop that were formally presented with the explanation that as the newest member of the court and, consequently, low man in the pecking order, I had to do the things that none of the more senior justices were willing to do—like sweeping out the court-room. I knew it was just a humorous routine they went through each time a new member was seated, but there was actually a bit of realism in it. No matter how important the position of justice was or how critical the work of the court might be, there was still a ranking order, and I was ranked below everyone else.

## Settling In

I adjusted rapidly and was happy in my new life on the court. Even though I had been something of an outgoing person with many acquaintances and several friends, the cloistered life didn't bother me at all. On the days when we heard oral arguments, we saw lawyers we knew from around the state. Our schedules were laced with speaking engagements, including commencement exercises at the law schools and activities of the Florida Bar. During the annual session of the legislature, members of the Supreme Court always played a special role in the ceremonies and social events.

The work load was surprisingly heavy. I found it necessary to take files home with me and spend time on them in the evenings to keep up. There was nothing dull or routine about the work. The cases on appeal were those involving death sentences, constitutional confrontations, advisory opinions to the governor, public utility rate cases that had a statewide effect, and other major litigation issues. Article V, the judicial article of the new constitution, deliberately restricted the kind of cases we were to decide so as to allow for thoughtful consideration, plenty of research time, and the opportunity to carefully write our opinions.

Everything went along without incident and I fell into the routine with ease. But the shock came when I received my first salary check. After deductions for Social Security, income tax withholding, insurance, and all the rest, I received less than $2,000 per month. All I could think of was the story about the drunk who confronted a doctor at a cocktail party and complained about the awful things his drinking was doing to him. The doctor was patient, and intending to help, asked the man, who at the time was holding a drink in his shaking hand: "How much do you drink?" "A lot," was the quick answer. So the doctor tried again: "Would you say you drink as much as a pint a day?" Holding up his hand with the drink in it so the good doctor could see the pronounced shaking of his hand, he said, "Hell, I spill that much."

Up until that point in my life, I had been accustomed to wasting as much money as the net of my new take-home pay. Life on the court was certainly different from the life that was afforded me by the practice of law.

## My Fellow Justices

There are seven justices on the Florida Supreme Court. When I arrived, Ben Overton, who had lived in St. Petersburg and was a circuit judge before being appointed to the court, was the sitting chief justice. James Adkins, who also had experience as a circuit judge, was someone I had known for a long time. I considered him to have the best legal mind of anyone on the court.

Joe Boyd was a former county commissioner from Dade County. He never forgot about his experiences on the commission or how to act like a county

Members of the Florida Supreme Court, front row, *left to right*: Justice James Adkins, Chief Justice Ben Overton, Justice Joe Boyd. Back row, *left to right*: Justices Joseph Hatchett, Arthur England, Alan Sundberg, and myself.

commissioner. He worked every group and shook every hand like a professional. He was very good at such things. Boyd was one of the justices investigated by the House Committee on Impeachment in 1975, and in my role as counsel to the committee I had interviewed the person who was alleged to have drafted an opinion for Boyd. I knew a different version of the facts of that incident than was accepted by the committee after I left to have the surgery that resulted in my long period of disability. I have to admit that thoughts of the investigation and the outcome of the procedure somewhat poisoned my mind and were ever present as I worked with Joe.

Alan Sundberg, a legal scholar, was a bit younger than most of us. He genuinely loved the law and was content to spend his time among the books in the library. Privately, his claim to fame was his capacity to drink martinis. He could hold more of them than anyone I had ever known, and I had known some real martini drinkers.

Arthur England was also there when I arrived. I envied Arthur because of his brain. He was at least a cut above the rest of us. His experience included working with legislative committees on problems in the state tax laws. He was considered to be an expert on state taxation.

The other member of the court at that time was Joe Hatchett, the person

Governor Reubin Askew had appointed to fill the vacancy I applied for in 1975. He was a fine justice and a fine human being. I respected him.

We all worked well together, each in our own way. There was no way to standardize the procedure because we dealt with an intellectual product. The case conferences were worth the price of admission. Discussions held in closed meetings are always interesting, but discussions among seven people who meet once a week to try to bring cases to a close and settle on an opinion for each one is a major challenge. We knew each other so well that we could anticipate the position each would take.

## Cases We Considered

Every case we considered was an interesting and important part of Florida jurisprudence. Our opinions decided the outcome of the particular case before us, but they also established the law of the state and served as precedent for future cases.

## Death Sentence

To illustrate, we should consider the Spenkelink case. John Spenkelink had murdered a man in a Tallahassee motel room. The two of them were ne'er-do-wells, and each had a criminal record. Their argument got out of hand and led to a violent end. No other lives were threatened nor was there any torture or deliberate, prolonged pain involved in the homicide. Spenkelink was arrested, there was a trial, a conviction, and a sentence of death.

The appeal to the Supreme Court is automatic and a right guaranteed by the Florida Constitution to every person sentenced to death. It is designed as a safeguard that prevents an execution until it can be determined that all of the defendant's rights have been accorded, including a fair trial. In addition to the appeal, the defendant can petition the court for relief on grounds not settled in the appeal.

During the review stage of Spenkelink's case another capital case surfaced and made its way to the U.S. Supreme Court. That court handed down an important opinion: the death penalty could not be used except in those cases in which the capital crime was more offensive than the typical cases. Thereafter the trial court would have to make a finding that the crime was committed under circumstances that endangered others (as in firing into a crowd) or that the murder was more violent or heinous than the usual crime of its type.

Most of the activity in Spenkelink's case preceded my election to the court, but after the U.S. Supreme Court spoke, Spenkelink returned to the Florida Supreme Court in 1977 and asked that his case be reviewed again in light of the new national precedent. He asserted, through his lawyers, that his crime could not be punished by death because it did not meet the test imposed by the U.S. Supreme Court. He had a valid point. Had he committed his crime the day he was in our court in 1977, he could not have been sentenced to death. How then could he be executed just because his timing was bad?

We thoughtfully considered his arguments and we did our own research. Finally, we held that the law existing at the time of the commission of the crime was the law that would be applied and, therefore, his sentence of death could be carried out. It was a very difficult decision for me. I knew that any other ruling would prevent the state from executing anyone because the law is a live entity and is constantly evolving. If every defendant could take advantage of every change that occurred in the law after their crimes were committed there would be no end to any case and the law of capital punishment would be ineffective. We did not want to legislate through our opinions, so we reached our conclusion and did the best we could to put aside our sympathy.

The day Spenkelink was put to death was a bad day for me. He had a low regard for capital punishment. It was reported that his last words were: "Capital punishment—them without capital get the punishment."

### Workers' Compensation

Workers' Compensation, another interesting part of Florida jurisprudence, was established by the legislature in 1935. In the ensuing years that law had been the subject of extensive litigation that refined both the form and substance of the complex system. There is general agreement that it is a workable, beneficial system that ought to be protected and kept current. Because of its importance, the law is a condition precedent to doing business in Florida. That is to say, a person cannot operate a business in this state unless he or she has this form of insurance protection for employees. Under such circumstances, it is not surprising that the law produced many cases for the justices to decide. The cases came to us after they had been heard by a judge of Workers' Compensation (an administrative judge with training and experience in this field) and after having been considered by an appellate authority. The system was created as an administrative process rather than an adversarial proceeding to be resolved in court. Nevertheless, in the final analysis the courts decide the ultimate, important, and fundamental issues.

One critical requirement was that for an injury or disease to be compensable under the Workers' Compensation law, it had to arise out of and in the course of employment. That part of the law was always under attack as workers had accidents or illnesses that didn't quite fit the language. For example, I once had a case in which two workers were sent from their hometown to Fort Pierce to work on a project. One evening they had a few drinks and drove into town at high speed. Their car went out of control and both were injured. They claimed that they were on duty twenty-four hours a day while in Fort Pierce and that whatever they did was in the course of their employment.

I successfully defended the case on the point that the injuries did not grow out of their employment. They had been drinking, which was a violation of the rules of their employer, and they were drinking and driving, which was a violation of state law. Therefore, they could not be compensated as though it was all in the course of their employment.

An important Workers' Compensation case decided by the court involved Tom O'Malley, the Insurance Commissioner of Florida. He suffered a heart attack and claimed it was compensable because there was tension in his job and because the heart attack occurred while he was traveling on official business. It was at the Atlanta airport, where he had to change planes with a connection so tight that he was forced to run to make the connecting flight. According to O'Malley, that tension and physical exertion caused his heart problem. Other cases had rejected the compensability of heart attacks because they usually grew out of circumstances unrelated to employment. However, O'Malley made a good case and was held to have a compensable injury.

Predictably, the skeptics asserted that the commissioner's status had some influence with the court and that if a regular employee had made such a claim, the typical rejection would have been forthcoming. I doubt there was any validity in the assertion, but after all, justices are mere human beings and each is the sum of his past. Anyway, the O'Malley case brought other heart cases to the court, and the law on that point was gradually refined and considerably narrowed.

## Cameras in the Courtroom

When I joined the court cameras were allowed in the circuit courts where trials were held, but not in the Florida Supreme Court where the most important cases were heard. There was a discernable mood in the state at that time which favored openness, and that had resulted in the passage of the "Government in the Sunshine" laws. We expected someone to fashion a lawsuit to put in issue whether there could be cameras in the Supreme Court, and sure enough it happened. The case was well prepared by supporters of the First Amendment to the U.S. Constitution. Their thesis was that the people of the state were entitled to some idea of how the justices handled the cases before them and arrived at their conclusions. The advocates admitted that the U.S. Supreme Court did not allow cameras in its courtroom. They argued that we could open our courtroom if we were willing to do so even though the U.S. Supreme Court didn't change its position. The oral argument was unusually informative, well planned, and professionally presented. Sandy D'Alemberte (who was later dean of the law school at FSU and eventually president of Florida State University) was active in the suit and oral argument. As anyone who knew him would expect, he did a wonderful job.

When members of the court met to discuss the case, there was a substantial difference of opinion. A concern was expressed that the cameras would cause the participants—including the justices—to "perform" and thereby waste the court's time. There was also the notion that the camera operators could distort the proceedings by focusing on one or two parties and leaving the rest out of the filming. All agreed that the cameras could change court decorum, and that they probably would do so. However, no agreement emerged as to whether the changes would be helpful or hurtful to the litigants who were, after all, the ones with the most at stake in the proceedings. Many were concerned that distractions and disturbances might also be caused by the cameras.

After thorough consideration an opinion was to be drawn for our discussions. In due time, the opinion was circulated to all of the justices. It went as far as the majority of the court was willing to go at that time. There were conditions, safeguards, and limitations. Subject to them, the court would allow cameras, but only in the main courtroom. None would be permitted in the conference rooms where the justices debated the cases and shaped the opinions. I dissented to the opinion and wrote that I not only favored opening the court to cameras, but felt that the mandated restrictions and limitations were excessive. I wanted to really open the process and believed that transparency would make the court more accessible to the people and increase its credibility with them.

Parenthetically, the system worked very well. The FSU Law School established a program to monitor, record, and broadcast oral arguments. Members of the public at first demonstrated an interest in what was being done, but then lost interest in all but the dramatic headliner cases. Students and legal scholars maintained an interest and found ways to benefit from the open proceedings.

While I was sitting on the Supreme Court we decided many death sentence cases, important utility rate cases, constitutional issues such as the time for appointment of members to a Constitutional Revision Commission, the enforceability of statutes, and a plethora of other types of cases. We also started the procedure to update and revise the rules for disciplining lawyers. As a matter of fact, I was named chairman of a committee of outstanding lawyers from around the state. The committee's charter required an in-depth review of the procedures that were creating an impression of a "Country Club Syndrome" in which misconduct was ignored or taken lightly because friends were exclusively in control of the entire disciplinary apparatus. The report and recommendations of the committee were approved, and in keeping therewith, history was made when non-lawyers were inserted into the process.

## Internal Issues

Each of us had a strong will, so there was no domination or bullying. There could be minor displays of temper and often tension in the air, but I judged the conduct to be gentlemanly and proper.

There came a time when Justice Arthur England and I had a fundamental disagreement on one procedural matter. Simply stated, I contended that the purpose of oral arguments was to give lawyers an opportunity to make their most important points and briefly explain why they ought to win on them. I argued that we should not interrupt them unless they strayed or seemed not to know what to do. That's what I was taught as to oral arguments as early as law school.

Each member of the court had his own position on the issue. Frequently, in informal discussions, we would talk about our respective opinions and argue the pros and cons. It was on this basis that I concluded I was in the minority. However, I maintained that I was right and would raise the issue from time to time.

Arthur, on the other hand, believed and argued that the sole purpose of oral arguments was to give the justices an opportunity to ask questions of the attorneys and make them defend the positions taken in their briefs. Thus, every week, right after the first lawyer introduced himself, Arthur would start with the questions. If the case was interesting or complicated, the questioning could take up all the allotted time. The other justices, regardless of their point of view, would follow Arthur's lead so they could be seen as involved in and knowledgeable about the issues, but often it was hard for any of us to get a question in edgewise.

It bothered me that the attorneys had to prepare their arguments as though there would be no interruptions, and then never had an opportunity to use them on behalf of their clients. The issue was never put to rest and may still be alive and well with the current court.

## Money and Health Issues

As the end of my first year on the Supreme Court approached, things were getting desperate in my personal life. There were the continuing health problems that had caused me such grief in the campaign and thereafter. They were not totally debilitating, but they were heavy baggage and affected almost everything I did.

However, the biggest problem was financial. That was no surprise. I knew the salary when I agreed to run, but it was so low considering the importance of the office and the changing economic environment that consequently I had the reasonable expectation that the legislature would adjust it by the time I took my seat. They did not do that, of course, nor did they adjust it during my first year on the court. The economy was in a slump; the value of my stock was down; and there was no market for a block of shares we owned in a bank. That situation only exacerbated the problems resulting from the prolonged campaign that used up my equity in the law practice and my meager reserves.

Seeing what was developing, we put our home up for sale. There were no buyers. Everything we had so carefully planned to make it possible for me to take a seat on the court did not work out.

After confiding the problem to one of my colleagues, he volunteered that his father would finance me until the market changed. I was touched and grateful; however, I couldn't ethically give up even a tiny bit of freedom to debate him on cases when we disagreed. Similarly, after the announcement that I would be leaving the court, a group offered to buy my home so I would have access to the substantial equity. I couldn't do that either.

I knew that one of the other justices had worked out an arrangement with a bank to gather up his debts and finance them at a low interest rate and no principal payments in order to buy time for the legislature to adjust the compensation, or for the market to get better. I had the same option, but I just couldn't take it. I couldn't live with the possibility that someone might think my decisions could be influenced because of the proffered help with my finances.

I resigned in 1978. To say I was disappointed would be putting it mildly. Words cannot explain how I felt.

What began as one of the happiest and most exciting periods of my life ended in unspeakable pain. This photo was taken the day I resigned from the Supreme Court.

# PART 4

## *The Operators*

## 15 *Speakers and Speeches* ——————

The legislature is a debating institution. Every member is a public speaker to some degree. In any given group of House or Senate members, there will likely be a few who are woefully inexperienced, notwithstanding that they have been through some kind of political campaign. There will also be a person or two blessed with some formal lessons in elocution that, when combined with the experience gained on the campaign trail, make him very comfortable and persuasive before a microphone. In any event, campaigning for public office is a good way for those who aspire to serve in the House or Senate to learn about speechmaking.

It naturally follows that all who become legislators become speakers. Speaking is what they do, and they do it and do it and do it. In fact, the excessive speaking prompted an old saying popular in those days: "In the legislature when all is said and done, there is a lot more said than done." On every occasion, whether a distinguished person visits, someone dies, or a hero emerges, a round of speeches is delivered.

Remember the Christmas story in which a child wanted to honor the baby Jesus, but didn't know what to do? The child was poor, so gifts were not a possibility. He was not an important person in government, so what he would say in a speech would have little credibility. The one thing he could do well was play his little drum, and that's exactly what he did. He played his drum to honor the holy infant. So it is with legislators: they speak.

A typical committee meeting where legislators discuss various bills. The meetings could become contentious, especially meetings of conference committees.

## Mean-Spirited Hecklers

Most audiences at political rallies (or "speakings" as they were often called at the time of the 57 Club) were polite and tolerant, but now and then a mean-spirited person would show up to heckle. Even that was a good experience for an aspiring politician because it helped prepare the candidate for the "no holds barred" debates that occasionally developed in the legislature.

At the end of my first term I had no opposition for reelection, but I regularly attended rallies in the rural areas so I could keep in touch with my constituents. On one such occasion, upon being called on, I climbed up on the back of a flatbed truck that was being used as a stage and prepared to make a well-practiced speech.

I was quite comfortable because my mother had given me lessons in elocution and dramatic art when I was a child and, of course, I had been through a tough campaign and had served two years in the House. So I took the microphone and with my best smile I said, "First I would like to thank you for not giving me an opponent." Just then, an old man who was sitting on the grass in front of me stood up and shouted at me, "We'll damn sure get you an opponent next time!"

I responded, politely, "That's fine, I'll welcome the competition." He didn't hesitate a moment and once again shouted as loudly as possible, "And we'll beat the hell out of you!"

## Civic Club Embarrassment

During a different campaign, I prepared to speak to a civic club in New Smyrna Beach, a city in the southern part of my House district. The person who invited me did not suggest a format for my speech nor otherwise limit my options. I made what I thought was a fine report on my legislative record and concluded with a promise to be grateful if those listening would vote for me in the coming election.

To my surprise, a member of the club stood and moved that the club turn in its charter and cease to exist because I had campaigned for public office at a regular meeting, something that was prohibited by their charter. His remarks were followed by a prolonged silence during which I wished I could disappear. I don't know if there was ever a decision made regarding the club member's motion, because the president adjourned the meeting and I meekly picked up my belongings and went home.

## The Oak Hill "Nonspeech"

Another incident occurred in my first campaign when I was soliciting votes in Oak Hill, also a community in the south end of my district. I had not done well there in the first primary, but I managed to enter the runoff without their support. So I was pleased to receive a call from a leader in that area inviting me to visit with him.

He asked me how many votes I had received in that precinct, and I replied, "I think I got three or four." He said, "Just for the record, you weren't supposed to get any. Some folks made a mistake. But, if you want our votes in the runoff, you can have them."

I assured him that I wanted every vote possible and then asked what I would have to do to get them. I had in mind speeches or meetings, but he told me with confidence that all I had to do was promise to give them a hearing on any major issue that affected their main business and speak with three local men.

"After you do that," he said, "you should stay out of here and spend your time speaking where the outcome may not be so secure." I said no more, nor did I make a single speech in Oak Hill, but I did receive almost all the votes cast on election day.

### Rescue Earns a Vote

And finally, there was a very short speech made on my behalf that was unusually effective. It was the result of a fishing trip with two friends in an inlet where currents were strong and boating was dangerous. As we were enjoying ourselves and thinking only about the fish, we saw a boat capsize and its two occupants go into the deep, swift water.

We moved quickly and carefully to get near them, take them aboard, and tie their boat to ours so we could tow it to safety. With heartfelt gratitude they asked what they could do for us. One of my friends spoke up with the best speech of the campaign. He said, "Vote for Fred Karl." They did far more than just cast votes. They worked hard in support of my campaign, and the simple comment from my fishing buddy was a good speech.

### Introductions

Outside of the legislature, most speakers are introduced before delivering a scheduled speech. The introduction is actually a speech in and of itself. It sets the tone, and in doing so the introducer can possibly poison the listening environment and ruin the whole event. On the other hand, a skillful introducer can serve as a "warmer upper" who makes the listeners hungry to receive the coming message.

All too often, the person making the introduction is ill prepared and either shoots from the hip in a flawed, extemporaneous presentation or reads some prepared biographical statement that turns out to be rich in facts but poor in delivery and often boring to the captive audience.

Throughout my public career I have been introduced countless times, and I have had opportunities to introduce others just about as often. The best advice I received with respect to introductions came from my senior law partner, Paul Raymond, a true scholar and great public speaker who had observed some of the best and some of the worst introductions. He passed on these rules:

1. Tell the audience something interesting about the speaker.
2. Be brief.
3. Emulate the advice given to young doctors: First, do no harm.
4. Never try to upstage the speaker.
5. Humor is a good thing, but only if it is done in good taste and in keeping with the other rules.

6. Prepare for the introduction as thoroughly as you would prepare your speech if you were the speaker.
7. Never read a canned introduction. If possible, memorize your remarks.

Once during my legislative career I was speaking at the University of Florida to a large gathering of students and faculty members. The president of the University introduced me, and in keeping with the seventh rule, he memorized all the facts he intended to use. Without notes or any other form of assistance, he went to the microphone, told a humorous anecdote about me, recited a few significant, relevant biographical facts, and brought me to the lectern for my speech. Those who came to hear me were in a relaxed and receptive mood and I was pumped up, too. I was pleased and flattered that he had taken the time to prepare so thoroughly, and the enthusiastic feedback I received from the guests was a pleasant stimulus. I made a great speech that day.

I am not certain where or from whom I first heard the introduction that came to be the one that I used more than any other over the years. I am certain that I did not originate it. I borrowed it from someone else, but I honestly admit that I wish I had thought of it.

I used it whenever I was introducing someone who was already known to the audience, as when the mayor was speaking to the Rotary Club. I would vary the introduction to harmonize with the occasion. For instance, I would say: "You can tell something about the importance of the speaker by the length of the introduction. When introducing our country's president, the introducer simply says, 'Ladies and Gentlemen, the President of the United States,' but when introducing someone else, as the importance of the person diminishes the introduction grows in length."

### An Error in Judgment

It doesn't pay to be too busy when there is an introduction to be made. Introductions are important, and I've always treated them as such. However, I overlooked this long-held belief during a conference at which I was obligated to introduce several speakers. The meeting had a long agenda, and I was really busy. For one of the introductions, I used a copy that someone else had composed in which Christopher Columbus was mentioned. For some reason or other, the script said that Columbus sailed from Portugal.

In my rush to commit the whole thing to memory, I didn't think about the accuracy and just accepted it as written. I knew better, but I let the error slip in accidentally and then recited the incorrect information in my introduction of the speaker. As soon as it came out, I realized what had happened, but I did nothing except call up the speaker and get off of the stage with the hope that nobody was paying attention. It didn't work. In the audience were people from the actual Spanish port from which Columbus had sailed and, following the conference, they wrote a very unflattering letter pointing out my error and suggesting that I needed a history lesson.

## A Strange Speech

Like me, a few of the 57 Club members completed their service in the House and eventually campaigned for, and were elected to, the state Senate. It was during our time there that we heard a strange speech eloquently delivered by Senator Wig Barrow of Crestview. Wig was unique. He had a good mind which manifested itself in many ways. He could tell stories or jokes like no one else. He also had a marvelous vocabulary—one that put him in a class of legislative speakers with Representative John Crews, Senator Mallory Horne, and a small group of others whose way with words gave them an edge in debate.

Wig was a lawyer, and I'll bet he was known for his courtroom capability in and around north Florida. He was also an outstanding fisherman, an attribute that kept him close to the well-known Senate leader, Dempsey Barron, and in touch with other senators with whom he had little in common, like Verle Pope, the Lion of St. Johns County.

When a debate started in the Senate, Wig could not restrain himself. He had to participate. He spoke extemporaneously, and observers never knew which side he would take. It was often said that he could make a great argument on either side of almost any issue, and that sometimes he spoke for both sides. When making a point about ethics or morality he regularly cited the "Yellow River Code." I gathered that Floridians living in the vicinity of the Yellow River in north Florida had a strict code of conduct that made them stand out from the crowd. Whether the rumor was true or not, Wig relied upon that code. He would speak of it with reverence and as though we all knew the details of its terms.

On the day in question, Wig had made a splash in the morning papers with a story about how he was arrested for playing poker for money, a violation of state law at the time. When the Senate convened for the morning session,

Senator Barrow was recognized by the president of the Senate to speak on a point of personal privilege.

With a flourish of humility and contrition, both seemingly sincere, he recounted the events of the late-night gambling adventure held in a place with overnight accommodations. At least there was a bed nearby, which became a point of interest. The game was raided by Tallahassee policemen, and Wig admitted openly that they had found him hiding under the bed. He spoke seriously, but the other senators could not hold back the smiles and smirks.

After the background explanation, he apologized profusely for embarrassing the Senate and concluded by saying, "When you are a senator, and decide to play poker, it is not whether you win or lose, but where you play the game."

## Lessons in Legislative Relationships

Ralph Turlington of Gainesville, Alachua County, and 57 Clubber Bob Mann of Tampa, Hillsborough County, should be rated higher than most with re-

Ralph Turlington and I were political friends, but that didn't prevent him from submarining one of my legislative bills.

spect to speaking ability and skill in debate. That, in my view, is a big compliment to both men. Both were smart, well educated, bold, and courageous. I respected them, and we had friendly relationships. One might even say we were friends, if it is understood that there were different degrees of friendship. Less was expected in the way of loyalty from those who were not close friends but maintained something like an arms-length friendship.

Stated another way, neither was a friend in the category of Bob Lee, my company commander in Europe during WWII, or Lester Force, my friend since kindergarten. Those friendships were tested many times and always found to be chock full of loyalty. The friendships with Bob and Ralph did not require them to give me any special treatment in the legislature, and neither did I owe them such consideration.

They had something other than credentials in common as well: each one gave me a lesson in legislative relationships. As I said, I didn't expect perfection in either of them, so I didn't feel betrayed when they challenged me.

Ralph was an agent for State Farm Insurance Company, and his main legislative goal was support of the University of Florida, including its proper funding and freedom from oppressive legislative interference. Like Bob Mann, he was an articulate debater who enjoyed emasculating someone's bill when the sponsor wasn't expecting an attack. My lesson from Ralph came first. At the request of a lawyer, I had introduced a bill that undid some aspect of tort reform but, unbeknownst to me, was unacceptable to Ralph. I had carefully worked it through the committee system and had succeeded in getting it on the House calendar for final consideration and passage.

I thought it was non-controversial and was already thinking ahead to what I could do to induce the governor to sign the bill into law. When the speaker asked if there were any amendments, I started to stand up and respond, but at that moment the clerk announced, "There is an amendment on the desk by Mr. Turlington."

The clerk was then ordered to read Ralph's amendment. I was taken by surprise and first assumed that it would be some friendly correction of a typo. But no, it was an unfriendly amendment that proposed to strike a paragraph that was the heart and soul of my bill and replace it with Turlington's words. He had drafted an amendment which enabled him to employ humor as his weapon.

The amendment made no sense at all. Ralph had taken a whole litany of terms that lawyers use and written them into a paragraph that did not contain one complete sentence. He wrote things like: "the party of the first part had joint and several punitive damages and writs of habeas corpus."

He had used anything that sounded technically correct, but the dense legalese actually formed a bunch of incoherent phrases. The members had a good laugh and, while still laughing, voted for the damnable amendment and destroyed my bill as I stood there dumbfounded.

That was a great lesson for me, and I learned to expect such treatment from certain legislative friends and to take nothing for granted. However, I did let my guard down once more, and Bob Mann killed another bill of mine. In retrospect, I have to admit that he was right on that particular issue. I never should have introduced and agreed to manage such a piece of legislation. Here's what happened:

Just around the corner from my law office in Daytona Beach was a respectable Mom and Pop liquor store that had been there for years. The owners were clients of our firm and had supported me with enthusiasm when I campaigned for my House office.

Along the way, they made me understand that big companies were establishing cut-rate liquor stores throughout the state and thereby destroying the small, privately owned stores, just as the supermarkets had done to the corner grocery stores. I could feel their pain and I sensed the fear they were experiencing as their main asset and sole source of income was being ruined right before their eyes. I expressed sympathy, assumed that my voiced concern had sufficiently validated their situation, and thought I had fulfilled my political obligation as their representative. That was wishful thinking on my part.

When I arrived in Tallahassee, one of the first to corner me was a lobbyist representing a statewide association of Mom and Pop liquor stores that were similar in size to the store owned by my friends. The lobbyist from this association produced a little bill and told me it needed a sponsor—and I was just the one to handle it. Moreover, he assured me, it would be non-controversial—sure it would.

I felt the need to further demonstrate my sympathy for my hometown constituents, so I rationalized my thinking. I did not like the notion of trying to limit or control advertisements—which this alleged non-controversial bill did—but liquor was already tightly regulated by the state. In fact, as mentioned previously, counties were permitted to outlaw liquor completely. So, I asked myself, how bad was it to have some limitation on advertising? There was also the convincing argument that curtailing advertising would constitute some kind of deterrent to youthful and new drinkers, so it was arguably a bill in the realm of public health.

Filled with these good intentions, I got the bill on the calendar and up for debate without serious incident. But Bob Mann was waiting to pull the trigger. He made a marvelous speech about our First Amendment rights and about how we should be fighting to protect them instead of trying to limit them.

Still, at that point I wasn't really worried about my bill. Bob sounded like a liberal and I just knew the small county guys wouldn't go for that stuff. Then came the sockdolager—the last and best statement.

Bob concluded with a political warning that went something like this: "This bill is for the small retail sellers of liquor. Remember when you vote on this bill that there are a whole lot more people who buy and drink that stuff than sell it."

I guess there was a whole lot of truth in his persuasive comment because my bill went down in flames.

## Bob Mann

Bob Mann was an outstanding advocate, and probably the brightest and best-educated member of the 57 Club. However, he was not an easy person to like because of his somewhat abrasive personality and his seeming preoccupation with his own thoughts and ideas. Oddly, his presence in the legislature tended to improve the image of that body.

Bob's legislative style was interesting to watch. He seldom managed a piece of legislation alone. It was a rare occasion to find his name first as the lead introducer of a bill. Yet he was always prepared to attack a proposal he didn't like. He seemed always to be on the move, striding around the chamber and stopping now and then to visit with another House member. It would be a mistake to label him a gadfly, and yet his restlessness and defensive approach argued for such a classification. Whatever he was, he was effective.

Bob and I got along well enough. There were differences in our personalities and I always felt a bit overwhelmed by the various college degrees he had earned (and proudly displayed), but we seemed to share the same general principles and ethical standards. In the end, we basically respected the expertise of one another, and that was enough to build a lasting legislative friendship.

Neither Bob nor I qualified as one of the "good old boys." We were seldom invited to the events sponsored by the most powerful lobbyists. And yet we both had many friends among the small county representatives. As a matter of fact, when E.C. Rowell, a notorious small county leader, became speaker, he appointed Bob chairman of the Education Committee and subsequently supported me in my campaign for a Senate seat.

Bob and I were both fairly effective in passing or stopping legislation. We learned that we could oppose the House leadership on issues and, so long as we fought them on the issues alone, we could remain on friendly terms and maintain their respect.

As we grew older and the days of the 57 Club drifted further and further into the past, we seldom met. Once in a while we would both be at a Rotary Club meeting or a library dedication, but we had little contact beyond those casual encounters. The last time I saw him was at the ceremony held in my honor by the County Commission of Hillsborough County during which the county's administration building was named the Frederick B. Karl County Center. I was surprised to see him in attendance because we were never really close personal friends. Moreover, he was in severe pain from arthritis, but had willingly tolerated his discomfort to congratulate me and wish me well. He died shortly thereafter and before I had an opportunity to reciprocate or tell him how much I appreciated serving with him over all those years.

In spite of our sometimes adversarial relationship, I had supported Bob when he ran for speaker, and he had gone all out for me when I ran my premature race for governor. Bob Mann was defeated when he ran for speaker, but served as a judge on the Second District Court of Appeal. He later served as a member of the Public Service Commission and ended his career as a professor in the law school at the University of Florida, where he taught my son constitutional law.

## A Man of Few Words

It is worth noting that my bill was not the only one that was murdered by a House member with a short, direct political warning. In a subsequent session, those of us advocating better financing for the public schools supported a one-cent tax on each bottle of soda. Cokes and the like sold for five cents at the time, so what we were asking for was a 20 percent tax. Even so, we thought we had it going our way. Then Homer T. Putnal was recognized to speak.

Homer T. was in the House for one or more sessions before 1957. He was from Mayo in Lafayette County. (The county's name, by the way, is pronounced La-FAY-ette.) Anyhow, Homer T. was a portly man who seldom spoke to the members of the House, so his desire to speak was reason for all to pay attention.

His remarks were short and to the point. He said, "All you who vote for this bill ain't comin' back here 'ceptin on a visit."

The bill died.

Homer T. Putnal: His speech was short but effective. (Photo courtesy Florida Archives.)

### Welcoming a Distinguished Visitor

There was an inexperienced representative from one of north Florida's sparsely populated counties who had a distinguished visitor, and he wanted to honor the visitor by having him escorted to the House rostrum to address the entire body. The privilege of speaking from the rostrum was reserved for truly distinguished people.

It was a big deal for that representative and he was very nervous, but determined to gain recognition not only for his guest but also for himself. So, with his outstanding guest beside him, he managed to be recognized by the speaker and he said: "Mr. Speaker, members of the House, it is my privilege to have this distinguished person as my personal guest. Therefore, I move that a committee be appointed to escort my guest to the restroom."

We laughed, of course, but understood that it was nervousness that caused the embarrassing error. The speaker, proceeding as though the motion had been properly made, appointed a committee to escort the visitor to the rostrum to make his remarks.

### Sound Arguments

Then there was a speech on the floor of the House that was delivered by use of a sign that the member from Hardee County held up to do the talking for him. It was quite appropriate when the debate was heated. The sign said: "Your argument is sound, all SOUND."

Another "sound" argument was accomplished with the use of a bugle. Everyone who watched the legislature in the mid '50s will remember the representative from Escambia County who had a bugle and knew a few calls. He would actually stand up and blow his horn in the chambers when he wanted attention.

## Lobbyists as Speakers

Many of the lobbyists were also talented speakers, and nearly all of them were good storytellers. I once attended a fundraising meeting conducted by one of Florida's all-time best lobbyists. He stirred his audience and motivated them to make generous contributions to the candidate he was supporting. Then he ended his presentation by reminding them that their active participation was essential to victory.

He said he was reminded of a speech that George Washington made on the banks of the Delaware River that cold night during the American Revolution. Washington told his soldiers that he knew the surest way to win the war. "All you have to do," he said, "is get in the boat!"

## A Lobbyist as Examiner

Another lobbyist who represented truckers told me about his experience examining the ability of truckers to react quickly. He told me that they checked periodically to be certain the drivers could think fast and respond logically. The examination they used was given orally, and an oral response was required immediately following the question that was posed.

The problem the lobbyist described was a typical one, and he told me how one prospective driver responded. Here's the way he told it:

The driver being examined was young and well trained. He sat quietly, listening intently. He was told to mentally place himself in the cab of his eighteen-wheel truck and trailer and imagine that he was on a mountain road, at night, with his truck fully loaded. His schedule was tight, so he was pushing as hard as possible to be on time. He went over a hill, and as he started down the other side he tried his brakes and found that they were not working. He had no braking power at all.

A quick look at the road told him that it was a two-lane mountain road with a long stretch going downhill. On his left was the hill with a natural wall close to the edge of the road, while on his right side there was a 200-foot drop to a field of rocks. Neither side offered him a way off of the road. As his truck was gaining speed, he was told to imagine that he could see a truck just like his coming up the hill toward him. And, at that moment, a second truck of the same size started to pass the first truck, so that both lanes of the road had oncoming trucks approaching him.

"Quick!" The examiner yelled at the man being examined, "Tell us what you are going to do!" Without hesitation the driver loudly declared: "I would wake up Barney."

The examiners were taken aback and said, "Who in the Hell is Barney, and why would you wake him up?" The driver explained, "Barney is my assistant driver, and he sleeps while I drive. I would wake him up because he ain't never seen a really big truck wreck."

## A Unique Orator

Welborn Daniel and I were about the same age, and we had a good many things in common, including our membership in the 57 Club. We were veterans, lawyers, politically ambitious, and we had each won a seat in the House on our first try. His county was in central Florida, about thirty miles inland from the east coast. Citrus groves and other agriculture activities were the principal economic factors in that part of the state.

Welborn was one of those young men who were deceptively smart. That is to say, he did not flaunt his intelligence and at times seemed to be hiding the fact that he was smart. But time after time, when there was a special need for above-average intelligence, he would answer the call and fulfill the need. Moreover, he had a great wit and a wonderful sense of humor.

Once during a special session with a limited agenda, he observed that there were hardly any lobbyists around to take the representatives out to dinner. Welborn suggested a game of "Who Ain't Here?"

The way the game is played, he explained, is for a group of legislators to look around to see which lobbyists are present and "who ain't here." Then the legislators introduce bills that would be hurtful to the clients of the absentees. It never failed to bring the lobbyists back to town.

And who could ever forget Welborn's casual remark to a group of legislative colleagues who were fascinated with the question of why a certain member took his wife to every single function, no matter what time of day or night it was held. That was unusual in any situation, but this member's wife was, unfortunately, regarded as the world's ugliest woman, which only deepened the mystery.

Not so for Welborn. He knew the answer and told us forthrightly: "She's so ugly," he said, "that our fellow legislator had to take her with him, because he couldn't stand to kiss her goodbye."

As a member of the House, Welborn quickly built a reputation as a fierce advocate and an equally fierce defender of his ideas and decisions. Those attributes were most evident in committee meetings, particularly conference committees. Presiding officers understood how resolute he could be, and they regularly appointed him to conference committees where representatives from both the House and the Senate were tasked to reconcile differences with respect to the same bill. Welborn was sent in to strengthen the position of the House.

In his debates, he would occasionally use humor; sometimes a well-prepared statement; and at other times he would apply political pressure as only he could. But in my view, his most effective technique was his grunt. When one of the opposing conferees would become passionate in his argument regarding an important point, Welborn would hear him out without reaction, except for an audible grunt followed by an awkward and prolonged silence.

His derogatory response was unnerving and, to some people, offensive. But whatever the adversary's reaction, Welborn's grunt was effective because there was nothing left to argue about. The adversary who was trying to make a point or elicit some helpful answer might as well talk to the wall.

When Welborn and I served on a conference committee to revise the judicial article of the new constitution during our Senate days, his grunt was at its best. Dempsey Barron was the designated leader of the Senate delegation and had very fixed ideas as to the end product he wanted. Welborn and I had a difference of opinion with Dempsey on one point that was important to the people of one of the counties we represented. We had mustered the vote to have our way on that point, and Dempsey set out to reverse the decision. All I had to do was defer to Welborn and watch him perform with his grunt. It was so effective that Dempsey could not win.

After Welborn and I left the House there was legislative turmoil over reapportionment as the courts attempted to institute the notion of one-man/one-vote, an expression that suggests equality in legislative power. A part of the judicial solution was a two-senator district—which was the district I represented—containing five counties: Volusia, Lake, Sumter, Citrus, and Hernando. In an off-year election, Republicans won both of those seats. Then in

1968, Welborn and I took on the two incumbent senators. Both of us won, but it was not easy.

We each endorsed the other and pooled our strengths. I helped him in Volusia County, which had about half the votes in the five-county district. He helped me in the rural areas of the other four counties. It was a good and successful effort, but he was never able to persuade the powerful Willis McCall, sheriff of Lake County, to support me.

The story of Sheriff McCall and his tenure in law enforcement is not so much an anecdote as a historical event. However, for this purpose let it suffice to say that he was powerful, genuinely feared, and seemed to detest LeRoy Collins, the former governor. I was never able to talk to McCall during the Senate campaign, and the only reason I was given for his unfriendly conduct was that I was a friend of Governor Collins.

In spite of Sheriff McCall's disagreeable attitude, the rest of the campaign went very well. In Citrus County, for example, there was a parade in honor of Welborn and me. The public high school band was there, and we rode on the top of a publicly owned fire engine.

An even greater mystery than how our supporters worked that out was how the local radio station was able to spend the whole day promoting the parade and rally and then do a play-by-play broadcast of our events without offering equal time to our opponents. At the county fairgrounds where the event climaxed, we were each given ample speaking time to let everyone know what we stood for and what we proposed to do if elected. There were about 2,000 votes in Citrus County, and we received around 60 percent of them.

In Sumter County, we both had the support of Representative E. C. Rowell, which was important to our victory in that part of our respective districts.

As previously mentioned, we each won a seat in the Senate and served four years together. I did not seek reelection, but Welborn did, and he won another term. Thereafter, he became a circuit judge and I, as a justice of the Supreme Court, had the pleasure and honor of administering his oath of office.

Ultimately, Welborn was seated on the Fifth District Court of Appeal, where he served with distinction for many years.

After a lifetime of public service, Welborn Daniel retired from the court. However, he did not just sit on his porch and watch the world go by. He became a mediator and continued to use his unique talents to solve problems. It is not always easy for a judge who has been successful as an adjudicator to change his approach to problem-solving and be satisfied to facilitate a process in which the adversarial parties craft their own settlement agreements.

Welborn, however, made the transition without difficulty. The very attributes that served him so well as a young man in the legislature made possible his success in the closing days of his very full political career.

## Speeches Tailored to Their Purposes

Every speaker must be able to tailor his/her speech to the purpose for which it is to be given. The best way for me to illustrate that rule is to cite examples of two situations which required totally different preparation techniques. On the one hand, a speech made in the legislature concerning a bill that provokes questions and requires extensive preparation—such as the bill to institute no-fault automobile insurance laws—is quite different from a speech made in opposition to a bill or resolution. Here is an example of each one.

## No-Fault Debate

In the session of 1971, I was chairman of the Senate Commerce Committee. Dempsey Barron and Welborn Daniel, both 57 Club members, were also senators at that time. Automobile insurance was a hot issue. Premiums were going up because some companies were reducing the number of policies they would write, thereby filling the residual insurance pool. There were the usual allegations of discrimination and red lining (refusing to insure residents of a geographic area or members of a particular class or classification, such as age or race).

When any regulated industry gets into that sort of controversy, an effort is made to correct the situation by tampering with the laws that govern it. Quite often a major overhaul of the key statutes governing the industry is undertaken on the notion that it is easier to birth a new statute than it is to clean up the one already on the books. That was exactly what happened when we needed to adapt our car insurance laws to the changing times and new insurance environment.

All of that developed in the period leading up to the decision to enact a no-fault automobile insurance law in Florida. The insurance environment during those days was terrible. Instead of tampering with the laws and putting bandages on them, it was decided by the principals that legislators should cast out the old system, take a new approach, and enact a no-fault law. The proposed legislation was filed in both houses and sent to my Senate committee. I planned to handle it in the committee and then take the issue to the floor and advocate its passage. The House version was sent to a committee chaired by William Gillespie of Volusia County, but Kenneth (Buddy) MacKay was the chief advocate because he was recognized as something of a specialist in the field of insurance. Buddy was appointed to handle it on the floor of the House.

MacKay and I set up an informal communication arrangement that involved some personal communication as well as technical coordination using staff people. I had a fine staff, but they had little in the way of insurance credentials. So I secured permission to hire an outstanding person well-known for his insurance expertise to work with my committee. His name was Harry Landrum, and he was good. I put him in charge of the no-fault bill and promised to stay close to him as we moved it through the Senate.

The bill was controversial. The main opponent was the personal injury lawyers association. We also had to contend with the Florida Bar, a powerful lobbying force that loaned its name and resources to the plaintiffs' trial bar. The lawyers in the Senate were pretty well divided along the lines of their private practices. That is, if a lawyer's practice was on the defense side of the automobile controversies, you could reasonably expect him to be supportive of a bill like the one that was contemplated. But, if he concentrated on the plaintiffs' side of cases in his office, he would likely be part of the opposition.

The swing votes appeared to be coming from the non-lawyers in the Senate and lawyers who practiced in other fields such as family law, real estate law, and probate. It was very hard to count the votes in advance. We, the proponents of the bill, thought we had enough for passage, but there was no way to be certain.

The Senate and the House each passed a bill. As usual, they were similar but not exactly alike. A conference committee was established and the differences in the two bills were reconciled. Again, as usual, there were more compromises, side deals, and a few wins and losses. The product of the conference committee was a complex and controversial bill.

The debate began with an explanation of the proposal. I had unanimous consent to have Harry Landrum on the Senate floor next to me so I could confer with him if need be. Basically, we proposed that every driver be covered by his own insurance so that in the event of an accident he/she did not have to prove that someone else's negligence was the cause of bodily injury or property damage. In return, the driver received a sort of immunity from being sued. The title, "no-fault," obviously meant no one had to prove fault. It seemed simple enough, but in fact raised many questions .

The law required the purchase of the prescribed insurance, but what about those who did not comply? What about non-residents of Florida? There were thousands of people driving in the state that were not bound by our law because they resided in Georgia, Alabama, Tennessee, or some other state. Would they have immunity from lawsuits when they were not in compliance with our law?

There were also questions about passengers who were injured. Were they covered by this new law even if they were non-residents? Were they to be treated differently if they owned their own cars that were insured in Florida? How would the law be applied if the driver of an insured car was guilty of gross negligence? What were the consequences if an owner allowed someone else to drive the car? What if the car was a rental vehicle? Were private passenger vehicles treated the same as commercial vehicles such as trucks?

The list of questions was infinite. Because of that, most of the debate consisted of questions, with the advocates of change answering them, rather than the customary debate with each side making speeches.

I was on my feet virtually the entire time the Senate considered that bill, which was just about seven hours. If I was not at the microphone, I was going to individual senators to lobby them while someone else answered a few questions. Then at the appropriate time we had a test vote on a motion to return the bill to the conference committee with instructions to change it. We knew that if that motion passed, it was all over. We held our breath waiting for the decision of the Senate. The motion failed by one vote. Thereafter, a motion was made to place the bill on third reading and consider it for final passage. Lo and behold, it passed.

## Resolution Opposition

In contrast to the question-and-answer format of the no-fault debate, we once actively debated the merits of a resolution through a series of speeches. This debate concerned a Senate resolution asking the president of the United States to pardon a young military man by the name of Lt. William Calley, who had been found guilty of ordering the My Lai Massacre in which hundreds of civilians—including children—were killed during the Vietnam War.

Several members of the 57 Club were senators at that time, but the speech to be considered was mine. As I understood it, Calley's defense at his trial was that he was ordered to massacre the Vietnamese villagers, and because he was so young, scared, and combat weary he just followed the orders. He was convicted, of course, and pending his sentencing someone thought that he should be pardoned because of his age and the conditions existing in Vietnam at that time.

The term used to describe the process the Senate was following was called "memorializing." In that effort, a resolution is drawn reciting the facts and concludes with the specific message or request. In this case, it was asking the president to exercise his constitutional power and pardon Calley.

When the resolution was ready, it was scheduled for debate in the full Senate. I had been pondering it since I first learned that such a resolution was being crafted. With some hesitation I decided that I would oppose it when it came up for the vote. I knew that some of the leaders were in favor and I knew that the proponents had lobbied the senators by asking them to support it. I would be virtually alone in my opposition. It was not a very pleasant position in which to find myself, but if one believes he is right, no amount of unpleasantness or pressure should deter him.

Prior to my taking the floor, it had been said that there were patriotic, humane, and sympathetic reasons to vote for the proposed resolution. The proponents had certainly done a persuasive job of convincing those present that this was the right action to take. There was no doubt that it was going to pass, and forevermore the Florida Senate would be on record favoring the pardon—if it was given—and our resolution could possibly be what would eventually tip the scales in Calley's favor. I could not, in good conscience, consider his actions a meaningless act. So, I stood and sought recognition for the purpose of opposing the resolution.

My speech was fairly short. I reviewed the facts as I understood them and tried to present them in a manner that neither evoked sympathy for Calley nor outraged the more sensitive listeners. And then I concluded with a personal story of World War II.

My story began in the Ardennes Mountains in Belgium, in early January 1945, shortly after the tide had turned in the Battle of the Bulge. My division had been the ground force that cut off the point of the bulge, and our next assignment was to move to the east and start a drive in the southerly direction toward Bastogne, which was under siege.

We would be fighting on a parallel course with other Allied forces to destroy those who had been the aggressors in that battle. Enemy troops were everywhere. Some even had American uniforms and a few had captured American tanks, so it was difficult to recognize the enemy. Also, the Germans were determined to hold the ground they had taken when they overran our troops. The fighting was fierce.

I was sick, as were some of my fellow soldiers, from some spoiled food we had eaten. I was cold. The temperature was so low and the tanks got so cold at night that we had trouble starting them in the morning. Since oil thickens in the cold, the engines could not turn over. However, when we finally got them going, we began the attack. We were led by Captain Bob Lee, who was fearless and a superior leader. Typically he did not say, "Go get 'em." Rather, his favorite command was, "Follow me." He would be the first on the objective. He was a very good friend of mine.

As we moved forward, Capitan Lee was to the right of me, and as he was going by an old house someone fired a bazooka round at his tank and hit it where the gas tank was located. The explosion blew a small hole in the tank and it set fire to his gasoline and ammunition. The resulting fire was so hot and spread so rapidly that the tank virtually exploded in flames. No one had time to get out, and all five occupants—including Bob Lee—died right before our eyes. They didn't have a chance.

The sight and smell of that tank and the crew burning, when added to my physical and emotional conditions that were already in the pits, almost drove me over the edge. I was so sick, so weary, so scared, and so angry that I was a menace on the battlefield.

I looked over near Lee's tank and saw an American infantry squad with three enemy soldiers they had captured. I left my tank and walked over to them and, pointing to Lee's smoldering tank, I asked, "Which one of you bastards did that?" One of the soldiers acted as though he understood my English, and he smirked. I drew my .45 automatic pistol from my shoulder holster and pointed it at his head. At that time, I believed he was the one who had hit Lee's tank, and I intended to take the top of his head off.

No one made a move to stop me, and my rage was still in full bloom, but somehow at the last moment, and just before the point of no return, I realized that what I was about to do was to commit murder. I returned the pistol to my holster and went back to my tank to try to control my anger and find the strength to go on with the mission in spite of the loss.

When I finished telling my story in the Senate I concluded by saying, "I was a young officer like Calley. I was at least as cold and scared as Lt. Calley, and I certainly had enough motivation, but I didn't pull that trigger. Calley pulled his trigger. In my book he is not a hero. He is a murderer. I cannot vote for the resolution."

A motion was made to return the resolution to committee and, to my surprise, it passed. The resolution went away and never surfaced again.

# 16 *Lobbying and Lobbyists* •————————————

There were many types of lobbyists in the late '50s. The popular negative image of patently corrupt, cigar-smoking roughnecks assembled in a smoke-filled room planning to bribe a public official does not apply to most of the lobbyists I knew. Oh, a few were thought to be something like that negative stereotype, but only a few.

However, the popular perception was that the halls were full of unscrupulous lobbyists, so a tendency developed to paint all who lobbied with the same brush. That was not fair. Most did all of their work with public officials on a high level of integrity. Some were skilled public speakers who made their cases to committees; others concentrated on one-on-one meetings; quite a few entertained; and a few used questionable tactics to gain the confidence of their targets. However it was done, it was a tough job.

Lobbying wasn't a job for anyone with a lack of energy, because it was pretty much an around-the-clock activity when the legislature was in session. Nor was it a job for a person who was sensitive, because, I am sorry to report, too many legislators could be demanding, rude, and overbearing. Unfortunately, some people elected to serve in the House or Senate promptly let the experience go to their heads. The things that I have heard a few of them say, and the conduct that I occasionally witnessed, was embarrassing. I sometimes wondered how a lobbyist could continue in that profession. It was not my kind of thing.

Fortunately, the few times that I was required to register as a lobbyist I never had any of those negative experiences. In my work with Hillsborough County, Tampa General Hospital, the Florida Bar, and to some extent while I represented insurance interests in my law practice, I helped my clients with strategy and committee appearances. In other words, I limited my lobbying efforts to non-social settings and never engaged in high-pressure arm twisting. In almost every instance, I had a professional lobbyist working with me to do the heavy lifting. Consequently, my relationship with legislators was very different from those of lobbyists who used entertainment and other similar methods to induce favorable consideration by senators and House members.

Today, lobbying is a more sophisticated profession than it once was. A good lobbyist today will do his or her preparations as carefully as a good lawyer works up an important case for trial, or the way a good surgeon readies for a major operation. It was different in 1957, with less sophistication and fewer rules to play by, but changes were coming, albeit very slowly.

Without a doubt, it may be asserted that the best and most successful lobbyists of that era studied all of those to be lobbied very thoroughly and knew what it would take to induce each one to vote for or against any given proposal. It is also fair to say that most of the entertainment activities sponsored by lobbyists were on a fairly high moral scale. However, if one believes rumors and secondhand testimony, a fair amount of the other kind of lobbying took place as well.

### John Germany

Probably the best example of a good lobbyist from the days of the 57 Club was John Germany. John was a veteran of World War II, having fought in Europe in General Patton's Third Army. He completed his formal education by earning a law degree at Harvard Law School. Governor LeRoy Collins met John in Tampa during the successful 1954 campaign to unseat Acting Governor Charley Johns. Collins found John to be a man of competence and high principles. Not surprisingly, the two of them hit it off at once.

The governor induced John to arrange a leave of absence from the law firm where he was practicing. John agreed, and soon after he went to Tallahassee to help Collins organize the Governor's Office and assist him with his legislative program. Technically speaking, those duties made him a lobbyist. Needless to say, he was not a smoke-filled room sort of lobbyist. He lobbied by talking to legislators one-on-one and by appearing on behalf of the governor at committee meetings.

Once in a while, for John's convenience, the governor would invite a few legislators to lunch at the Governor's Mansion, but there were none of the traditional entertainment-style dinners usually held at one of the favorite restaurants such as the Silver Slipper or Joe's. Certainly, there were no yachts, hospitality suites, or trips to championship sports events where legislators were guests of honor. John Germany's type of lobbying depended on the merits of his argument and thorough preparation designed to convince legislators to vote a certain way. His kind of lobbying effort was helpful in 1957, and I would wager that it still is helpful and effective today.

John Germany took a leave of absence from his law firm to help Governor Collins.

John helped Governor Collins with his legislative program and then returned to Tampa, where he served as a circuit judge, civic leader, and partner in the prestigious law firm of Holland and Knight. The public library in downtown Tampa was appropriately named the John Germany Library in recognition of his meaningful public service.

### Howard Friedman

Another example of a lobbyist who did not fit the shady stereotype was a man named Howard Friedman. He did for the Department of Education what John Germany did for the governor. When I chaired the Education Committee of the House, Howard was wonderful. He knew the existing law, and he studied and researched all serious proposals to change any part of the law. He also knew all key legislators, and he understood the system and how it worked.

Howard had no entertainment budget, so he hosted no parties or special events. However, he could be found any weekday evening at the Silver Slipper Restaurant that was so popular with legislators. He was usually with his wife, and they sat at the same table every night. I can honestly say that I never saw him pick up a check for anyone's dinner, including his own. I never figured out how his bill was paid, who might be paying for his meals, or even why he was so persistent about being at the same place night after night.

I came to know Howard very well, and when I ran for governor he took a leave from the Department of Education and gave his full time and attention to my campaign.

## Harry Landrum

Among the best commercial lobbyists was Harry Landrum. He was prepared for his career by education, self study, and extensive experience. He was easy to like, warm and friendly, and, of course, trustworthy. To my knowledge, he was never known to lie or mislead anyone with whom he was doing business.

I first met Harry when he was employed by the Insurance Department and had worked his way up to the position of deputy, or chief assistant. The year was 1957, and the entire insurance code was being reviewed and updated. The bill—with all its revisions—was referred to the House Committee on Insurance and also had to go through the Appropriations Committee before being considered by the entire House of Representatives. As luck would have it, I had been appointed to the Appropriations Committee and the Subcommittee on Insurance and, until my exposure to that bill, I had no clue as to how complex the insurance code really was. Although new to the process, I did understand that Harry was managing the entire effort.

The insurance code was a part of the Florida Statutes. It provided that the executive branch of state government, by and through the Department of Insurance, would regulate all insurance companies, agents, claims adjusters, and department executives. There were sections on surety bonds, substantive issues, and a lengthy section defining unfair insurance practices and how violators would be punished.

One had to read the early sections on regulatory power and the later sections on solvency and ratemaking to understand how premiums were to be calculated and approved. For a layperson like me, it was a mass of confusion. But not for Harry Landrum. He understood how the code worked and the purpose of every nuance.

I had no role to play regarding the code as it went through the Insurance Committee. However, when that committee completed its work and the issue moved to the Insurance Subcommittee of the Appropriations Committee, I was asked to handle the bill. My mission was to move it through the subcommittee intact, with no amendments attached. That was an unusual request for a freshman, but I was too proud to admit that I didn't know enough to do a good job. However, I was not too proud to ask Harry Landrum to help me prepare for the enormous task that had been assigned to me.

Harry stepped up and devoted his life, for the next several days, to preparing me for my debut. I learned more about the regulation of the insurance industry than anyone needs to know, and when the legislative "Day of Judgment" arrived, I was ready—and excited about being in the limelight for the first time. I had visions of emerging as something of a hero. But, to my chagrin, it didn't happen that way. As it turned out, Harry was the only hero.

The chairman of the Appropriations Committee knew Harry Landrum, and he matched my degree of confidence in Harry's knowledge and integrity. When the time came for the consideration of the revised code, he turned to Harry Landrum and said, in effect, "Are there any appropriations implications in this bill?" Harry answered with his usual candor that there were a few, and he proceeded to briefly explain them. Most of the committee members knew Landrum, so no one offered challenges or asked significant questions. The ordeal was over, and the bill was approved without an amendment.

Being a freshman, I was tempted to volunteer additional information so that the subcommittee would be a little better informed and my colleagues would know how much preparation had gone into my non-presentation. But to my credit, I held my tongue. If I had spoken, the final vote might have been quite different. The wisdom I demonstrated at the end of the meeting I had learned early on in my legal career. Very wise lawyers taught me to fold up my books and notes and leave the hearing room just as soon as the judge announced his favorable ruling on my motions before him. It was said that if the winning attorney lingered for small talk, there was always a chance that the ruling might be changed, but if the victor left, the argument was over.

I never continued arguing or tried to enhance my position after a favorable ruling, and I always left without delay. It proved to be a sound policy that day when the approval of the subcommittee was so critical.

Harry and I learned in that exercise that we could work well together. As circumstances developed, it was a blessing for both of us that such was the case. Harry's boss, the Florida Insurance Commissioner—an elected officer at the time—was defeated at the polls in the next election. Harry, being a straight arrow, couldn't work for the man who beat him, so he resigned. He had no other job waiting for him, and as a state employee he had no sizeable cash reserve. He needed a job. To my knowledge, he had several good overtures, but he was skeptical of them and concerned that they might try to improperly use his experience with the Insurance Commissioner.

At that juncture, I was in the Senate and had been appointed chairman of the Senate Commerce Committee, which was responsible for examining all insurance legislation and making recommendations to the full Senate regarding such. Harry agreed to be a special staff advisor to my committee and the rest, as they say, is history. We handled a load of bills on Workers' Compensation, recommended and steered to passage the state's first health maintenance organization (HMO) regulatory law, and were responsible for all aspects of the Senate's actions in successfully passing the automobile no-fault law. Then Harry became a full-time lobbyist.

## Rumors

One of the strongest rumors tied to lobbyists and some not-so-ethical activity concerned a group known as the Cuban Navy. A small group of lobbyists, so the story goes, sponsored a hospitality suite at the old Floridan Hotel on Monroe Street, near Tennessee Street. What distinguished it from other, classier hospitality rooms were the young, attractive women who served the visitors while wearing nothing but underwear. It was said—fairly or unfairly—that the young ladies were from Cuba and were willing participants in almost any activity suggested by visiting legislators.

Another rumor concerned an ongoing party at a place known as the Trailers. It was located somewhere west of Tallahassee in a sparsely populated area. Models of mobile homes were on the site. Delicious steaks were cooked to

It was rumored that parties hosted by the Cuban Navy were held on the top floor of the Floridan Hotel on Monroe Street, shown on the left of this photo.

order over red hot coals every evening, and there were free drinks and other tasty goodies dispensed by a set of attractive servers.

Stories of the exciting parties at those venues will have to remain in rumor status all these many years later, because I was never invited, nor did I ever go to either place, and those who told me about them passed away without authorizing me to use names.

Parties of what could be considered a more acceptable kind were scattered throughout the session, along with a wide variety of receptions, buffet dinner events, and daily hospitality get-togethers wherever lobbyists lived. However, by far the most popular form of evening entertainment was dinner at one of Tallahassee's restaurants. Legislators never seemed to get tired of good steaks.

## Borrowed Bourbon

With further reference to lobbyists, an example of how they were always nearby occurred on that enjoyable fishing trip, mentioned earlier, at Nutall Rise. As Representative George Anderson, his invited friends and I fished, we grew tired of beer and agreed that a bottle of bourbon would have to be secured. George remembered that a well-known lobbyist had a lodge nearby and used it to entertain legislators, principally senators. George volunteered to go there and see if the man would lend him a bottle of the required nectar. I did not know the lobbyist, nor did I know of the lodge, but I offered to go with George and he accepted.

George knew exactly where the lodge was located, so I assumed he had been there before. Whether by luck or hidden skill, our boat missed the dangerous rocks partially hidden beneath the water and we arrived safely at our destination. The lodge was rustic but decorated in good taste. We were greeted warmly by the lobbyist, given a quick tour, and told that he would "lend" George the bourbon. I was out the front door when I realized that the man had held George back to talk with him.

I stopped to wait and I believe I heard George being asked if he needed cash. In any event, the conversation seemed to be along the line that it was a financial hardship to serve in the legislature and that the lobbyist didn't like seeing young legislators worried about grocery money. I lingered just long enough to hear George, to his everlasting credit, decline the offer. We returned with the bourbon and resumed our party. Neither of us ever mentioned the incident at the lodge.

## Mandatory Sunday Work

Contrary to common belief, lobbyists are very important to the legislative process. In fact, without them there would be many more mistakes than are normally made during legislative sessions. Oftentimes, seemingly innocent bills can have unexpected, serious, and far-reaching effects on other areas of interest. One personal example comes to mind.

Early in my service in the House, a person came to me with a reasonable question. He asked, "Do you believe that supermarkets ought to be able to require, as a condition of employment, young mothers to work on Sundays and holidays?" He then proceeded to explain how grocery chains made young women work behind the cash registers, standing for hours even if they were pregnant.

I allowed as how I thought that was unreasonable, and he produced a proposed bill that would stop it. "Sign here," he said. I did, and by doing so became a co-introducer of the bill. The next morning a lobbyist for one of the public utilities was at my desk on the floor of the House asking me to have lunch with him. I agreed. It was a good lunch and a pleasant break from the hectic pace of life as a legislator.

After our enjoyable meal, the lobbyist asked if I realized that the bill I had signed the day before applied to his company. I replied that I hadn't thought about it one way or another. He explained how his company and others in the telephone, gas, and electric businesses were required, by statute, to be open and serve the public on Sundays and holidays.

If my bill should pass, he said, there would be no way to get people to work during those times, so the companies couldn't function and would be in violation of the existing law. I withdrew my name as a co-introducer. The bill did not pass.

## Dead in the Senate

On another day, a man I had met and liked approached my desk just before the House was called to order. He gave me a lesson in a lobbyist's control and confidence. He told me of a bill which was on our agenda that day that would hurt his business if it passed and became law. I readied myself to say no to him because I knew his business was a dog track, and I assumed he was there to ask for my help in killing a bill that he thought was offensive.

I must have given my intentions away with something I said or with my expression or some other manifestation of negativity because he surprised me by saying that he didn't stop by for the purpose of soliciting my help. He just came to my desk to say hello, he said. But, as long as we were talking about the bill, he told me not to worry about it. I should vote any way I wanted. He said that he didn't care what the House did because he had commitments in the Senate to kill it. He appeared to be very sure that he had enough votes to do the job. Sure enough, the bill died in a Senate committee just as he said it would. That's the sort of situation a legislator remembers, and I carefully tucked that knowledge away for another time. Someday he might be opposing one of my bills, and I would know what to expect—and what I would have to do to save it.

As he walked away, the only thing I could think about was something my father told me years before. He said, "If you discover someone is a S.O.B., don't do anything about it. Don't even be disillusioned or disappointed. But do remember the incident, because one day you may need a S.O.B. and you'll know just where to find one."

### A Friend of Lobbyists

It should come as no surprise that certain legislators were very close to one or more lobbyists. A member of the 57 Club who had a tight relationship with many of the most entrenched lobbyists—and eventually became one himself—was E. C. Rowell. His home was in Sumter County, a small county about fifty miles north of Tampa. As an indication of how small Sumter was at the time, less than 1,500 people voted in the 1956 election.

Wildwood was the most prominent town in the county because it had a railway facility and was located at the intersection of US 301 and State Road 44. There was a huge farmers market in Webster, another community a few miles from Wildwood.

I knew E.C. from our meeting at the caucus in St. Augustine in the summer of 1956 until his death. He was a prominent member of the House and at one time served as its speaker. Following his legislative service, he was a lobbyist for truckers and was regularly in the state Capitol.

I never learned whether E.C. was his name or the initials of his first and middle names. Recently, I read his biography, *E.C.: Mr. Speaker, E. C. Rowell*, written by Ormond Powers. In that biography, E.C. is quoted as saying, "That's all the name I've got. It doesn't stand for anything." As far as I'm concerned, he wanted to be called E.C., and that was that.

In the early days of our acquaintance, we learned that we had something in

E. C. Rowell and I seldom agreed on issues, but when we did it was a powerful combination. (Photo courtesy Florida Archives.)

common. Before World War II, when I was in high school in Daytona Beach and delivering newspapers to customers along and near Main Street, I frequently stopped by a small but popular drive-in restaurant for an early morning snack after delivering my newspapers. The restaurant was called the Red Pig. It was next door to an Amoco service station operated by Bill France, later of NASCAR fame. It seems that at the same time, E.C. was an all-night, short-order cook in that very same drive-in restaurant and was on duty at the times I regularly stopped there.

I often stopped at the Red Pig early in the morning before going to school, but neither of us recalled meeting the other. It just gave us something to talk about as we learned how very little else we had in common.

Early in the '57 session, the speaker appointed E.C. to chair a committee to see that portraits or pictures of all past speakers were displayed on the walls of the House chambers. He was given a respectable budget and he worked hard on his assignment. It was my observation that he worked hard at whatever he agreed to do, whether he was hanging pictures or presiding over the House as speaker.

E.C. was an active participant in the Small County Bloc. In the first place, his county was small in population, so he had a commonality of interests with others who represented counties of similar size. But more than that, E.C. was personally in harmony with those who found it advantageous to exercise a degree of control over the House and have influence with the members. He was a farmer who raised cattle as well as crops. He was also in the small loan business. Both of those ventures relied on the legislature for their financial well being.

And, speaking of the small loan business, I was quite impressed with their lobbyists. They were well organized and participated in all the forms of lobbying with which I was familiar. Successful lobbyists studied each lawmaker and knew exactly what made them tick. They got the information they needed from various places and, in some cases, tested legislators as I was tested in 1956. As noted earlier, just after I had won the Democratic primary, a person offered me a retainer just to be available. I would also be paid for any work I did for them. Under the circumstances it appeared that they were making the offer because I was a legislator. I saw that arrangement as creating a legislative conflict of interest and declined the offer.

### Help from an Unlikely Source

Without a doubt, E. C. Rowell left his mark on the state, just as many others did. Through a strange set of circumstances, my casual acquaintance with him led to a deeper and more complex relationship when I was a candidate for a Senate seat in a district comprised of five counties, including Sumter County. Indeed, in a way, he even left something of a mark on me.

In 1968 I decided to try to unseat an incumbent Republican—a strong, brilliant lawyer who played the role of the "good old boy" very well. My opponent would probably have been able to carry the four small counties if E.C. had supported him, but E.C. didn't.

One morning early in my campaign I received a call from E.C. asking me if I would like his help. First, I asked what I would have to do to get it. When he assured me that there were no strings attached, I said, "Hell yes!"

His conversation with me that day and his subsequent actions say a lot about him. E.C. was brief and to the point. He explained that just so there would be no misunderstanding between us, he would not be helping me because he liked me, for we had never become friends. Nor would it be because he liked my voting record, because it was quite different from his own. The way he put it was: "I can't stand that guy you're running against." I understood and had similar feelings. We symbolically shook hands over the phone, and thereafter my race took a turn for the better.

History tells us that I won the Senate race and served for four years. E.C. lobbied for the truckers for many years, in fact, until he died.

## Associated Industries of Florida

No discussion of lobbying and lobbyists in Florida would be complete without including a bit about Associated Industries of Florida and the people who represented that organization in the capital city. The Association was in Tallahassee when the members of the 57 Club arrived, and it was there when we left. In fact, it is still there and remains a dominant part of the governmental scene. For as long as I have known about the organization, it has had a lot to say about everything that goes on in the legislature.

I never really knew what the terms of membership were. In the beginning I only knew that some of the largest and most influential businesses in my area were members. Over time I learned about other significant businesses around the state that belonged, and I developed a deep respect for the organization. It was the voice of business and was dominated by the most successful and reputable businesses in the state. It was obvious that the members paid sizeable dues, because officials of the organization traveled first class wherever they went. That is to say, every element of the organization from lobbying staff to legislative services was first class.

I had very little contact with their people in my early years. I didn't bother them, and they had no reason to court me. However, one of our law firm's good clients was an active member of Associated Industries of Florida, and before each session he would talk to me about the program Associated Industries was going to advocate. He did it correctly. He was not demanding or threatening. It was a high level and professional discussion. Their program always seemed reasonable in those early days, so there was very little friction. Once, however, I wouldn't vote the way they asked, and someone in the organization called our client. The client, in turn, called me, and after I explained my position and complained about the unfairness involved in the call to him, he did not pursue it further. No one in the group ever reported me again as far as I know.

## Jon Shebel

In 1974, Jon Shebel took over Associated Industries as its president and managed all its programs, focusing primarily on Workers' Compensation disputes. Of course, Workers' Comp reform was just one subject in Jon's stable of responsibilities, but it was an important one. The Florida Statutes include an entire chapter on this subject.

Every business is required to carry this kind of insurance for the protection of its workers. In 1935, when Workers' Comp was introduced in this country, it was the device that allowed legislators to severely limit the rights of workers to sue their employers for damages resulting from on-the-job injuries.

Workers' Comp laws are designed to ensure that employees who are injured or disabled on the job are provided with fixed monetary awards, eliminating the need for litigation. These laws also provide benefits for dependents of those workers who are killed because of work-related accidents or illnesses. Some laws also protect employers and fellow workers by limiting the amount an injured employee can recover from an employer and by eliminating the liability of coworkers in most accidents.

State Workers' Compensation statutes establish this framework for most employment. Federal statutes are limited to federal employees or those workers employed in some significant aspect of interstate commerce.

It was, in my opinion, a very progressive and badly needed program. Because Workers' Comp is expensive, mandatory, and important to all involved, it is an issue in nearly every session of the legislature. Parenthetically, Creston Nelson-Morrill has authored a comprehensive review of this interesting and controversial subject. The name of the book is *Workers' Compensation in Florida, 1935–1995*. It is a readable account of the issues and many of the players. I predict that it will become a most valuable research tool and an authority on Workers' Compensation.

Incidentally, Creston Nelson-Morrill features Jon Shebel in her book and writes about his fearsome demeanor, summing up all that is said about him by picturing him with a caption that labels him "The Enforcer."

Workers' Comp is featured here because, from the time of the birth of the 57 Club to the present, it has occupied the attention and used the energy of some of the best lobbyists. One of them was Jon Shebel.

Shebel was not your typical lobbyist. He did many of the same things as other lobbyists, but performed better than most. He was also a cut above most lobbyists in terms of success.

He was, by his own description, a very private person. He was not a glad-handing, back-slapping kind of person as so many lobbyists are, but rather was quite serious and always seemingly preoccupied with his business mission. That is not to say that he avoided public appearances, for he did not. He regularly attended legislative committees. Sometimes he did not speak—his 6-foot-6 stature and his military bearing making clear that there was no nonsense about what was going on. Other times he did speak, and he was articulate and forceful. He was an outstanding lobbyist who made a record of successes that is the envy of most lobbyists.

I only had limited contact with Jon during my legislative days, but I watched him as much as possible. He was the kind of person I learned from, and he was known to be such a strategist that every time he showed up for one of my meetings, I became wary and tried to figure out what he was planning.

Shebel did not seem to care much for lawyers generally. But he saved his strongest feelings for lawyers whose practices included litigation involving insurance. There were lawyers who represented the plaintiffs—those who are damaged in an accident or some other incident. There were also lawyers who represented defendants, or people who were alleged to be at fault in accidents. And, of course, there were lawyers who represented the insurance companies, and they were on all sides of insurance-related controversies.

Jon had little use for any of them. That, I understand, was in spite of the fact that he had a year or more of legal education. For those reasons, Dempsey Barron—a lawyer whose firm specialized in representing insurance companies and was the chairman of the 57 Club—was not one of his favorites. Furthermore, I feel certain that Jacksonville attorney Jack Mathews, another Club member, fell into the same category as Barron. But strangely, it was my observation that Welborn Daniel, a lawyer who also arrived on the Tallahassee scene in 1957, got along very well with Shebel. But then again, Welborn wasn't a typical kind of insurance lawyer.

After the adjournment of the 1979 legislative session, in which many of us were involved because of drastic changes in the Workers' Compensation law, there was an article in the Florida Bar's newspaper about the revised brand of compensation that went under the name of "Wage Loss." The newspaper headlined its story "Wage Loss: Is There Anything Left For the Practitioners?" Shebel surely must have enjoyed that moment.

### Mary Ann Stiles

In the course of my regular legislative work, I had limited contact with Mary Ann Stiles, a lawyer and lobbyist. The principal reason was that she wasn't really a part of the legislative scene until she finished her work in higher education and took a position with a committee when Terrell Sessums was speaker. That was well after I had finished in the Senate and had gone back to my law firm.

During that time I moved my family to Tallahassee and opened a branch of the law firm there. Concurrently, I served on various boards and as counsel to the House Impeachment Committee. I was privileged to be Florida's first public counsel. Because of those assignments, coupled with the fact that a few of my good clients had business with the state, I spent a good bit of time in the Capitol. That was how I came to know Mary Ann Stiles.

There weren't many female lobbyists when she started that part of her career, so I guess she felt the oppressive hand of prejudice. However, one would never know it from watching her at work. She never allowed such things to get in her way. She always seemed to be up, and was forever confident and optimistic. She believed that she could take on the best lawyers, lobbyists, or legislators and beat them at any time in any game. As I began to know her, I came to believe that she could do all those things and that she was a winner.

She started with duties involving Workers' Comp, and for years a part of her time was dedicated to some aspect of that law. She is without a doubt the most knowledgeable lobbyist in that field. She is recognized as an expert on the subject and knows an equal amount about the legislature, its members, and its culture.

In Tallahassee almost everyone gets a nickname or two. I've heard her called the "Lightning Rod" and I know she has often been referred to as the "Tigress." I am sure that considering how active and effective she has been in the legislative halls, there are other nicknames. The one I like best is "Friend."

## A Compensable Illness

At some point, when it seemed that the whole world was involved in the struggle to bring order to the Workers' Compensation system, a novel idea was floated. It seems appropriate that we memorialize it today. Members of the group that listened to the new idea were all knowledgeable about Workers' Compensation, so they knew that the goal of the law was to provide assistance to those workers who sustained an injury or contracted a disease that arose in the normal course of employment. However, the actual scope of eligibility for benefits was somewhat limited in the name of economy. Moreover, case books were full of opinions defining "employment" and deciding whether a specific incident in which a worker was injured or contracted a disease qualified as having arisen out of and in the normal course of employment.

The presenter of this new idea was a lobbyist who knew the law. He asserted that there was a gross oversight in the compensation law, and it related to lobbyists. He argued that all lobbyists should not only be covered by the law, but should be entitled to compensation for alcoholism. He explained that drinking with legislators was normal work for lobbyists, and that made lobbyists susceptible to alcoholism. Insofar as alcoholism has been defined as a disease, any lobbyist who became an alcoholic would be entitled to the same consideration as any other worker.

He proposed a change in the law to accomplish that wholesome purpose.

Upon a motion duly made and seconded, the meeting was adjourned and his proposed bill was left on the table.

# 17 *End of Story* ———————————

And so, after more than fifty years, it has been a pleasant task to scroll back through the years from the birth of the 57 Club and record something of those who were members, what it did, and what became of it.

The 57 Club melded into and became a part of the legislature, so it is difficult to identify specific legislative achievements. However, certain generalities are true and relevant.

The members of the Club were active and relatively aggressive. Some of them were involved in every major issue for many years. As a matter of fact, Dempsey Barron served in the legislature continuously from 1957 to 1988, always in a leadership role. So the Club's influence existed to some extent for thirty-one-plus years.

During that time, the state made it safely through the troubled waters of racial turmoil. The legislative branch of state government was transformed from a citizen legislature to a professional body with enough amenities and high-tech equipment to facilitate interaction with the modern world.

The changes resulting from court-ordered reapportionment, along with new rules providing for single-member districts and term limitations, caused extreme bitterness and raised a serious expectation of violence. However, no acts of violence developed. In fact, the official response to these changes can be described as reasonable. The state coped with the changing economic situation and enormous population growth. A fairly decent record was established with respect to all levels of education, as well as protection of wetlands and other natural habitats. In all respects, the state is better off for the legislative oversight it has had.

As for me, I am satisfied with my record. I spent myself and most of my resources on public service, but I was able to prove that my parents were correct when they taught me that there is no higher form of public service than the honest practice of politics. When I was preparing to leave the House after eight years of fighting the good fight, I was both surprised and pleased to be visited by a group of small county legislators who asked me to run for Speaker of the House. I had to say no because, at that time, I was committed to run for governor.

At the time of their visit, I had no idea how much support was available to me from their small county colleagues and, at this point, it doesn't really matter. The significance of that gesture was that a delegation of legislators I had fought with about segregation, reapportionment, education, spending, taxation, and more, were asking me to take a position of control over their legislative careers. The incident reinforced my belief that one can disagree with others—even those in control—and if done honorably, can continue to have their respect.

## What Became of the Club?

The 57 Club existed and is a part of Florida's history, although there never was a formal charter. It served as a valuable thread linking the lives of the thirty-nine members in perpetuity.

Only those who were elected to serve in the legislature for the first time in 1957 could be members, so there can never be new members and, sad to say, there never can be a female, racial, or ethnic minority member.

There were some very fine people among that group of thirty-nine freshmen legislators and, as we have seen, they had a lot to say about what the state government of Florida accomplished in the years since 1957. All of them are aging rapidly, and many have already gone on to a better place. I don't know why, but as you can see I am fortunate enough to still be here and able to tell these tales. God isn't finished with me yet.

One won't find much of anything about the 57 Club in textbooks or libraries because it died in its infancy. Moreover, this would have been much easier to write if the Club had been a secret society or even an organization with some lofty purpose, but it never rose to those levels. It merely came upon the scene and then, at some echelon in the control structure and for reasons never announced, the decision was made to let it go—and it was gone.

For my part, I don't play the "What if?" game, so I do not wonder what might have happened if the Club had actually functioned. I am content to salute it, recognize it as about the only thing the thirty-nine of us had in common, express my gratitude for the privilege of serving with the other members, then pick it up ever so gently and place it on the table of history.

I am glad I was a member of the 57 Club. May it rest in peace.

## Epilogue

There were thirty-nine freshmen members of the 1957 session of the Florida Legislature, and for the next thirty-two years they had a hand in making, executing, enforcing, and interpreting laws.

A few did not stay involved very long. In fact, four served only one session. Along the way others left the legislature and went into other government service or just dropped out and did not pursue a career in any venue of public service. George Anderson, for example, became a Methodist minister.

However, the longevity record is impressive. After eight years, seventeen of the thirty-nine were still active in the legislature. After twelve years, ten Clubbers remained in the legislature, six of them in the Senate and four in the House. The ten were further reduced over time, and at twenty years there were still four remaining. Eventually, Dempsey Barron was the only one of the original thirty-nine left. One would think that he would be lonesome, but he wasn't. Neither was he impotent with respect to political power. He grew stronger over time and honed his skills to a fine edge. Given his personality, experience, institutional memory, and determination, he usually had his way in the Senate and imposed his will on the others more than anyone else serving with him.

The group that stayed in the House provided one speaker and four who were elected to serve as speaker pro tempore.

Of those who departed the legislature but participated in state government in some way, seven became judges. There were four circuit judges; two made it to district courts of appeal and one went all the way to the Supreme Court. One 57 Club member served on the Public Service Commission and then became a professor and taught law at the University of Florida. I had the distinction of being Florida's first Public Counsel.

The Club members won all kinds of honors while in the House and thereafter. There is even a law library named for one member and a twenty-eight-story building in Tampa named for another.

Recently it was noted that on a national level, veterans of WWII are dying at the rate of about 1,000 a day. Since many in the Club served in that war, it follows that Club members are also leaving. In fact, at last count fifteen of the thirty-nine have passed on.

It is fair to say that the members of the 57 Club, as a group, were active, effective, and influential in state government for more than thirty years.

# Appendix A

## The 1957 Freshmen in the Florida House of Representatives

George H. Anderson (Jefferson County)
T. H. "Tommy" Askins (Nassau County)
John L. Ayers (Hernando County)
Dempsey J. Barron (Bay County)
Ralph J. Blank Jr. (Palm Beach County)
Thomas M. Carney (Pinellas County)
C. Welborn Daniel (Lake County)
Gordon V. Frederick (Seminole County)
Ben Hill Griffin Jr. (Polk County)
William E. Harris (Bay County)
George L. Hollahan Jr. (Dade County)
Frederick B. Karl (Volusia County)
Morrison Kimbrough (Santa Rosa County)
Howard Livingston (Highlands County)
Robert T. Mann (Hillsborough County)
Wayne O. Manning (Holmes County)
John E. Mathews (Duval County)
Ray Mattox (Polk County)
Richard O. "Dick" Mitchell (Leon County)
Sam Mitchell (Washington County)
Richard B. Muldrow (Broward County)
William G. O'Neill (Marion County)
J. Troy Peacock (Jackson County)
Otis R. Peavy (Madison County)
Edwin H. Peters (Calhoun County)
J. Y. Porter (Monroe County)
C. A. Roberts (Union County)
E. C. Rowell (Sumter County)
Bobby Russ (Wakulla County)
A. J. Ryan Jr. (Broward County)
Rupert J. Smith (St. Lucie County)
George Stone (Escambia County)
Allison R. Strickland (Citrus County)
John A. Sutton (Orange County)
L. B. "Buck" Vocelle (Indian River County)

W. L. Wadsworth (Flagler County)
James Lorenzo Walker (Collier County)
B. D. "Georgia Boy" Williams (Columbia County)
James H. "Jimmy" Wise (Okaloosa County)

# Appendix B

## Jack Orr's Speech

Explanation of Vote by John B. Orr Jr. Representative from Dade County, on Senate Bills Nos. 10-xx, 11-xx, 12-xx, 13-xx and Senate Concurrent Resolution No. 17-xx (from the *Journal of the House of Representatives*, July 26, 1956).

Gentlemen, I wish to explain my votes on the several segregation bills which have been passed during this Special Session. Due to the delicacy of the subject matter, I have written this speech.

I appreciate and understand how strongly many of you feel about the necessity of preserving segregation even though it has been declared to be violative of our basic law. I trust that you will attempt to understand my position. I will state it as succinctly as my control of language permits.

First, I favor the gradual integration of our public school system. In view of the fact that our custom of segregation is one of long standing, I realize that this cannot be changed overnight as the consequence of governmental edict, but I do not understand the decision of the Supreme Court of the United States to require that abrupt a change. I believe, moreover, that had we devoted as much energy, time, and talent to discovering means to live under the law instead of in defiance of it, we could have discovered a way.

I believe segregation is morally wrong. The existence of second-class citizens is repugnant to our great democratic principles. The fact that the custom is one of long standing makes it no less wrong. Surely not many of you would argue today that slavery was morally justifiable, and yet this was a custom of long standing.

The pigmentation of one's skin is no rational basis for setting him apart. But proponents of segregation say that God intended this; that He created the European continent for the White man, the Asian for the Yellow, the African for the Black, and the American for the Red Man. Of course the logical inference from this type of reasoning is that we should give the country back to the Indians. No, I believe that God intended us to live in harmony under the Brotherhood of Man, and that His plan has been sidetracked from time to time by humans who have felt the necessity of having someone to look down upon. I believe that most of our problems, most of our wars, are a consequence of this type of inferiority complex.

Examine the effect of our Southern attitude on international affairs. We of the White race are a minority group. Our diplomats preach, and are backed up by our Constitution, that we do not discriminate on the basis of race, color, or creed. Each time that we do not practice what our officials preach, the Communists score a propaganda victory. They have used this with alarming success against us in Asia. We have provided them with ammunition more effective than the hydrogen bomb in this Special Session. If we hope to maintain our leadership among the free peoples of the world, if we hope to give hope to those subjugated peoples behind the Iron and Bamboo Curtains, we must demonstrate by our acts as well as our words that our democratic form of government places no artificial barriers on the opportunity to live and work with our fellow man.

Passing from the moral and international problems, what has been the effect on our economy?

We have not provided equal but separate educational facilities, and I don't believe this is possible. As a consequence of the disparity in educational facilities, we in the South have had over the years a large segment of our population which has been poorly educated. The result has been that the living standards of all of us have been pulled down. Our wage rates are lower, our disease rates are higher. Every facet of our life has been adversely affected by the artificial barrier we have created and maintained.

In recent years we have made much economic progress in the South. I believe this has been due, in part, to the elimination or reduction of discrimination in many fields. More Negroes are participating in our political life. They serve on our juries; they vote in our elections; they serve on our police departments and serve as judges. It might be well to mention here that they fight beside us in time of war.

To continue to progress, I believe we have an obligation, not just to the Negro, but also to ourselves to provide the same educational facilities to all children, regardless of race or color or creed. This cannot be accomplished in a segregated system.

I predict that none of the measures passed or proposed will accomplish the result you seek. Despite the clever language employed, the Supreme Court will surely see through the Fabisinski Committee Bills and will strike them down.

Neither will interposition work. Interposition is that doctrine which requires one side to put on blue uniforms and the other side gray ones. We tried that before and I doubt that General Lowry will be able to accomplish what General Lee failed to do.

None of these attempts will succeed ultimately and furthermore upon their failure, complete integration may be imposed immediately upon us without our having made adequate plans to orient our people to the change.

But perhaps the most dangerous by-product of our activity in this Special Session and of the political campaigns that preceded it, and are responsible for it, is the attitude of disrespect for our laws and the principles of common decency that is developing. To defy the highest court in our land is unthinkable to me. As a lawyer, I've frequently disagreed with decisions of all of our courts—most particularly when they rule against me—but I wouldn't think of telling my clients to ignore the decisions. Neither would you.

You wouldn't cheat on an examination and you wouldn't condone cheating of graders. Yet the efficacy of the student admission plan to maintain segregation depends on who grades the papers or who gives the tests. This is demonstrated by the colloquy that occurred during the committee hearing. One member expressed doubt that this plan would prevent integration because some colored children would be as bright as the white children and would come from homes of comparable backgrounds. His doubt was dissipated when reminded by another—"who will be giving the tests."

The development of this kind of attitude will surely weaken the moral fiber of our government and of our community life. For us to set an example of hypocrisy and deceit—of disrespect for our laws—will surely do more harm to our children than will result from their being seated in a classroom next to one whose skin is of a different hue.

It is not my intention to condemn any of you personally.

I have great respect and personal admiration for most of you. I simply felt constrained to point out what I believe to have been a grave mistake.

When we finally have to face up to this problem, and we surely will be required to, I hope that God gives us the wisdom and strength to conquer prejudice and bigotry and to renew our faith in our Constitution.

Meantime, I will take solace in the prayer our chaplain delivered last Tuesday: "Help us, thus, to see that it is better to fail in a just cause that will ultimately succeed, than to succeed in an unrighteous cause that will ultimately fail."

# Appendix C

## Toby Simon's Case

*THE FLORIDA BAR v. SIMON Fla. 1964*
Supreme Court of Florida.
THE FLORIDA BAR, Complaint, v.
Tobias SIMON, Respondent.
No. 33893.

Original proceeding on motion by an attorney for an order requiring that all matters and proceedings before grievance committee under pending charges against him be made public information. The Supreme Court held that proceedings before the grievance committee under Integration Rule, 31 F.S.A. Integration Rule of The Florida Bar, art. II, rule 11.04, are confidential and that, until the grievance committee made a recommendation of probable cause, the only parts of such proceedings which attorney was entitled to have made public information were the notice served on him of the nature of conduct being investigated and his right to be heard and, if committee so determined, the notice of determination not to recommend probable cause.

Ordered accordingly. West Headnotes

[1] Attorney and Client 45 €=48

45 Attorney and Client

451 The Office of Attorney 451(C) Discipline 45k47 Proceedings

45k48 k. Notice and Preliminary Proceedings. Most Cited Cases

Except for notice of nature of conduct under investigation and opportunity to be heard, attorney under investigation is not a party to grievance committee proceeding and has no right to participate therein, though he may be required to testify and produce evidence as any other witness. 31 F.S.A. Integration Rule of The Florida Bar, art. 11, rule 11.04 and subd. (2).

45 Attorney and Client

451 The Office of Attorney 45I(C) Discipline 45k47 Proceedings

45k48 k. Notice and Preliminary Proceedings. Most Cited Cases

Determination of grievance committee not to recommend to board of governors a finding of probable cause terminates the matter and if attorney has been notified of investigation, he is entitled to notice of finding of no probable cause. 31 F.S.A. Integration Rule of The Florida Bar, art. 11, rule 11.04 and subd. (5) (a).

45 Attorney and Client

451 The Office of Attorney 45I(C) Discipline 45k47 Proceedings

45k48 k. Notice and Preliminary Proceedings. Most Cited Cases

Purpose of proceedings before grievance committee is solely to determine whether there is probable cause to proceed further and such proceedings are confidential in order to insure proper conduct of investigation as well as for the benefit of attorney under investigation. 31 F.S.A. Integration Rule of The Florida Bar, art. 11, rules 11.04 and subd. (2), 11.12 and subd. (1).

45 Attorney and Client

451 The Office of Attorney 451(C) Discipline 45k47 Proceedings

45k48 k. Notice and Preliminary

Proceedings. Most Cited Cases

Until grievance committee made recommendation of probable cause, only parts of proceedings before committee which attorney under investigation was entitled to have made public information were notice served on him of nature of conduct being investigated and right to be heard and, if committee so determined, notice of determination not to recommend probable cause. 31 F.S.A. Integration Rule of The Florida Bar, art. 11, rules 11.04 and subds. (2), (5) (a), 11.12 and subd. (1).

45 Attorney and Client

451 The Office of Attorney 451(C) Discipline 45k47 Proceedings

45k48 k. Notice and Preliminary Proceedings. Most Cited Cases

If grievance committee recommends probable cause, all matters and things required to be served on attorney under investigation may be made public information at instance of respondent attorney. 31 F.S.A. Integration Rule of the Florida Bar, art. 11, rules 11.04 and subds. (2), (5) (a), 11.12 and subd. (1).

1. Lewis, Hall, Tallahassee, for The Florida Bar, complainant.

Cody Fowler, of Fowler, White, Gillen, Humkey & Trenam, Miami, and Frederick B. Karl, of Raymond, Wilson, Karl & Conway, Daytona Beach, for respondent.

PER CURIAM.

Respondent, Tobias Simon, a member of The Florida Bar, has filed in this Court a motion stating that charges alleging professional misconduct by him have been filed with The Florida Bar and that the Seventh Judicial Circuit Grievance Committee 'B' is now investigating said charges. Respondent further alleged that he had been served with a notice of hearing by said Grievance Committee, which notice advised him that he was charged with the solicitation of legal business. The notice also advised respondent of his right to either appear before said committee, in person or by counsel, for the purpose of explaining, refuting or admitting the charges, or to submit a written statement explaining, refuting or admitting the charges.

Respondent also alleges that pursuant to Rule 11.12, Article 11, Integration Rule of The Florida Bar, 31 F.S.A., he has filed with The Florida Bar a request in writing that the proceedings against him be made public information.

Respondent's motion prays that this Court enter an order requiring that all matters and proceedings against him under the pending charges be made public information.

We have heard argument by counsel representing respondent and The Florida Bar, following which we entered an order continuing further action and hearings by said Grievance Committee and The Florida Bar until further order of this Court.

*374 Article 11, Integration Rule, contains the rules relating to discipline of members of The Florida Bar. It provides first for an investigatory procedure conducted by a Grievance Committee. After conducting its investigation a Grievance Committee may make either a finding and recommendation of probable cause or no probable cause, but before recommending to the Board of Governors a finding of probable cause the attorney under investigation must be advised in general terms of the nature of the conduct under investigation and be given the opportunity to appear before the Grievance Committee, personally or by counsel, to explain, refute or admit the charges, or to file a written explanation, refutation or admission thereof. Rule 11.04 (2).

[1] Except for this notice and opportunity to be heard the attorney under investigation is not a party to the Grievance Committee proceeding and has no right to participate therein, although he may be required to testify and produce evidence as any other witness.

[2] If the Grievance Committee determines that it will not recommend to the Board of Governors a finding of probable cause the matter is ended and the file is disposed of as directed by the Board of Governors. If the accused attorney has been notified of the investigation he shall also be notified of the finding of no probable cause. Rule Il.04(5)(a).

We think it necessary now to rule on respondent's motion only as it pertains to his right to make public information the proceedings before the Grievance Committee. If the Grievance Committee shall recommend probable cause and the respondent's rights not be accorded him we can then determine any further questions presented to us.

[3] The proceedings before the Grievance Committee are closely akin to proceedings had before a grand jury. Their purpose is solely to determine whether there is probable cause to proceed further. Such proceedings are confidential. This confidentiality is not only for benefit of the accused attorney, but is required for other reasons, one being to insure that the investigation may be conducted unhampered by possible interference with witnesses or other action of the person under investigation. We do not by this imply that the respondent here involved would attempt to hamper an investigation of himself.

Rule 11.12 specifically provides that all disciplinary proceedings are confidential except as provided therein. Rule 11.12(1) specifies that upon written request of the respondent attorney, as was done in this case, 'those parts of the proceedings prior to trial which are required to be served upon an accused, and the record of the proceeding as elsewhere defined, shall become public information.'

Until the Grievance Committee recommends probable cause to the Board of Governors the only part of the proceedings required to be served on the respondent seems to be the notice of the nature of the conduct of the respondent under investigation by the Grievance Committee, or the notice of a finding of no probable cause.

[4][5] Therefore we conclude that the only document, thing, or part of the proceedings which the respondent may make public information at this time is the notice, a copy of which is attached to the motion filed before us, given to the respondent pursuant to Rule 11.04(2), Article II, of the Integration Rule. If the Grievance Committee determines not to recommend probable cause the notice thereof required to be served on respondent under Rule 11.04(5)(a) may also be made public information. If the Grievance Committee recommends probable cause the respondent may make public information all matters and things required to be served on him under the Rules.

As stated above, if the proceedings progress beyond the Grievance Committee we will on appropriate petition or motion consider*375 any further aspects of this matter as may be required to protect the rights of the parties.

DREW, C. 1., and THORNAL, O'CONNELL and CALDWELL, J1., concur.

ERVIN, J., concurs specially with opinion. ERVIN, Justice (concurring specially).

I concur in the opinion and judgment. However, I take note that the majority opinion did not pass upon the right of the respondent to an open and public hearing in the event the Grievance Committee shall find probable cause and the matter is referred to a referee for trial. By way of caveat, it is my view that under such circumstances, and if requested by him the respondent would be entitled as a matter of right to a public hearing before such referee.

Fla.1964

*The Florida Bar v. Simon* 171 So.2d 372

# Appendix D

## Governor Collins Veto Message of the Last Resort Bill

June 6, 1957
Honorable Doyle E. Conner
Speaker, House of Representatives
Capitol Building
Tallahassee, Florida
    Sir:
    Pursuant to the authority vested in me as Governor of Florida, under the provisions of Section 28, Article III, of the Constitution of this State, I hereby transmit to you, with my objections, House Bill No. 671, enacted by the Legislature of 1957, and entitled:
    "AN ACT RELATING TO PUBLIC FACILITIES AND INSTITUTIONS; AUTHORIZING LOCAL AUTHORITIES TO SUSPEND UNDER CERTAIN CIRCUMSTANCES ANY PUBLIC FACILITY OR INSTITUTION WITHIN ITS JURISDICTION AS AN EMERGENCY MEASURE IN THE PUBLIC INTEREST PURSUANT TO PETITION AND REFERENDUM; PROVIDING PROCEDURES FOR THE REACTIVATION OF A SUSPENDED PUBLIC FACILITY OR INSTITUTION; PROVIDING AN EFFECTIVE DATE."
    Contrary to the impression which has been given, this bill is extremely broad and is by no means restricted to integration in the public schools. It seeks to authorize any local governing authority to suspend the operation of any public facility or institution in any area over which such authority has jurisdiction when the "standards, of health, or safety, or welfare, or peace, or morals of the community . . ." are threatened.
    The impression has been given that the law is to be resorted to in order to close the public schools of a community only after integration occurs. Actually, all that is required under its terms is that there be a mere "threat" and that the threat be to the "standards, health, safety, welfare, peace or morals of the community." This, in my opinion, would be a come-on to the professional agitators and extremists and on many issues other than integration could result in a community being torn asunder under a siege of hysteria emanating from mere suspicion and propaganda. Any of our fine communities could see its school system wrecked by the handiwork of a scandal monger. The act would be the spring board and stimulant not only for race baiters and bigots, but even worse, it could be the weapon of vindictive, scheming and unscrupulous elements bent on venting their spleen for personal reasons only.
    For the reasons aforesaid it occurs to me that this should not be referred to as

the "Last Resort Bill" but actually the "First Resort Bill," that is, the first resort for the agitator.

Insofar as the public school system is concerned, I view the bill as wholly unnecessary. Under the present school code (Section 230.23(4)(F), the respective county boards of public instruction of this State have the express power to "adopt regulations for the closing of schools during an emergency and to provide for the payment of salaries of the members of the instructional staff on such occasions." Furthermore, Chapters 313.89 and 312.90 of the laws of this State, enacted by the Legislature in the Extraordinary Session last year, specifically vest in the Governor the power to promulgate emergency rules and regulations with respect to the use of public facilities, including schools.

In addition to the foregoing reasons, sound legal counsel have advised me that the title to the bill is clearly defective and that the tenure and retirement rights of the teachers of this State may be placed in jeopardy as a result. I have also been advised by the State Superintendent of Public Instruction that it would be next to impossible to administer the legislation. Children from closed schools would have to be transferred to nearby public schools, which in turn would have to transfer pupils because of overcrowding, and the result well could be a chain reaction resulting in the closing of school after school.

I also regard the proposed legislation as a definite threat to the validity of the program passed in the recent Extraordinary session, which to date has been completely effective.

Therefore, if allowed to stand, it is my opinion that the bill would be the unnecessary stimulant for discord among our people, that it may place in jeopardy the tenure and retirement rights of the teachers, that it is unworkable and that it places in serious jeopardy our whole program to meet the serious problems presented to us under the unfortunate decision of the Supreme Court of the United States.

This measure ignores a workable approach to vexing problems and encourages the substitution of a chaotic abandonment of reason.

It pours across the face of a great State the highly combustible fuel of racial hatred and beckons to firebrands and the irresponsible to come and ignite the flames.

When men harbor hatred in their hearts for the fellowmen, it is a regrettable thing.

But when government is used as an instrument for translating racial hatred into a force to destroy the very institutions which nurture and sustain it, then such is an even more serious wrong, and I condemn it.

For the foregoing reasons, I, therefore, withhold my approval from House Bill No. 671, regular Session of the Legislature, 1957, and do hereby veto the same.

Respectfully

Leroy Collins

Governor

# Appendix E

## Interposition Resolution in Response to *Brown v. Board of Education,* 1957

(From: *Acts of the Territorial Legislature and Acts of the Legislature, 1822–Present,* Series S 222)

The Florida State Legislature passed this resolution in opposition to the 1954 U.S. Supreme Court decision in the *Brown v. Board of Education of Topeka, Kansas,* case that ended legal segregation in public education. Racial segregation was originally found to be constitutional by the U.S. Supreme Court in the landmark *Plessy v. Ferguson* case in 1896.

That decision laid the legal foundation for what became known as Jim Crow laws throughout the nation, and especially in the South, by declaring segregation legal only if the facilities were "separate but equal." But the Brown decision removed that foundation, and many segregationists saw the case as an opening wedge to ending all segregation. Therefore, the Florida Legislature argued that the decision usurped the state constitutional powers, and passed the resolution to declare the court's decision in 1954 as null and void.

Although he initially condemned the *Brown* decision, as did the majority of southern elected officials, Governor LeRoy Collins fought with the Florida Legislature to prevent them from passing the Interposition Resolution. Such a resolution was intended to "interpose" itself between the citizens of Florida and the United States government in order to prevent what the legislature contended was an illegal intrusion by the federal government upon the right of the state by imposing integration.

Governor Collins used a little-known provision of the state constitution by unilaterally adjourning the legislature to prevent it from passing the resolution. After the legislature returned and passed the resolution, he had no power to veto it, because it was not a law but only a resolution expressing the opinion of the legislature on the matter of racial integration. However, as it passed through his office, Collins hand-wrote the following at the bottom of the Interposition Resolution:

This concurrent resolution of 'Interposition' crosses the Governor's desk as a matter of routine. I have no authority to veto it. I take this means however to advise the student of government, who may examine this document in the archives of the state in the years to come that the Governor of Florida expressed open and vigorous opposition thereto. I feel that the U. S. Supreme Court has improperly usurped powers reserved to the states under the constitution. I have joined in protesting such and in seeking legal means of avoidance. But if this resolution declaring the decisions of the court to be 'null and void' is to be taken seriously, it is anarchy and rebellion against the nation which must remain 'indivisible under God' if it is to survive. Not only will I not condone 'interposition' as so many have sought me to do, I decry it as an evil thing, whipped up by the demagogues and carried on the hot and erratic winds of passion, prejudice, and hysteria. If history judges me right this day, I want it known that I did my best to avert this blot. If I am judged wrong, then here in my own handwriting and over my signature is the proof of guilt to support my conviction.

LeRoy Collins, Governor.

May 2, 1957.

A RESOLUTION TO DECLARE THE UNITED STATES SUPREME COURT DECISIONS USURPING THE POWERS RESERVED TO THE STATES AND RELATING TO EDUCATION, LABOR, CRIMINAL PROCEDURE, TREASON AND SUBVERSION TO BE NULL, VOID AND OF NO EFFECT; TO DECLARE THAT A CONTEST OF POWERS HAS ARISEN BETWEEN THE STATE OF FLORIDA AND THE SUPREME COURT OF THE UNITED STATES; TO INVOKE THE DOCTRINE OF INTERPOSITION; AND FOR OTHER PURPOSES.

BE IT RESOLVED BY THE HOUSE OF REPRESENTATIVES OF THE STATE OF FLORIDA, THE SENATE CONCURRING:

That the Legislature of Florida doth hereby unequivocally express a firm and determined resolution to maintain and defend the Constitution of the United States, and the Constitution of this State against every attempt, whether foreign or domestic, to undermine and destroy the fundamental principles, embodied in our basic law, by which the liberty of the people and the sovereignty of the States, in their proper spheres, have been long protected and assured;

That the Legislature of Florida doth explicitly and pre-emptorily declare that it views the powers of the Federal Government as resulting solely from the compact, to which the States are parties, as limited by the plain sense and intention of the instrument creating that compact;

That the Legislature of Florida asserts that the powers of the Federal Government are valid only to the extent that these powers have been enumerated in the compact to which the various States assented originally and to which the States have assented in subsequent amendments validly adopted and ratified;

That the very nature of this basic compact, apparent upon its face is that the ratifying States, parties thereto, have agreed voluntarily to surrender certain of their sovereign rights, but only certain of these sovereign rights to a Federal Government thus constituted; and that all powers not delegated to the United States by the Constitution, nor prohibited by it to the States, have been reserved to the States respectively, or to the people;

That the State of Florida has at no time surrendered to the General Government its right to exercise its powers in the field of labor, criminal procedure, and public education, and to maintain racially separate public schools and other public facilities;

That the State of Florida, in ratifying the Fourteenth Amendment to the Constitution, did not agree, nor did the other States ratifying the Fourteenth Amendment agree, that the power to regulate labor, criminal proceedings, public education, and to operate racially separate public schools and other facilities was to be prohibited to them thereby;

And as evidence of such understanding as to the inherent power and authority of the States to regulate public education and the maintenance of racially separate public schools, the Legislature of Florida notes that the very Congress that submitted the Fourteenth Amendment for ratification established separate schools in the District of Columbia and that in more than one instance the same State Legislatures that ratified the Fourteenth Amendment also provided of systems of racially separate public schools;

That the Legislature of Florida denies that the Supreme Court of the United States had the right which it asserted in the school cases decided by it on May 17, 1954, the labor union case decided on may 21, 1956, the cases relating to criminal proceedings decided on April 23, 1956, and January 16, 1956, the anti-sedition case decided on April 2, 1956, and the case relating to teacher requirements decided on April 9, 1956, to enlarge the language and meaning of the compact by the States in an effort to withdraw from the States powers reserved to them and as daily exercised by them for almost a century;

That a question of contested power has arisen; the Supreme Court of the United States asserts, for its part, that the States did in fact prohibit unto themselves the power to regulate labor matters, criminal proceedings and public education and to maintain racially separate public institutions and the State of Florida, for its part asserts that it and its sister States have never surrendered such rights;

That these assertions upon the part of the Supreme Court of the United States, accompanied by threats of coercion and compulsion against the sovereign States of this Union, constitute a deliberate, palpable, and dangerous attempt by the Court to prohibit to the States certain rights and powers never surrendered by them;

That the Legislature of Florida asserts that whenever the General Government attempts to engage in the deliberate, palpable and dangerous exercise of powers not granted to it, the States who are parties to the compact have the right, and are in duty bound, to interpose for arresting the progress of the evil, and for maintaining, within their respective limits, the authorities, rights, and liberties appertaining to them;

That failure on the part of this State thus to assert its clear rights would be construed as acquiescence in the surrender thereof; and that such submissive acquiescence to the seizure of one right would in the end lead to the surrender of all rights and, and inevitably to the consolidation of the States into one sovereignty, contrary to the sacred compact by which this Union of States was created;

That the question of contested power asserted in this resolution is not within the province of the Court to determine because the Court itself seeks to usurp the powers which have been reserved to the States, and, therefore, under these circumstances, the judgment of all of the parties to the compact must be sought to resolve the question. The Supreme Court is not a party to the compact, but a creature of the compact and the question of contested power should not be settled by the creature seeking to usurp the power, but by the parties to the compact who are the people of the respective States in whom ultimate sovereignty finally reposes;

That the Constitution of the State of Florida provides for full benefits to all its citizens with reference to educational facilities and under the Laws of Florida enacted by the Legislature through the Minimum Foundation Program its citizens under states' rights, all are being educated under the same general law and all teachers are being employed under identical educational qualifications and all are certified by the State Board of Education alike, which enables the people, themselves, in Florida to provide an educational establishment serviceable and satisfactory and in keeping with the social structure of the state. The people of Florida do not consent to changing state precedents and their right by having doctrines thrust upon them by naked force alone, as promulgated in the school cases of May 17, 1954, and May 31, 1955;

That the doctrines of said decisions and other decisions denying to the States the right to have laws of their own dealing with subversion or espionage, and criminal proceedings, and denying the States the right to dismiss individuals from public employment who refuse to answer questions concerning their connections with communism by invoking the Fifth Amendment, and denying the States the right to provide for protective "right to work" laws, should not be forced upon the citizens of this State for the Court was without jurisdiction, power or authority to interfere with the sovereign powers of the State in such spheres of activity;

That the Court in its decisions relating to public education was without jurisdiction because (1) the jurisdiction of the Court granted by the Constitution is limited to judicial cases in law and equity, and said cases were not of a judicial nature and character, nor did they involve controversies in law or equity, but, on the contrary, the great subjects of the controversy are of a legislative character, and not a judicial character, and are determinable only by the people themselves speaking through their legislative bodies; (2) the essential nature and effect of the proceedings relating exclusively to public schools operated by and under the authority of States, and pursuant to State laws and regulations, said cases were suits against the States, and the Supreme Court was without power or authority to try said cases, brought by individuals against States, because the Constitution forbids the Court to entertain suits by individuals against a State unless the State has consented to be sued;

That if said Court had had jurisdiction and authority to try and determine said cases, it was powerless to interfere with the operation of the public schools of States, because the Constitution of the United States does not confer upon the General Government and power or authority over such schools or over the subject of education, jurisdiction over these matters being reserved to the States, nor did the States by the Fourteenth amendment authorize any interference on the part of the Judicial Department or any other department o the Federal Government with the operation by the States of such public schools as they might in their discretion see fit to establish and operate;

That by said cases the Court announces its power to adjudge State laws unconstitutional upon the basis of the Court's opinion of such laws as tested by rules of the inexact and speculative theories of psychological knowledge, which power and authority is beyond the jurisdiction of said Court;

That if the Court is permitted to exercise the power to judge the nature and effect of a law by supposed principles of psychological theory, and to hold the statute or Constitution of a State unconstitutional because of the opinions of the Judges as to its suitability the Sates will have been destroyed, and the indestructible Union of Indestructible States established by the Constitution of the United States will have ceased to exist, and in its stead the Court will have created, without jurisdiction or authority from the people, one central government of total power;

That implementing its decision relating to public education of May 17, 1954, said court on May 31, 1955 upon further consideration of said cases, said; "All provisions of Federal, State, or local law. . . . must yield" to said decision of May 17, 1954; said Court thereby presuming arrogantly to give orders to the State of Florida;

That it is clear that said Court has deliberately resolved to disobey the Constitution of the United States, and to flout and defy the Supreme Law of the Land;

That the State of Florida, as is also true of the other sovereign states of the Union, has the right to enact laws relating to subversion or espionage, criminal proceedings, dismissing public employees who refuse to answer questions concerning their connections with communism and "right to work" protection, and has the right to operate and maintain a public school system utilizing such educational methods therein as in her judgment are conducive to the welfare of those to be educated and the people of the State generally, this being a governmental responsibility which the State has assumed lawfully, and her rights in this respect have not in any wise been delegated to the Central Government, but, on the contrary, she and the other States have reserved such matters to themselves by the terms of the Tenth Amendment. Being possessed of the lawful right, the State of Florida is possessed of power to repel every unlawful interference therewith;

That the duty and responsibility of protecting life, property and the priceless possessions of freedom rest upon the Government of Florida as to all those within her territorial limits. The State alone has this responsibility. Laboring under this high obligation she is possessed of the means to effectuate it. It is the duty of the State in flagrant cases such as this to interpose its powers between its people and the effort of said Court to assert an unlawful domination over them;

THEREFORE, BE IT FURTHER RESOLVED BY THE HOUSE OF REPRE-SENTATIVES OF THE STATE OF FLORIDA, THE SENATE CONCURRING:

Section 1. That said decisions and orders of the Supreme Court of the United States denying the individual sovereign states the power to enact laws relating to espionage or subversion, criminal proceedings, the dismissal of public employees for refusal to answer questions concerning their connections with communism, "right to work" protection, (and relating to separation of the races in the public institutions of a State) are null, void and of no force or effect.

Section 2. That the elected representatives of the people of Florida do now seriously declare that it is the intent and duty of all officials, state and local, to observe, honorably, legally and constitutionally, all appropriate measures available to resist these illegal encroachments upon the sovereign powers of this State.

Section 3. That we urge firm and deliberate efforts to check these and further encroachments on the part of the Federal Government, and on the part of said Court through judicial legislation, upon the reserved powers of all the States' powers never surrendered by the remotest implication but expressly reserved and vitally essential to the separate and independent autonomy of the States in order that by united efforts the States may be preserved.

Section 4. That a copy of this Resolution be transmitted by His Excellency the Governor to the Governor and Legislature of each of the other States, to the President of the United States, to each of the Houses of Congress, to Florida's Representatives and Senators in the Congress, and to the Supreme Court of the United States for its information.

HOUSE CONCURRENT RESOLUTION NO. 174

ORIGINATED in and adopted by the House of Representatives on April 5, 1957

Doyle E. Conner

SPEAKER OF THE HOUSE OF REPRESENTATIVES

Lamar Bledsoe

CHIEF CLERK, HOUSE OF REPRESENTATIVES AND EX-OFFICIO EN-ROLLING CLERK

ADOPTED by the Senate on April 18, 1957

M. A. Shands

PRESIDENT OF THE SENATE

Robt. W. Davis

SECRETARY OF THE SENATE AND EX-OFFICIO ENROLLING CLERK

# Acknowledgments

I certainly am not an island. I do very few things alone. I am truly a people person, and I rely on people to give me strength, encouragement, and constructive criticism. Without helpful suggestions, I would flounder. Many came to my aid during the writing of this book, and I feel certain that some of them were not even aware they were helping. I am grateful for all their good wishes and their gracious and meaningful encouragement.

As is often the case, a few provided such unique help, and in such quantity, that they deserve more than being identified on an acknowledgment page. But on this project, that is about all there is to give. Consequently, as evidence of my appreciation, I have mentioned them here. I acknowledge my indebtedness to them and I tender my heartfelt thanks.

Among the many friends who helped and probably had no idea that their friendship and demeanor provided needed encouragement included my Rotary Club friend Charles Banks, my long-time friends and clients Robert Thomas and Bill Poe, Mayor Pam Iorio, Rhea Law, Bridget McCormick, and Michael Maher. Somehow I will find a way to reciprocate by helping each of them.

From the onset of this project, all my children and grandchildren voiced their confidence in my writing ability and encouraged my storytelling urges. I am deeply grateful for all their confidence in my creative aptitude. Tami, Cynthia, and Brad gave much of their precious time and talent to the project, and they deserve an extra measure of recognition.

My friend Steve Otto, columnist for the *Tampa Tribune*, was supportive and suggested that I tell my story in a series of anecdotes. I willingly took his advice.

My colleague Michael Foerster, a veteran newspaper person and retired Hillsborough County official, drew on his expertise and devoted an enormous number of hours of his time, advising me about aspects of the project with which I had little or no experience. He helped me with chores of editing, formatting, and critiquing, and he was particularly helpful with the technique of moving from one subject to another. For applying his professional ability and for his friendship I am, and always will be, grateful.

John Belohlavek is a historian who teaches history at the University of South Florida. He has been helpful in many important ways from the beginning of my book project. He voluntarily assumed the roles of mediator, agent, advisor, technical consultant, and mentor. His willingness to commit his intelligence and acquired knowledge to assist me has increased the public's confidence and enhanced the credibility of my efforts. He never intruded or suggested that he could do a better job of composing any part of it himself. He was able to be critical of parts of my work product without shaking my confidence. Not once did he raise doubts about the overall quality of my work or cause me to question the wisdom of going forward, yet I am certain that it is better as a result of his participation.

My regret is that these poor words do not adequately express the depth or magnitude of my gratitude to all who assisted. The saving grace is that they all know me well enough to understand how strongly I feel and how sincerely I wish I had the ability to properly describe what I am feeling.

Finally, there is no way I can appropriately thank my wife, Merci. She has been not only my wife, but also my soul mate, my nurse, my advisor, my sounding board, my computer person, my proofreader, my best friend, and my partner throughout this entire project. As a token of my gratitude, I dedicate this book to her.

# Index

Chiles, Lawton M., Jr., 48–51, 96, 191, 202–4; as governor, 8, 202; as U.S. senator, 85

Chiles, Rhea, 48, 335

Civil War, 7, 96, 102, 156–57

Clark, Dill (senator), 14, 121

Clendenin, James, 188

Cleveland, Mack, 90

Cleveland, Mrs. Mack, 91

Cobb, Thomas T. (representative), 10, 112

Collins, LeRoy (governor), 8, 14–15, 19, 166–68, 183–85, 327–30; appointment of, 30, 120; books about, 214; and campaign support, 235; as candidate, 8–9, 158; and ethics code, 22; and integration, 124–26, 129, 157–58; and Interposition Resolution, 329–34; and Last Resort Bill, 123–26; at National Association of Broadcasters, 186; and reapportionment, 146; and secret sessions, 206; in Selma, 187; as senator, 9, 132, 176, 178, 182; and separation of powers, 157–58; and turnpike, 166–68; as Undersecretary of Commerce, 186; veto message, 327

Collins, Mrs. LeRoy, 185

Collins administration, 190, 238

Collins/Johns race, 182

"Colored," 70, 105, 115

Commissioner of Agriculture, 19, 33

Commissioner of Education, 19

Comptroller, 19, 65, 194

Confederacy, 101, 157

Confederate states, 102

Conference Committee, 80–81, 145, 148, 161, 276, 289, 292–93

Conner, Doyle (Speaker of the House), 32, 34, 131, 327, 334

Constitutional Revision Commission, 269

Constitution of 1885, x, 144, 161, 197

Constitution of Florida. See Florida Constitution

Constitution of 1968, 12–13, 22, 54, 86, 149–50, 160–61, 165, 197

"Country Club Syndrome," 269

"Courthouse Gang," 10

Court-ordered reapportionment, 312

Crews, John, 42–44, 191, 253; as representative, 280

Cross, Emory "Red," 149

Cuban Navy, 301

Currier, Florence (Jane Morgan), 233

Dade County Teachers Association, 257

D'Alemberte, Sandy, 234, 268

Daniel, Welborn (senator), 160–61, 196

Dansby, Grace (widow of Pete Gibson), 94

Davis, Amos (sergeant at arms), 153

Davis, Marguerite, 156

Davis, Robert W., 334

Daytona Beach News Journal, 105, 207, 212

Daytona International Speedway, 87, 89, 229, 230

"Dean of the Senate," 26

Deep South, xi, 101

Dekle, Justice, 155–56

DeLand newspaper, 206

De la Parte, Louis, 44–46, 221; as president pro tempore, 46; as senator, 46, 85

Democratic Party Caucus, 19, 121

Department of Beverages. See State Beverage Department

Department of Community Affairs, 234

Desegregation, xi, 124, 183; order for, 118; of public schools, 183

Dickinson, Fred O. (Bud), 65; as candidate for governor, 174, 191–93, 195, 222–23, 239–40; as state comptroller, 194

Doctrine of Interposition, 157, 330

"Dream Team," 202

Durden, Bob, 10–11

Duval Hotel, 64

Dyckman, Martin, 186, 213–14, 247

Early, Lloyd, 208–10

E.C.: Mr. Speaker, E. C. Rowell (Powers), 304

England, Arthur (justice), 264, 269

Equal Rights Amendment, 24

Ervin, Richard (attorney general), 125

Expulsion of a House member, 165

Fabisinski, L. L. (retired circuit judge), 16, 18

Fabisinski Committee, 320

Fabisinski report, 134

Fair, Jim, 197

Fair apportionment, 14, 34, 145–46

Farrish, Joseph, 209

57 Club, 1–2, 22, 87, 173, 205, 313, 315; formation of, 2; as informal fraternity, xiii; members running for governor, 194; and oath of office, 56–57; as original member, 1; at the Piney Z farm, 150; and relationship with Governor Bryant, 190; and relationship with the press, 211–12; and work on constitutional revision, 165–66

57 Club members, 8, 128; George Anderson, 121; Dempsey Barron, 23, 25, 27, 309, 312; Welborn Daniel, 160, 288; Gordon Frederick, 90; Ben Hill Griffin Jr., 127, 129; Bob Mann, 281, 284; Jack Mathews, 28–30; Bill O'Neill, 151; E. C. Rowell, 304; A. J. Ryan, 30–32; Baldy Strickland, 159; Buck Vocelle, 136

First Amendment of the U.S. Constitution, 205, 257–58, 268, 284

First District Court of Appeal, 156, 209

Flagler, Henry, 19

Florida Agriculture and Mechanical University, 70

Florida Bar, 28, 309; award, 105; and judges, 256, 258; and lobbying, 204, 292, 297; and Toby Simon case, 323–24

*Florida Bar v. Simon, Supreme Court of Florida*, 104, 323–26

Florida Cabinet, x, 7, 19, 191

Florida Constitution, 8, 12–13, 28, 46, 125

Florida Education Association (FEA), 221

Florida Industrial Commission, 136

Florida Insurance Commissioner, 300

Floridan Hotel, 64, 301

Florida Power and Light Company, 22

Florida Road Department, 64

Florida State College for Women, 71

Florida State University, law school, 51, 268

*Florida State University Law Review*, 156

Florida Supreme Court, 214; cameras in, 267; opinion of, 9, 164, 183–84; and Toby Simon case, 104; and Spenkelink, 266

Florida Supreme Court justices, 155–56, 263–64; and impeachment, 153

*Florida Trend*, 228

Florida Women's Hall of Fame, 48

*Floridian of His Century* (Dyckman), 186, 214

Force, Lester, 233, 282

Fowler, Cody, 104, 324

Fowler, White, Gillen, Humkey & Trenam, 104, 324

France, William (Bill), Sr., 87–89, 229–31, 305

Frederick, Gordon V., 90, 317

Frederick B. Karl County Center, 285

Freshman class of 1957, 25, 115

Friedman, Howard, 298

Future Farmers of America, 33

Gambling, 119, 198; facilities, 14, 146; taxes, 37

Game and Freshwater Fish Commission, 159

Georgia Code, 164

Germany, John, 297–98

Gibbons, Sam (representative), 34–35

GI Bill of Rights, 25

Gibson, Grace (Dansby), 94

Gibson, Pete (senator), 94

Gillespie, William (Bill), 204, 291

Glenn, John, 5

"Good old boy(s)," 121, 196, 284, 306

"Government in the Sunshine" laws, 95, 149, 267

Governors, 7, 19, 329; Askew, 27, 53–54; Bryant, 190; Chiles, 8; Collins, 19, 30, 157, 185, 290; first Republican, 196; Graham, 136; Johns (acting governor), 8; Kirk, 52, 78, 82, 208; Martinez, 201–2; McCarty, 8

Governor's mansion, 185, 201, 203, 246, 298

Governor's office, 12, 196; and rules of succession, 8
Governor's race of 1964, 219, 251
Graham, Catherine (publisher), 200
Grant, John, 237
Great Depression, 114, 206
Griffin, Ben Hill, Jr., 3, 127–28, 317
Grove, the, 168, 185

Hatchett, Joseph (Joe) (justice), 53, 247, 254, 264
Health Maintenance Organization (HMO), 301
"He-Coon," 51, 96
High, Robert (Bob) King, 174, 192–95, 235, 240; as mayor, 191
Holland and Knight, 298
Holly, Charles (Charlie), 191, 194, 251
Home Rule, 12–13, 150; powers of, 12, 151, 233
Homophile Institute, 140
Homosexuality, 118, 139
Homosexuals, 130, 132, 139–41
Homosexuals Anonymous, 140
Horne, Mallory, 39–40, 90; as president of the senate, 39, 46; as representative, 87, 94; as senator, 280; as Speaker of the House, 39
Hospital at Chattahoochee, 148
House Committee on Appropriations, 148
House Impeachment Committee, 155, 214, 247, 264, 309
House Journal, 17–18

*If It Takes All Summer* (Warren), 10
Impeachment, 153–56, 214; articles of, 153–54; grounds for, 154; of a judge, 165; process, 154–55, 247; power of, 154; trial, 153
"Impeachment in Florida" (Davis), 156
Insurance companies, 78, 119, 299, 309
Integration, 15–16, 17, 70, 72, 114–18, 125, 130, 132, 134, 184–85, 193, 320; advocates of, 3, 16; of armed forces, 109, 110; imposing, 329; integrated dances, 107–8,

mandated, 15; movement, 16, 72, 109; opposition to, 123, 157; prevention of, 120, 321; of public facilities, 8, 16; of public schools, 16, 18, 118, 123, 124, 147, 190, 319, 327; of the races, 205; racial, xi, 16, 38, 43, 110, 124, 174, 178, 190, 219; of residential areas, 192; and social gathering, 108; and sporting events, 123
Integration Rule of the Florida Bar, 323–26
Interposition Resolution, 156–58, 320, 329–30

Jim Crow laws, 329
Joe's Spaghetti House, 60
John Germany Library, 298
Johns, Charley, 8–9, 36, 131–33, 137, 179, 180–83, 185; as acting governor, 8, 181, 297; as senator, 131–32, 141, 178–80
Johns Committee, 5, 85, 118, 130–35, 137–38; bills of, 136
Johnson, Beth, 46–48
Jones, Daryl L., 102
Jones, Leo C., 141
Judicial Article V, 165–66
Judicial Nominating Committees, 186

Kalfas family, 60
Karl, Cynthia (daughter), 92, 335
Karl, Debbie (daughter), 254
Karl, Jim (son), 74, 254–55
Karl, Mercedes (wife), 53, 254–56, 262, 336
Karl, Rick (son), 75, 120, 254, 256
Karl, Tami (daughter), 254, 335
Kelly, Richard (judge), 155
Kelly, Scott, 174, 191–93, 222–23, 240
Kennedy, John F., 5–6, 186, 192–93, 235–36
Kennedy, Robert (Bobby), 5, 236–37
King, Larry, 214–15
King, Dr. Martin Luther, Jr., 5, 10, 103–4, 187
Kirk, Claude, 48, 53, 84; as governor, 52–53, 78, 82, 195–99, 208–9
Ku Klux Klan, 102

*La Gaceta*, 216
Lake Mystic, 65–67

Frederick B. Karl's career in law and public service spans more than fifty years. He is one of a select group of individuals to have served in all three branches of state government. His public service career also extended to municipal and county governments in Florida.

Fred Karl was born in 1924 in Daytona Beach. Upon graduation from Seabreeze High School, he enrolled at the University of Florida, but left his studies in 1942 to join the Army.

At the age of eighteen, he was commissioned as a second lieutenant and saw action as a tank platoon leader in Europe, where he was wounded during the Battle of the Bulge. He was awarded the Silver Star, Bronze Star, and Purple Heart medals.

After the war, Mr. Karl continued his education at Stetson University. He opened a law practice in Daytona Beach upon earning a law degree and later became the City Attorney for Daytona Beach and Ormond Beach.

He ran successfully for the Florida Legislature, serving eight years as a state representative and then four more years as a state senator.

In 1974, Mr. Karl became Florida's first Public Counsel, with the responsibility to represent consumers when public utilities requested rate hikes.

In 1976 Mr. Karl was elected to the Florida Supreme Court, the last justice to be elected to the state's highest court. He resigned from the court and returned to private practice in Tallahassee.

Moving to Tampa in 1988, Mr. Karl answered yet another call to government service, first as the County Attorney for Hillsborough County and then as the County Administrator. As its chief executive officer from 1990 to 1994, he led Hillsborough County through a period of rapid improvement in county services and modernized governmental processes and procedures.

One of his legacies was the purchase of a new but vacant downtown high-rise office building, which he turned into an efficient and cost-effective county government center. The building now bears his name.

Leaving public service in 1994, Mr. Karl was immediately asked to take the helm of Tampa General Hospital, a major health care facility in Hillsborough County which was undergoing financial and administrative problems. He is well remembered for stopping the effort to sell the institution.

After stabilizing the hospital, his third retirement was short lived, being asked in 2003 by newly elected Tampa Mayor Pam Iorio to serve as the City Attorney.

He "officially" retired in 2004 at age eighty.